Emotional Intelligence Mastery

(7 Book Box Set)

Ryan James

Table of Contents

Book #3 - Cognitive Behavioral Therapy: Complete Guide

Book #4 - Cognitive Behavioral Therapy: 21 Most Effective Tips and Tricks

Book #5 - How to Analyze People

Emotional Intelligence

The Complete Step-by-Step Guide on Self-Awareness, Controlling Your Emotions and Improving Your EQ

Introduction: A Step-by-Step Guide to Developing Emotional Intelligence

To define emotional intelligence (EI) as being aware of one's emotions and knowing how to control those emotions to build fruitful and empathetic relationships doesn't give you the full picture. The beauty in studying EI is to understand how to develop and use that emotional intelligence to improve your life. My goal in this book is to take you through the steps of how to do just that—to identify, develop and heighten your emotional intelligence to create stronger personal and professional relationships.

For clarity, let's take emotional intelligence beyond its definition and step into a greater understanding of what EI can do for you. Perhaps the best way to bring clarity to the term "emotional intelligence" is first to dispel some of its mysteries and myths. Emotional intelligence is NOT a personality trait. People who have high EI aren't necessarily optimistic, agreeable, or always happy. EI goes deeper than your outward personality; it's almost like having an inherent ability to perceive emotions and respond in a way that benefits all parties. It's learning how to feel emotions, not just be able to identify or recognize them. Having high emotional intelligence is knowing how to harness emotional energy and turn it into predictable and positive outcomes.

In my book, *Emotional Intelligence: The Definitive Guide to Understanding Your Emotions, How to Improve Your EQ and Your Relationships,* I spent lots of time describing the term and the importance it played in your personal and professional relationships. So, for some of you, it might be a good idea to first read that book and my second book *Emotional*

Intelligence Mastery: How to Master Your Emotions, Improve Your EQ, and Massively Improve Your Relationships. They both offer a firm foundation on what is introduced in this book. Now that you've learned what Emotional Intelligence is and how it can influence your life, we're going to take you through a step-by-step guided tour of how to improve your emotional intelligence through a robust analysis of your emotions and that of those with whom you surround yourself.

In this step-by-step guide to emotional intelligence, you'll learn how to assess your EI, observe others emotions with a heightened awareness, practice control and focus on improving your EI, and create predictable outcomes that bring you greater success in life. Instead of ignoring or scoffing at the evidence of emotions, you'll learn how to follow the steps to change the course of your life and others by using those same emotions to make you more decisive and attractive.

Often, the best way to better understand a topic is to begin questioning your feelings on the matter. So, let's get personal, shall we? Let's make it all about you. Ask yourself the following:

1. What will develop a high emotional intelligence in you?
2. How will you know if you have a high emotional intelligence?
3. Why is it important to know what your emotional intelligence is, anyway?
4. When will you notice a difference in your life?
5. Where can you expect this greater emotional awareness to take you?

To know what developing a high emotional intelligence can do for you, it's helpful to know what it has done for others. Developing a high emotional intelligence has helped CEOs run huge corporations, national leaders gain public support, and creative artists reflect the values and truths of their times. As you work through the steps of this book, you'll begin to examine your personal EI and determine the things you'll need to do to climb to a higher standard of emotional communications. Some of you who already have high EI may not notice a significant difference, merely a little improvement here and there to lighten the load. However, those of you who have been ruled for decades by emotional outbursts or suffered social isolation because of poor EI, the changes you'll experience will be immediate.

As to where you can expect this greater emotional awareness to take you? Well, the possibilities are limited only by your ability to practice these steps daily to become an emotional intelligence mensa. Improving your EI can lead you to more stable relationships, greater professional achievements and a more intuitive understanding of how to respond to others and predict how they will react to you. In short, increasing your emotional intelligence can be life altering.

You don't have to be a road scholar to have high emotional intelligence. In fact, there is no correlation between having a high IQ and a high EI. The size of your brain has little to do with your ability to recognize and build your emotional intelligence. It's more about the size of your heart than the size of your brain. When you approach others, how do you perceive them? What feelings do you leave them with when they leave your presence? It's more about feeling with your heart than knowing with your mind. That's what the following steps will show you—how to control and apply your feelings and emotions so that you will be perceived and will see others in their absolute best light.

As you learn and follow the steps presented in this book, you'll begin to see yourself and others differently. Instead of jumping to conclusions before knowing all the facts of the situation, you'll find yourself stepping back and observing the other person's emotions. When, before, you would have made a rash decision based on irrational feelings, now you'll start to mull things over a bit more and imagine how your behavior might negatively impact others. That's called having emotional intelligence. So, join me on this tour, this step-by-step guide to helping you discover and develop your emotional intelligence.

Chapter 1: Step #1—Assessing Your Emotional Intelligence

If we can agree that Emotional Intelligence is important, how can you assess your EI? We have designed a little test for you that will give you an accurate idea of your Emotional Intelligence. Take a few moments to answer the follow questions, and then let's talk about your scores.

Emotional Intelligence Assessment

Answer the following questions and then tally up your score. At the end of the test, you'll know your Emotional Intelligence level.

1. You're riding in a taxi. You notice that the driver is taking many side streets, and you fear your charge will reflect his poor sense of direction. What do you do?

   a. Tap him on the shoulder and tell him you don't appreciate his attempt to rack up a higher tab.
   b. Let him know you are familiar with the area and ask him what he believes is the quickest route to take to get to your destination.
   c. Ignore him and decide never to use this company again.
   d. Refuse to pay the bill.

2. Your daughter has a friend in the neighborhood come over to play. When the friend leaves, your little girl begins to cry because she has no more money in her

piggy bank. It appears the older child next door took advantage of your daughter and stole the money from her piggy bank. What would you do?

e. Listen to your daughter's story, and then share with her how something similar happened to you when you were little so she wouldn't feel so bad.
f. March right over to the neighbor's house with your daughter to tell the girl's mother and demand she gives back the money.
g. Let your little girl express her anger over her loss, and then together discover a way to prevent this from ever happening again.
h. Reprimand your daughter and refuse to give her any more allowance until she learns to take better care of her money.

3. You are trying to impress your boss and win the "salesperson of the year" award, but you're getting discouraged because the last 20 calls you've made have been hang-ups. What do you do?

a. Try a different call tactic.
b. Quit
c. Stop trying to get so much attention for your performance.
d. Stop and consider what you are doing that could be hindering your opportunity to make the sale, and then try something you've learned that might be more efficient.

4. You're on your way to the movies with your significant other, and the driver in the car next to you cuts you off. Your significant other starts to fume—what do you do?

a. Encourage him to pull beside the other drive so you can yell obscenities.
b. Turn the radio up and sing to drown out your partner's swearing.
c. Tell him he gets way too mad when drivers cut him off, and then share with him how it happens to you all the time and you don't lose it.
d. Let him express himself, and then point out that the other driver could have been an out-of-towner or someone headed for the hospital.

5. You are trying to learn some new software on your computer, but the tutorial is not helping, and you're getting quite frustrated. What do you do?

a. You give it a rest for a while, and then ask a friend who is good with computers for help.
b. You vow never to use the computer again and shut it down.
c. You decide to wait until you're in a better mood to try learning the new program.
d. You choose to take a class on the software and be patient with yourself during the learning curve.

Scoring: Give yourself five points for every correct answer.

1. Correct answer is b = 5 Points
2. Correct answer is c = 5 Points
3. Correct answer is d = 5 Points
4. Correct answer is d = 5 Points
5. Correct answer is d = 5 Points

If you scored 25 points, you have the highest Emotional Intelligence.

If you scored 20 points, you have more Emotional Intelligence than many.

If you scored 15 points, you need to work on your Emotional Intelligence.

If you scored 10 points or below, you have little awareness of your or others' emotions.

So, let's think about this brief assessment for a moment. How do you "feel" about the emotions this test stirred in you? What if I told you, no exact five-question test could demonstrate the level of your emotional intelligence? The five-question assessment has no validity, but now you're probably feeling a whole other set of emotions. You could be feeling frustration, confusion, tricked even. Any way you look at it, there are some emotions you have to deal with right now. So, now we can truly assess how you're thinking about these emotions.

Most people tend to over-rate their Emotional Intelligence level. Have you ever had bosses who considered themselves to be very tuned into their emotions and those of their employees, but who were actually living in an emotional wasteland? All this thinking about emotions leads us to a different definition of Emotional Intelligence. Emotional Intelligence is how you think about and express your feelings. Taking it one step further, how do you use that information about your feelings to change your behavior and the behavior of others?

Taking a test isn't going to provide answers about feelings and emotions. Contemplating your feelings and how to control your emotions is what will give you an accurate gauge on your Emotional Intelligence. Not all emotions are black or white—many fill up that gray area of complex feelings that need more than a label to define them. For example, it's easy to identify a feeling of sorrow when your pet dies. However, can you distinguish the difference between frustration and anger? Do you know when you're feeling shame or is it embarrassment you're experiencing?

Complex emotions need reflection and thought to sort through and assess. That reflection is what eventually improves and strengthens your Emotional Intelligence. Learning to deal productively with your emotions helps you to identify and assess others emotions. Emotions are not to be confused with moods. Moods are, by nature, flighty and erratic. Emotions are truer, easier to think through and assess. Have you ever awakened in a bad mood, as if for no reason? You've had no conversation, no event yet in your day that could cause you emotional turmoil—you're just in a mood, right? It's helpful to understand as we go through these steps that we're not speaking of mood swings here, but rather discussing one's inner emotions.

Since Emotional Intelligence requires thought about your feelings, let's do that to develop a more accurate measurement of your EI. I'm going to give you some situations, and I want you to think about how you typically feel when you find yourself enmeshed in them. The first step in assessing your feelings is simply recognizing or identifying them.

What did you feel when...

- Your best friend, once again, stood you up for a get-together?
- Your employer broke his/her promise to give you a pay increase?
- Your family member was very ill and in the hospital?
- You heard someone at your door at midnight, and you were all by yourself?

- Your significant other said they had a confession to make?
- Your mother or father expressed pride in your achievement?
- You wanted something so desperately but knew you could never have it?
- You lost your job or failed to get that promotion?
- Your sister or brother received rewards for something you knew you could do better?
- Your husband or wife forgot your birthday?

As you go through these issues, you will notice that some emotions are clearly defined, and others fall in that gray area. Emotions that you must think about are usually ones with layers of unresolved issues, ones that you have repeatedly stuffed down or ignored so as not to have to deal with them. By not pausing at the time to think through your emotions, you have stunted the forward progress of your Emotional Intelligence.

Assessing your Emotional Intelligence means asking yourself if you truly have a handle on your feelings. When you are emotional, do you react or stop to think things through? If your friend is hurting, do you avoid her company until she has worked through her problem, or do you stand by her and help her to resolve the emotional issue? All this is a part of your Emotional Intelligence. Every time you feel emotional, or you sense a high emotional state in others, think about what you are feeling and how best to manage those feelings to help yourself and others reach a positive outcome to the issue. It's the thinking that positively contributes to one's Emotional Intelligence. It's important to know how you process all the emotional information you absorb each day because it's in that processing that you can better asses your EI.

There are all sorts of tests that say they measure your Emotional Intelligence, but if your perception of self is somewhat skewed, isn't the information just more of the same? Most of us can't trust ourselves to be honest when it comes to evaluating our EI, so how valuable are any of these tests? If you're reading this book, you probably either sense that you need help with your emotions, or you have a desire to learn how to become more emotionally intelligent when it comes to making decisions. Either way, it doesn't matter. You've already taken the first step—you're thinking about the emotions you and others are feeling—you've worked through Step #1!

Chapter 2: Step #2—Creating Emotional Awareness

Since our childhoods, most of us have been taught to categorize and judge our emotions and the emotions of others. What is omitted in our early training is how to be more aware of our emotions and how they affect our decisions, behaviors, and beliefs about ourselves and others. For example, you may have learned as a child that crying was bad. Consequently, as an adult, you rarely cry and especially not in public. If someone you trusted had taught you that crying was only a way your body allows you to let off some built-up steam and stress, then perhaps you would be more capable of handling your own tears and feel more comfortable around others when they feel the need to cry.

That's the first step in creating more emotional awareness. Let go of your past judgments and categories where you have conveniently tucked away the emotions with which you feel uncomfortable. When you have tears or see someone else tearing up, grab a tissue and experience the waterworks. You'll be surprised at how refreshed you will feel when you let yourself experience the honesty of your emotions without the need to try to explain or rectify the situation. Just feel the raw emotion. As you think about what you are feeling with the tears, most of them will probably just dry up on their own, and you'll be consumed with wonder about the feelings associated with the tears.

There's No Right or Wrong Time to Feel Emotions

The process of awareness is enhanced when you close the door on judgment and criticism. Keep in mind; there's not a right or wrong time to feel your emotions. The only thing that is wrong is deciding not to feel at all. When you allow yourself to feel and think about the emotions you are feeling; you have increased awareness of how to use your feelings to positively impact your life.

Emotional awareness also reveals patterns in behaviors and thoughts that help you to identify and link similar emotions to events that may be triggers for you. When you are aware of emotional patterns in yourself and others, you can teach yourself to use this emotional information in your relationships, decision-making, and know when you are reacting irrationally to a situation. Then, instead of experiencing the typical "knee jerk" actions that may have challenged you in the past, you'll know to pause and give yourself a bit more time to think things through. You'll use your emotions in a more logical manner.

Learn to Listen and Observe

While awareness is necessary, it's not the end-all to gaining more Emotional Intelligence. Okay, so you're aware that every time you sit down at your desk at work, you feel a knot in your stomach. So, what? If you have identified the feeling but haven't given yourself time to think about why you feel this way, then there's no hope of resolving the underlying issues.

Listening and observing your body's reaction to emotions enhances your awareness and increases the likelihood that you'll seek a remedy for the discomfort. What must you do to dissolve the knot in your stomach? Well, if your feelings are telling you that you don't like your job, then it may be time to choose another company or perhaps a different career path. If you break out in a sweat every time you give a presentation, maybe you need more practice to increase your confidence. Some emotions cannot be avoided or ignored, but when you are aware of their influence, you can take steps to manage them better. That's practicing higher Emotional Intelligence.

As you become more aware of your emotions, you'll want to ask yourself some questions during the "think through" process. Some of the questions that are helpful are as follows.

- How are these feelings contributing to my setbacks or successes?
- Am I unduly distracted by these feelings or emotions?
- How am I being challenged by these emotions to allow myself to move forward in a more positive manner?
- What will enhance my ability to manage these emotions and use them to create stronger personal and professional relationships?
- What positive responses and behaviors do I see from others who might be experiencing similar emotions?

As you learn to listen and observe yourself and others' outward display of their feelings, use the time to reflect on the emotions you are witnessing. Think about how you would have handled the emotional situation. Give yourself time to consider alternative behaviors. Suddenly your Emotional Intelligence has changed from being an "inside" thought process to an external action that causes you to behave differently in future situations. You've successfully linked your previous thoughts to future outcomes, making it easier to predict favorable results. Greater Emotional Intelligence is an amazing thing, don't you think?

Breaking the Habits of Low Emotional Intelligence

Having low Emotional Intelligence is habit forming. You've become accustomed to ignoring yours and others emotions and so it's easier to continue to do what you've always done—turn away and distract yourself with other things. If you give emotions any thought at all, it's usually to pass quick judgment and then busy yourself with another activity. This can be a habit that is challenging to break.

There are two common habits that those with low Emotional Intelligence frequently practice. They are either easily offended, or they easily offend. Either way, these two habits block your ability to become more emotionally aware and use your emotions to benefit yourself and others. Pay attention to your thoughts when you witness the emotions of others. Do you say to yourself, "Oh for heaven sake—suck it up?" If so, learn to reprogram your self-talk. Start by thinking to yourself, "I wonder what is causing them to feel this way? What can I do to help?" This is called empathy or putting yourself in another's shoes so that you can open new avenues of understanding. If you get your feelings hurt at the drop of a hat, take notice of your feelings. Ask yourself, "Did I do something wrong? What can I do next time to improve my response to this type of situation?"

Deriding yourself for your feelings doesn't work, and it does nothing to help you break either of these two habits that inhibit greater Emotional Intelligence. There is a message in every emotion, so you must search for the message. What are your feelings telling you? How will being more aware of these feelings in the future help you to change your behaviors and improve your relationships? Now you've established new habits, making it much easier to eliminate the old ones.

Learning to Hear Your Emotions

Once your awareness has increased, you'll notice that emotions can be quite apparent in your voice as well as your body. Many people who are feeling fearful or are experiencing a lack of confidence will get a shaky voice. Of course, anger will make your voice increase in volume and speed. Frustration, on the other hand, often raises your voice a few octaves. Sorrow or disillusionment usually lowers your pitch and volume. When someone is attempting to control their emotions, their voice can become slower, more stilted and pronounced.

Couple the voice with body language, and you'll soon be reading a whole novel of emotions in others as well as yourself. For example, if someone is holding their body rather stiffly and their rate of speech is slower with their words pronounced more distinctly, you can almost bet they are feeling some strong emotions—usually anger or frustration. When you have successfully read the emotions lurking just beneath the surface of your conversation, you can act accordingly to defuse the emotion. Take a deep breath, accept that there is something wrong, and then take the appropriate action. What a transformation. Now you've used your Emotional Intelligence to set a higher standard of behavior than you would have previously exhibited.

Getting Comfortable with Your Emotions

Did you ever think that you'd be using the words comfort and emotions in the same sentence? If you're not quite a believer yet, that you can become comfortable with your feelings and emotions, keep practicing. Like anything else, the more you allow yourself to think and experience your emotions, and the more empathy you have for others, the easier Emotional Intelligence becomes.

At first when you have increased your emotional awareness, expect a flood of emotions to come streaming through your previously damned-up wall. Not to worry! Take one emotion and feeling at a time and give yourself time to think about it— identify it—manage it. Then you'll be ready for the next one and the next one until you've managed to work through an entire parade of emotions. It also takes some energy, so be patient with yourself. Enhancing your Emotional Intelligence takes effort, and allowing yourself to fully feel your emotions for the first time can be a bit draining. Trust me; it'll get better.

Once you get comfortable with your emotions, it will be much easier to deal with the emotions of others. Empathetic understanding will be second nature to you, and you'll earn the respect and admiration of others who may have previously been out of reach. People are attracted to those with high Emotional Intelligence, even those who pride themselves on being quite logical minded. Everybody likes to be heard, understood, valued and appreciated. That's what Emotionally Intelligent people do, and that's why others seek to have what they recognize in Emotionally Intelligent people.

Very little else sets you apart more than your Emotional Intelligence. It is as powerful and persuasive as having an extremely high IQ. In fact, studies show that Emotional Intelligence is more likely to bring success and well-being than those with high IQs. The Center for Creative Leadership (CCL) studied why seemingly intelligent corporate leaders found their careers stalled when their abilities and skills should have dictated otherwise. After a study of more than 20,000 individuals in 2,000 organizations what they discovered was that there were three main reasons for this phenomenon—all related to Emotional Intelligence.

1. They had challenges handling change.

2. They found it difficult to work as a team.

3. They were incapable of developing strong working relationships.

Many CEOs have been relieved of their positions, not because of their lack of competence, but because of a lack of Emotional Intelligence. Furthermore, studies done by the Carnegie Institute of Technology showed that 85% of our success financially was due to how well we had learned to communicate, negotiate, and perform skills that required an awareness and understanding of others feelings and emotions. Just 15% of our financial success was due to our technical expertise and abilities.

Now that you're becoming more aware of the need to address your emotions and allow yourself to feel, let's look in the next chapter how you can move from chaos to control.

Chapter 3: Step #3—Moving from Chaos to Control

People of high Emotional Intelligence experience just as much chaotic emotions as the next person, the difference is they have learned how to control the chaos of emotions that others let run amuck. They are aware of their emotions and feelings, but instead of burying them, they take a breath and examine their feelings to determine how best to manage the emotions in a positive and constructive way. Sure, they feel all the emotions with the exception that they don't react impulsively and let their emotions create chaos. They practice self-control.

The truth is, as humans we experience the emotions before we have time to think about why we feel as we do. Those with a high degree of Emotional Intelligence give themselves permission not to have all the answers, to search for another alternative to the problem that would be more positive and productive. Emotional Intelligence requires that we take a moment to analyze how the emotions we are feeling will influence the outcome of the situation and impact us and those around us. Emotionally Intelligent people are confident enough to give the issue some time to simmer—time for them to contemplate different perspectives.

Exercise C.O.N.T.R.O.L.

Let me share with you what I mean by C.O.N.T.R.O.L.

C = Consider the Consequences

What will be the result of your actions? If you react without thinking about the consequences, your choices may not provide you with the desired outcome.

O = Optimism

Practicing optimism allows you to get in front of the emotion with positive thinking, even a little humor if necessary. People with positive outlooks almost always get more positive results from the decisions they make.

N = Neutralize the Emotions

Thinking about emotions neutralizes their power and calms the feelings. Most extreme emotions carry quite a punch, so when you can take the power out of the punch, your emotional state calms down, and you can think more rationally.

T = Take Ten

Take ten seconds to pause and consider the what and why of your feelings. This brief little pause along with a few deep breaths will position you to think calmly and make all-around better choices.

R = Regulate

Regulate your reactions in emotional situations. Apply all the elements of control, and help yourself and others to move away from the chaos of emotionally charged situations.

O = Openly Accept

Openly accept that you are going to experience emotionally charged situations. It's how you respond in these circumstances that will enhance your Emotional Intelligence. Be open to doing things differently, to accepting your own and others' emotions, to a willingness to admit your mistakes and hold yourself accountable for the decisions you make.

L = Look for Alternatives

Look for alternative behaviors, actions, and solutions to problems rather than giving into the chaotic emotions that have ruled you in the past. When you reach a higher degree of Emotional Intelligence, the alternatives will present themselves more clearly, and you'll be much more open to trying something different.

How Do You Get Control?

Good question! You get to control one moment at a time—one emotion at a time—one action at a time. As difficult as it might seem, there are some definite steps you can take to move from chaos to control.

1. Assume responsibility for your emotions and actions.

   - Here's that word "consequences" again, but you must learn to accept the consequences of your actions. Hold yourself accountable. Admit you've made mistakes so that you can correct those things next time.
   - Stop blaming others for your circumstances or dicey situations. Nobody should have the power to control your success but you. If you think they do, then you've given away too much of yourself—you've lost your inner strength and confidence.
   - Put yourself in an emotional place that enables you to earn the respect of others. It's an incredible boost

to know that others look up to you, that they depend on you to help them grow emotionally.

2. Know what's most important to you.
   - What do you value? What do you believe? What are you absolutely not willing to compromise?
   - Know what you believe to be morally right, and then refuse to cross that line.
   - What is your ethics? Do the decisions you make reflect high morals and ethical behavior?

3. Reap all the benefits of calmness.

   - Pay attention to your emotions. Know what creates stress in your life, then decide how you plan to remove the stress. Take action to come to calm.
   - Stop the negative self-talk. If it takes writing down all your negative talk on a piece of paper to enable you to visualize the influence negative emotions have over your well-being, then write them down, rip them up, and dump them in the circular file.
   - Practice deep breathing. Get some physical exercise. Do whatever it takes to spend some of that emotional energy. Then enjoy the calm.

You'll know you've reached greater levels of Emotional Intelligence when the decisions you make are rarely rushed or filled with emotional baggage. When your self-talk is positive, and you stop judging and stereotyping others, that's a clear indication that your Emotional Intelligence is gaining ground. When people are drawn to you and share their situations with you in hopes of guidance, then you'll know you've made great strides in improving your Emotional Intelligence.

Some people are born more intuitive, and feeling than others and some learn to have greater Emotional Intelligence at an early age, but no matter how old you are and what your position in life is, you can strengthen your ability to control and manage your emotions. There is nothing that is so permanent that it cannot be changed even if it's just by a little here and there. Perhaps the situation cannot be changed, but you can modify the way you perceive it, the way you plan to handle it. On the other hand, if there is something that happens that you feel changes everything, there are ways to face that battle as well. Those with high Emotional Intelligence see possibilities when others see problems; they see opportunities when others see obstacles. The choice is yours. So, what's it going to be? Well, it depends on your Emotional Intelligence, which provides you with great motivation to improve your EI.

I've heard it said that the greatest predictor of future outcomes is past behaviors; however, I'm not so sure that's true. I believe the more accurate predictor of future outcomes is the level of your Emotional Intelligence. Are you willing to look at your emotions in the eye and say to yourself, what can I do differently today that will give me better results than I had yesterday? How can I use the emotions and feelings I am having to influence my life's outcomes and bring me greater success? The choices you make and the actions you take as a result of these questions are truly life altering. Improving your Emotional Intelligence is what will be the best predictor of your future success.

Satisfaction in both your personal and professional life is more linked to Emotional Intelligence than almost anything else. More so than riches, IQ, or great careers, you'll find that Emotional Intelligence isn't too far behind the scenes of successful people. Our most memorable moments are teaming with individuals who have a high level of Emotional

Intelligence. Think about when you felt the most loved, appreciated, valued, cherished, and needed, and then reflect on those who surrounded you in those moments. I'll bet you can identify many who had a high degree of Emotional Intelligence, right?

The Best Way to Control Yourself is to Help Others

Few things create more desire to perform at your peak, to reach heightened self-awareness, or to share the most love as others in your life who are willing to give the same back to you. Whether you have high Emotional Intelligence or yours is rather lacking at the moment, the people you find most attractive are usually those with high Emotional Intelligence. They somehow have the ability to draw people to them like wanderers to a warm fire on a cold winter's night.

We recognize Emotional Intelligence in others and want that for ourselves. You may not know what to call it, but you know there's something different about them that makes you enjoy their company. To examine your emotions and apply control over what might have been a turbulent past, observe and listen to those whom you recognize to have Emotional Intelligence. Watch how they monitor their emotions and express their feelings. Listen to how they encourage others to do the same. Do they take a little time to think things through before trying to resolve a problem? Do they value what others contribute in a meeting or a personal relationship? Then ask yourself how! How do they do what they do? Better yet, ask them to share their feelings with you. Emotionally Intelligent people don't mind opening up about their feelings. In fact, they usually welcome the opportunity.

Looking at the World through a Positive Lens

There was once two young men who were twins with entirely different outlooks on life. Although they had been raised by the same parents, in the same neighborhood, under the same economic situation, their futures reflected two completely different outlooks on the world. When asked why the one twin left home at such an early age and turned to using drugs, he responded, "Well, it was because of my parents and the neighborhood in which I lived." When asked why the other twin went on to college and became a successful businessman, he replied, "Well, it was because of my parents and the neighborhood in which I lived."

Each twin was raised in the same environment under the same circumstances, but with obviously different degrees of Emotional Intelligence. Each chose how they felt about their life's circumstances and how those feelings would influence the decisions they made in their lives. They even experienced the same emotions. What was different was how they chose to think about and control those emotions that set each twin's life path.

So, let me ask you—what will you choose? Will you choose chaos or control? Then ask yourself, what influence will these choices have over the rest of your life?

Chapter 4: Step #4—Redirecting Your Focus

What you choose to focus on is one of the most critical elements to being able to manage your emotions effectively. Whatever emotion you are focusing on at the time, you are actually feeding it, making it more powerful, and giving it enduring strength. By focusing on the negative feelings in your life, you not only strengthen them, but you weaken the positives. What you feed becomes stronger; what you starve gets weaker. Your emotions are rarely stagnating; they are either growing stronger or becoming weaker. The main part of the word "emotion" is "motion."

Your body feels the emotion before your mind comprehends its intensity or purpose. To prove my point, try a little experiment. Turn the corners of your mouth in a smile and begin to chuckle. Now strengthen that chuckle into full-blown laughter. It won't take long before your mind begins remembering something that gave you a giggle, and in just a matter of minutes, the positive is set into motion. Admit it; you weren't necessarily thinking about a happy moment before you began to laugh, right? As you focused on the real laughter, your thoughts followed with a happy memory.

The same can be said for clapping your hands and singing a happy tune. There's something about clapping your hands that won't allow you to feel depressed. Focus on the motion of clapping and the happy words to the song, and soon your outlook will be happy. It's like putting the positive in motion. Whatever feeling you focus on and feed becomes stronger. You don't necessarily have to be right in the middle of a positive experience to feel positive emotions; you just need to engage your mind and decide to be happy and remember something that makes you smile.

Have you ever had a shared story or joke with a family member or best friend and every time you begin to talk about it around others you just can't control your laughter? Because many in the group didn't experience the same event you did, they might not get the humor in the story, but it doesn't really matter because you and your friend are both so into the memory you turn into dribbling idiots and end up needing a tissue to wipe away the tears of laughter.

I shared one of these memories with my mother about a time my father wanted to go swimming but didn't have a suit. So, Mom and I went to the store and purchased a one-size-fits-all canary yellow swimsuit for him. What we discovered was that the clerk wasn't exactly truthful about the one-size-fits-all thing. After 30 minutes of desperate pulling and stretching, with a myriad of loud grunts and groans, my father exited the bathroom with a suit that showed every vulgar bump and wrinkles imaginable. With each step, the suit began to roll and creep down until he then resembled the Norge refrigerator repairman with his exposure getting more critically dangerous by the moment.

Oh, and I forgot to mention that my x mother-in-law was also witness to this bizarre event, and the expression on her face was that of shock and awe. To this day, I cannot share this story, especially in the presence of my mother, without doubling over with laughter. In fact, even seeing a one-size-fits-all sign in a clothing store is enough to set us off.

My point in telling this story is that you can decide to experience whatever emotion you focus on at the time. When I want to alleviate stress or depression, I often dredge up the memory of dad's most unflattering swim attire. If I really want to cement the feeling, I pick up the phone and call Mom, and we sputter on the phone for half an hour about the incident. If you want to magnify your focus on a feeling, share it in a story with others.

In Tony Robbins' book "Awaken the Giant Within," he presents the idea that the only reason people are motivated to do anything is to change the way they feel. They want to feel powerful, so they purchase a luxury car or a big house. They want to feel beautiful, so they lose weight or buy an expensive suit or dress. What many people fail to realize is that you can feel those emotions right now. Just decide to feel. You are already powerful and beautiful; you don't have to wait for something to happen to create those feelings. It's an amazing thing, but you can feel all those things with nothing changing in your life except your perspective.

If you want to feel like a giving person, give. If you want to be perceived as powerful, act powerfully. Not long ago, there was a young man who conducted an experiment. He hired a bunch of people to follow him through the streets of New York City with camera crews and act like an enthusiastic entourage. Thinking he must be a celebrity, complete strangers approached him on the street and began asking for his autograph. Viola, he was a star because he acted like a star.

Another example of creating emotions was when a man stood before marathon runners wearing a t-shirt that said "Free Hugs." People were approaching the end of the marathon and were worn out from the experience. They visibly wore the look of exhaustion on their faces and bodies. As they crossed the line almost ready to collapse, the young gentleman approached them with his arms held out and a huge smile on his face, ready to celebrate their efforts with a free hug. Their physical transformation was stunning. After they had got over the initial confusion, they shared the young man's big smile, held out their arms to welcome the hug, and shared a warm embrace that was both fun and energizing. Suddenly, their focus was on the hug of celebration instead of their aching bodies. Their focus was on the accomplishment instead of sore muscles and tired feet.

Let your body lead the way to open your mind's focus on all the possibilities of achieving greater Emotional Intelligence. Redirect your focus and let it lead the way to create Emotional Intelligence. Instead of burying your feelings, celebrate them, use them to push you to maximum performance, more meaningful relationships, and greater satisfaction in life. If it's up to you to forge your own path, why not make it a positive experience by focusing on all that is right and good. It doesn't mean that you will never feel the negatives, but they won't be strong enough to take control of your destiny.

Make Slaves of Your Negative Emotions

Just like you can use your positive feelings and emotions, you can also learn to use the negative emotions when they arise. For example, if you are aware of your negative emotions and recognize their patterns, then use them to improve yourself. Like that knot in your stomach, we discussed earlier that happened whenever you sat down at your desk at work, use it to motivate you to get another job or change your career to one that is more pleasing.

It takes courage to make slaves of your negative emotions. Why? Because negatives can be strong motivators for change, and change rarely happens without some struggle. Once you have a clear grasp on your feelings and understand how they can influence your life, you'll be willing to go through a time of discomfort to get to a better place. Suddenly, the tables will turn. Instead of being a slave to your negative emotions, you make them slaves to your actions and behaviors. Use them to push you to excellence.

First, you need to focus on the emotion, then on how you need to change your perspective, and lastly on your desired outcome. If you let the negative emotions control you, your focus will be limited and stifled. Remember, what you focus on becomes stronger, and everything you focus on is your choice. It's quite a freeing notion, this whole focus idea, wouldn't you say? If you want to wallow in self-pity, it's your choice. If you want to enjoy the positive feelings of a higher level of Emotional Intelligence, that's your choice as well.

Improving Your Ability to Focus

Remember the story of that marathon runner? When you are exhausted, your inability to focus will be evident in the choices and decisions you make. To improve your focus, get lots of sleep. It's difficult to feel positive when you're getting only a few hours of interrupted sleep each night. Your mind becomes foggy, and you begin to question every decision.

Next, eat properly. If your body is the first to indicate your feelings, then make sure it's strong. Eat healthy food that feeds the mind and muscles. Avoid overeating and creating a sluggish system that can barely focus on getting out of bed in the morning. There are certain foods that fuel thought—eat more of those. I can tell you; they usually don't come prepackaged or in the form of frozen dinners or salty snacks.

Get plenty of exercise to burn off the unwanted negative emotions and encourage you to focus on a healthier lifestyle. It's much easier to feel positive emotions when you know you're looking your best. Exercise and healthy food create "feel good" reactions in the mind and body. Being physically fit released chemicals and endorphins that expand your thinking and encourage better focus and greater cognitive thought.

Whatever you do, do it now. Don't wait until you look better, feel better, have achieved more success in your job, or have found that one-in-a-million relationship. Remember, it's a decision, so decide now to focus on feeling positive and rejuvenated. Focus on where you want to be instead of where you are. Focus on what will happen when you achieve Emotional Intelligence.

Chapter 5: Step #5—Practicing a Daily Dose of Emotional Intelligence

We're such an instant society, always so busy running here and there that we rarely take the time to simply sit and reflect upon our feelings. In fact, just reading it might make some feel like they've returned to the '70s era where people walked the streets passing out flowers and sitting on the curb chanting. Who knows, perhaps that was the beginning of us thinking about Emotional Intelligence, and we lost touch with our feelings somewhere along the way.

As much as I believe Emotional Intelligence plays a significant role in all our lives, I too let my busy life get in the way of taking a few moments out of each day to focus on my feelings. Most people's lives are consumed by family, friends, careers, financial worries, and just everyday stuff that gets in the way of taking a little time for ourselves. At the end of a busy day, all we can think about is unplugging and turning into mindless little television zombies. The only emotions we want to reflect on at the end of the day is how we're going to address our exhaustion.

Well, here's a thought. What if that exhaustion is caused by your inability to take time for yourself? What if your day flowed much smoother and your energies were revived because you gave yourself a daily dose of Emotional Intelligence? You'd be amazed at how a few minutes escape each morning and afternoon would make such a difference in your energy level. Unresolved or misunderstood emotions can take their toll on your energy level.

There are three ways to deal with your feelings. Some people are clueless when it comes to understanding their emotions. They don't deal with their feelings because they refuse to consider the fact that they even have any emotions. Instead, they plow through life telling themselves they're loners, that they feel entirely comfortable being alone. Then, there are those people who are aware they have emotions and feelings that sometimes may be getting in the way of their relationships, but they don't know what to do with them. Instead of discovering how to deal with their emotions, they push them aside and make weak promises that things will get better when they are more financially stable, or when they lose weight or when they get a better job or a nicer car. What they don't realize is that their low Emotional Intelligence is what could be keeping them from greater achievement. If you've been putting off dealing with your emotions until tomorrow, consider this, tomorrow never comes. You're always in today—today is the time to practice Emotional Intelligence.

Then there are the ones, maybe just like you, who are seeking to improve your Emotional Intelligence by learning how to practice empathy, understanding, and awareness of yours and others' emotions. Stop reacting every time you have an emotional crisis, and start responding by giving your emotions some further thought. That's the difference between reacting and responding. When you respond to an emotional situation, you have already given it some thought. You have compared the feelings you are now having to others you have had in the past. You had already asked yourself when you experienced similar feelings how you planned to handle them in the future. Now, the future is here, and you are better prepared for the successful management of your emotions. You have just increased your Emotional Intelligence.

Practice Makes More Perfect Practice

It's important to understand that increasing your Emotional Intelligence is a lifelong endeavor. It's not something you "get" today, wipe your brow and let out a sigh of relief that you have finally reached your peak. Emotional Intelligence is a mountain or understanding and awareness that has no peak. You will never reach the top; however, each day brings you new vistas of serenity and calm experiences that clear your vision and prepare you for your next climb.

This is a tough one for those who pride themselves on perfection because you will never reach the perfect level of Emotional Intelligence. What is possible is that each day you think about your feelings and allow yourself to contemplate how you will do things differently next time, then place yourself in social and professional environments that enable you to practice dealing with yours and others emotions; you gain ground. If it helps you, think of Emotional Intelligence as being a mountain with many lookout points, and you get to see a whole new, panoramic view every day.

Talking about practicing Emotional Intelligence isn't enough; now it's time for some sound practice. First, practice on yourself. Once you've given some thought to your feelings, to why you reacted a certain way in an emotionally charged situation, then step out and practice your Emotional Intelligence on others. Observe the facial expressions and body language of a group you are in, and when someone seems stressed question them further about what is causing their hurt or pain. It could be they are on an emotional high, and that's a good time to ask them to share their experience as well. Celebrate their happy event with them. Enjoy their success or experience, their joy, and laughter. Emotions aren't always bad, you know. Some are over-the-top fantastic, and you can now share those feelings while you practice your Emotional Intelligence.

Creating a Safe Environment

If practicing your Emotional Intelligence is going to be a complete turn-around for you, make sure you create a safe environment. Begin practicing with people you trust. You may even share with them how you are feeling, that's a wonderful way to practice. Choose individuals who care about you and want to see you succeed. A word of warning, these may not be your bar buddies or your co-workers. If you are going to explore your feelings and share your goals with another, make sure it is someone with high Emotional Intelligence. They will be the ones who will show you empathy and understanding, and you will be able to learn from them how to handle your emotions.

It can be difficult to trust your emotions when you've never even admitted you have any, or when you've prided yourself on not showing them. So, when you first come out, so to speak, do so with people who are not emotionally starved or isolated from their feelings. Once you have thought about your feelings, you'll need to trust them so that you can be encouraged to step outside your routine and show empathy to yourself and others.

You're on the precipice of change, and change requires things of you that might be difficult and challenging. Keep at it; the payoff is incredible. Once you experience successful strides in building your Emotional Intelligence, you'll never want to go back to that person you were yesterday who felt something was missing. There will be a void that finally begins to close, and a completeness within yourself that you've never had before.

That's one advantage of transformation; you can look back and see how far you've come; enjoy the journey. Others who have always had a high degree of Emotional Intelligence might never appreciate what they have quite as much as those who have to work hard to get it. What takes more work to accomplish is usually appreciated more than what comes naturally or easily. You've worked hard and earned your success, and that's a plus in my book.

Expect the Unexpected

What will begin to happen will be just short of miraculous. If you have been a loner in the past, and you start to gain ground with your Emotional Intelligence, you'll soon find yourself attracting friends, and people that you previously felt were out of your league. If you felt trapped in a "go nowhere" job, you'll be more willing to take a risk and step out to search for something that is more suitable to your newly gained Emotional Intelligence. In fact, you may have people come to you wanting you to join their team. The more Emotional Intelligence you get, the more you understand and empathize with yourself and others, the more you'll change into that person you always wanted to become.

Reaching greater heights of Emotional Intelligence is directly proportionate to how much you practice empathizing and understanding yours and others feelings. Practice a little and gain a little ground each day. Practice a lot, and you grow by leaps and bounds. It's all about choice, and the choice is yours. You set your limits and boundaries.

When you build your Emotional Intelligence, you will experience the most unexpected occurrences. People will begin asking for your opinion, and "surprise—surprise," you'll look forward to sharing your ideas and feelings. You may become the "go to" guy in office meetings. You might get brave and introduce yourself to an attractive stranger at a party, and he or she welcomes the intrusion with open arms and enticing conversation. You might be able to save the rocky relationship you are currently in, returning to your first feelings of love and admiration. Emotional Intelligence brings more surprises than you can imagine, so take a deep breath and get ready for the ride of your life.

Chapter 6: Step #6—Predicting & Preventing Outcomes

In every aspect of our lives, it has been studied and proven that those with higher Emotional Intelligence can predict more positive outcomes in their personal and professional endeavors. Let's examine the influence of Emotional Intelligence from early adolescence to adulthood.

Predicting Academic Success

When children move into puberty, their hormones spur on the whole gamut of emotional experiences. To say that these emotions and feelings can be somewhat distracting is an understatement. If you begin to develop Emotional Intelligence at an early age, you are better prepared to manage these emotions and focus on academics successfully. Students who have a high Emotional Intelligence are calmer, more satisfied with their social networks, feel more supported by their family and friends, and can successfully handle the anxiety that comes with test taking and peer pressure.

Because early positive perceptions and beliefs about yourself are the most important elements in the development into stable adulthood, those who learn Emotional Intelligence in their youth are more likely to continue to gain more EI as they mature. Emotional Intelligence positions them for future management and leadership roles as they enter the workplace.

Influence of EI on Your Health and Well-being

Doctors Schutte and Malouff, researchers in the area of Emotional Intelligence conducted a study in 2007, where they researched the correlation between Emotional Intelligence and physical health. What they found was that people with high Emotional Intelligence made better decisions and were less likely to use alcohol, drugs, and food as a way to self-medicate and handle unresolved emotional issues. Continual unresolved emotional issues cause a great deal of physical and mental stress, which can take its toll on your overall health. Learn how to address your feelings and emotions, and your physical health gets a giant boost. The less stress you feel, the more you can focus on the positive goals you want to achieve.

Developing More Complex Relationships

What has been developed, whether low or high Emotional Intelligence, in school, will be a good indication of what to expect as you begin to seek more complex personal and professional relationships. Those with higher Emotional Intelligence are more likely to build secure, stable, and more satisfying interpersonal relationships, says a study by Yale professors Mayer and Salovey, in 1999 study.

It stands to reason, that when you have a high Emotional Intelligence, you are more able to avoid arguments and fights with your significant other. Your outlook on life is more positive, and you are in touch with yours and your partner's feelings. Most people with high Emotional Intelligence are less aggressive and have a calm, peaceful manner, which is much more conducive to a long-term, rewarding relationship.

Emotional Intelligence in the Workplace

Emotionally Intelligent people tend to make better choices when they decide on a career path, so they avoid much of the job-hopping and career changes that plague others whose decisions are impaired by emotions and feelings of which they are unaware. The benefit to making positive initial choices is that they experience greater job satisfaction and have more years to climb that ladder of success and to grow into a leadership role that brings with it more power and financial gain.

People enjoy being close to those with high Emotional Intelligence; therefore, they receive greater peer support and higher supervisor reviews. This also brings with it more pay increases and higher commissions. Salespeople with high Emotional Intelligence usually experience less rejection and more sales because they sell with empathy and understanding. It's a proven fact that people buy from those they like, and people like those with high Emotional Intelligence. There is also less burnout experienced by people with high Emotional Intelligence. Their energy levels are higher and they are more positive about their position in life, so there is less complaining and exhaustion at the end of their workday.

Emotionally Intelligent Leaders

Professors Freshman and Rubino, who was also Director of the Health Administration Program at California State University, held a study in 2002, showing that high Emotional Intelligence is a critical component of those in management and leadership roles. They discovered that people with high Emotional Intelligence experienced less turnover in the workplace and benefited from more productivity. When workers are not distracted or discouraged by overbearing and unsupportive leaders, they are much more positive and productive.

Here are a few examples of companies that have significantly benefited by incorporating Emotional Intelligence into their corporate structure.

- Sheraton—when Sheraton decided to include an Emotional Intelligence program, guess what happened? Their market share climbed by a whopping 24 percent.
- Pepsi—as Pepsi began to study the results of executives with high Emotional Intelligence, what they found was that their productivity was 10% greater than those with low Emotional Intelligence. They also discovered that they benefited from 87% less turnover. To put these figures into dollar amounts, what this meant to the Pepsi Corporation was an incredible 3.75 million in value and a 1,000% increase in their return on investment.
- Loreal—Loreal was another company who stepped out to examine what all the fuss was about regarding this Emotional Intelligence thing. What they found when investigating their salespeople was that those with high Emotional Intelligence sold 2.5 million more than those with lower EI.

When managers and leaders focus on good communications and pay attention to and support the feelings of their people, these reported financial gains make perfect sense. Executives who not only pay attention to what is said but also to what is not said, are far ahead of the game. When they can clearly see the stress on the faces of their employees and read the body language of workers who may be suffering from overwork or a lack of recognition, they can remedy these situations before the emotions can negatively impact production.

Managers and leaders who proactively engage their employees instead of reactively trying to put out the fires can spend more time in visionary pursuits that maintain their executives and company position as the industry's top dogs. It's no accident that Pepsi and Loreal have been leaders in their respective industries for over a hundred years. It's by design; it's by incorporating the ideas of those with high Emotional Intelligence that have given them marketplace longevity.

Taking Preventative Measures

As much as high Emotional Intelligence can predict positive outcomes to people's future, it should also be the encouraging element for you to take preventative measures to ensure you experience greater success. If you have suffered setbacks in your relationships or career, isn't it great to know that you can now take preventative measures to put you on a more successful path? Taking just a few minutes from your day to practice thinking about your feelings and how you can apply Emotional Intelligence in your decision making is being proactive in taking preventative measures that can help you to have more positive outcomes.

If you want to be more productive, then deal with the emotions before they deal with you. Do a little preventative maintenance and be one minded. When it's time to think about your feelings, do that. Then, when it's time to work you can do that without being distracted by anger or frustration that interferes with your job.

Ten Way to Prevent Negative Outcomes

1. Speak your mind. Be honest with yourself about your emotions and feelings. Don't interrupt your self-talk with negative comments. Refuse to trivialize your feelings; they are real and they can be used to create more positive outcomes.

2. Live in the present. Stop worrying about yesterday, and give your feelings and emotions your full attention right now. The only time you should think about the past in when making decisions on how to better handle your current feelings. If you practice Emotional Intelligence and you have poor results, give yourself time to improve. Don't quit!

3. Find connections between past emotions and current feelings. How you feel about today is probably a result of what happened to you in the past. Allow yourself to make the connection so that you can prevent more adverse outcomes.

4. Take thought breaks. Make a habit of taking breaks to think—just like some people take a coffee break. It will relax and rejuvenate your mind. You've heard that some executives take power naps. Why not take a thinking nap? Let your mind focus on your feelings and then find a solution to a pressing problem. Decide how to use your feelings to create more positive outcomes in your life.

5. Let your body speak. Listen to what your body is trying to tell you. If you are getting frequent headaches and stomach aches, it might mean that it's time for you to use your Emotional Intelligence and deal with your

feelings in a way that will relieve your body of having to do all the work.

6. Clear your self-perceptions. If you aren't sure you are getting an accurate reading on yourself, ask a trusted friend to help you out with your self-analysis. Take an inventory of your perceptions. Ask a close friend how they perceive you. You might be surprised when you hear what is said.

7. Emotions are powerful. Sometimes, if emotions are not properly dealt with, they express themselves in other ways. One of the ways is in our dreams. You may want to try recording your dreams. What are your dreams trying to tell you? Do you have a recurring dream that might have some significant meaning?

8. Daily inventory. Take a daily inventory of your feelings. This is a good way to begin thinking about your emotions and gaining Emotional Intelligent. Ask yourself how you are feeling today? What is different about today than yesterday? What will be different about tomorrow than today? Doing this allows you to plan how you can create more positive future outcomes.

9. Create a thought journal. If you are having trouble focusing on your feelings, write down your feelings in a reflection journal. There's something about writing that makes your mind slow down and focus.

10. Don't dwell on the negatives. Concentrate on the feelings, not the adverse event or outcome. If the feelings are negative, deal with the feelings—not the event or result of those feelings.

If all this is a bit too touchy-feely for you, if you think that thinking about feelings sounds weak, then consider this. Scientists, professors, national speakers and authors, even presidents have used Emotional Intelligence to achieve greatness. There was nothing soft about their positions or methods of leadership. Those same leaders with high Emotional Intelligence have helped us treat severe mental illness, taught us physics and calculus, led their industries in production, written books that helped thousands of people reach peak performance, and led us through wars. You'll be in good company when you chose to use higher Emotional Intelligence.

Conclusion

Thank you for purchasing *Emotional Intelligence: The Complete Step-by-Step Guide on Self-Awareness—Controlling Your Emotions and Improving Your EQ.* We've given you a lot to think about—most importantly, how you can use your Emotional Intelligence to achieve greater successes in your life. Practicing these six steps to success will help you build positive personal and professional relationships, make better decisions, and find greater satisfaction in your career choices. A new and exciting world of opportunity is about to open up to you as you gain Emotional Intelligence.

I hope we have helped to change your perceptions and to think about how to manage your emotions and feelings. Emotions can cripple you or empower you; the choice is yours. The steps you have learned in this book will help you as you journey through some of your unresolved feelings and emotions. If the reading of this book leaves you hungry for more information, you might want to read some of my other works. Check out *Emotional Intelligence: The Definitive Guide to Understanding Your Emotions, How to Improve Your EQ and Your Relationships,* and *Emotional Intelligence Mastery: How to Master Your Emotions, Improve Your EQ, and Massively Improve Your Relationships.*

Obviously, there is a recurring theme in these works, and that is my belief that emotions and feelings matter. Feelings are core to our most basic needs. Feelings drive us, motivate us, and inspire us to achieve. Emotions created by those feelings also have tremendous influence in our life's outcome. Emotions in themselves are not good or bad; it's how we deal with them that determines whether they have a positive or negative impact. The important thing for you to remember is that you are in the driver's seat. The feelings belong to you. Either you chose to control your emotions, or you chose to let them control you. What's it going to be?

We are all born with different degrees of Emotional Intelligence, just as we are born with different levels of IQ. Even though our Emotional Intelligence is inherent, it doesn't mean it cannot be increased and improved. That's what this book was all about, adopting ways to create high Emotional Intelligence. You are now victim to your knowledge. After reading this book, it will be most difficult for you to return to an emotionally devoid life. Having journeyed with me through the pages of this book, the most logical progression will be to put these six steps into action and follow these proven strategies to lead you to a greater empathy and understanding of yours and others emotions and feelings.

As you focus on your future of higher Emotional Intelligence, I look forward to hearing from you about all the positive outcomes you'll be experiencing. It will also be interesting to hear you share your feelings and emotions about all the unexpected things that will happen to you along the way. The growth won't be immediate and you'll have your share of challenges, but your increased Emotional Intelligence will help you to weather the storms that working through some of these emotions may create.

Don't wait to work on the steps presented in this book; do it today. As soon as you finish reading, set this book down and take a moment or two to reflect on your feelings. Ask yourself how you are feeling after having finished the book. Where do you expect this information to take you? What do you think will change when you begin to practice more Emotional Intelligence in your personal and professional life?

Don't be surprised when your friends and family members notice a real difference in your manner and outlook. Basque in the added attention you will receive when you put these steps to work for you and begin to make choices and decision based on sound emotions and feelings.

I hope you're ready to enjoy all the benefits of increasing your Emotional Intelligence, of becoming more aware of yours and others feelings, and reaping the rewards in store for you as you move through life with more empathy and understanding. Who knows, sharing your feelings might become so second nature to you that you'll want to share how you felt as you read these books and encourage others to read them as well.

Thank you for taking the time to read this book. If you believe it helped you to get in touch with your feelings and emotions, to gain more knowledge about how to improve your Emotional Intelligence, please take just a few more moments to post a review on amazon. It would be so appreciated, and you'd be in a position to help others raise their Emotional Intelligence as well.

Thank you once again, and congratulations on all the improved relationships, better decisions, and greater opportunities I know you will experience after having practiced these six steps to improve your Emotional Intelligence.

Emotional Intelligence

21 Most Effective Tips and Tricks on Self-Awareness, Controlling Your Emotions, and Improving Your EQ

Introduction

Do you get stressed easily? Do you have difficulty asserting yourself and your needs? Do you often make assumptions? Do you do everything to assert that assumption? Do you hold a grudge? Do you get into a lot of arguments? Do you often feel misunderstood? Do you have a hard time understanding other people? Do you think that other people are just too sensitive? Do you refuse to listen to other people's point of view? Do you blame other people for your mistakes? If you answered yes to most of these questions, you may have low emotional intelligence.

People with emotional intelligence are not afraid of change. They are not afraid to ask tough questions. They are patient and yet persistent. They also easily develop relationships that are based on trust and respect. They are also able to resolve conflicts positively.

Today, it's not enough to have a high IQ to succeed, you need to have high emotional intelligence, too. According to leading psychologists, emotional intelligence affects performance. It has a huge impact on your professional success. A study conducted by TalentSmart shows that emotional intelligence or IE (popularly known as EQ) is the biggest predictor of job performance. That's because emotional intelligence is the foundation of all critical skills – empathy, anger management, assertiveness, flexibility, accountability, communication, presentation skills, and stress tolerance. Over ninety percent of the people who are doing well at work also have high emotional intelligence. A study also shows that people with high emotional intelligence earn more money. There's no job that does not require high emotional intelligence.

Hence, every individual should develop the mature emotional intelligence skills needed to better empathize, understand, and deal with other people.

The good news is that emotional intelligence is something that you could develop over time. This book contains practical and easy to follow steps that will help increase your emotional intelligence.

In this book, you'll learn:

What emotional intelligence is

Traits of people with high emotional intelligence

Traits of people with low emotional intelligence

21 practical tips that will help you increase your emotional intelligence

How to set personal boundaries

How to get to know yourself deeply

How to increase your optimism and resilience

Real stories of people with low and high emotional intelligence

30 empathy statements

100 techniques to help you beat stress

And more!

Emotional intelligence helps you make good life decisions – in a sense, it helps increase the quality of your life.

It's time to get out of the emotional roller coaster that you're in. This book will help you understand and manage your emotions. This book will help increase your self-control, conscientiousness, adaptability, motivation, and trustworthiness. Most of all, this book helps you understand other people more so that you can build deeper and more meaningful relationships

Thanks again for purchasing this book and I hope that you enjoy it.

The Truth About Emotional Intelligence

We all know what IQ is – it is the measurement of your intelligence. Having a high IQ is like having a high cognitive capital in the information economy. It helps you solve problems and learn things quickly. It also helps you overcome attention disorders. High IQ is associated with occupational status and success, perceptual abilities, emotional sensitivity, artistic preference, altruism, achievement motivation, linguistic abilities, and practical knowledge.

But, many experts say that having a high IQ is not enough. You also need to have high emotional intelligence to thrive in this modern world.

Emotional intelligence is often referred to as EI or EQ (emotional quotient). The term was popularized by Daniel Coleman in his 1995 book entitled *"Emotional Intelligence"*. Since then, the word "emotional intelligence" has become a buzzword amongst psychology and behavioral science experts.

EQ is defined as the ability to identify and understand our own emotions and those of others. Emotional intelligence is associated with important life skills such as self-management, social awareness, ability to beat stress, accountability, listening skills, open-mindedness, communication skills, trustworthiness, conscientiousness, self-motivation, and likeability.

To understand this definition better, let's take a look at the case of Jackie – a middle manager of a software development company. She's got a degree at Harvard University and she's exceptionally intelligent. She has a strong passion for coding and she can create and read codes in multiple languages.

She's driven and she has the ability to drive excellence. She definitely has high IQ. But, her life is out of balance. She's too obsessed with work that she compromises her relationships and health. She also lacks humility. She believes that she's the only one who can do it all so she micromanages her employees.

She doesn't listen to her employees and she dismisses ideas that are not her own. She also lacks empathy and has no accountability. When things go wrong, she looks for an escape goat – someone to blame for her mistakes and shortcomings. She's close-minded and she steals credits for completed tasks and projects. She bullies her employees into seeing things her way.

Because of this, she is unable to get the best from her people. She fires people at whim and often engage in a power struggle with her co-managers. When she's stressed, she lashes out on her team. The firm was sued for emotional torts such as intentional infliction of distress on employees, defamation, and abuse of process. Jackie's boss didn't have a choice but to let her go.

Jackie has low emotional intelligence. People with low intelligence are impatient and they often feel like other people don't get their point. They think that being liked at work is unnecessary and overrated. They do not understand how other people feel and they try to downplay other people's feelings. They have a hard time maintaining a good relationship and can't cope with negative emotions. They lack accountability and empathy. They have the tendency to trivialize emotions in general. They lack compassion and they like to play games.

Now, let's look at another person with low emotional intelligence – Christine. She's a computer programmer. She's generally a nice person to the point that she allows people to take advantage of her. She's unable to say no, so she spreads herself too thin. She also easily gets overwhelmed and stressed. She's also close-minded and not open to new ideas. She constantly interrupts other people and she has poor listening skills.

Although she's the goody-goody type, Christine is unable to forgive. Five years ago, his fiancé, Kurt, left her at the altar. It's been five long years, but Christine is still bitter. She's unable to establish new relationships. She's also prone to emotional breakdown when exposed to stressful situations. She's stuck in a job that she doesn't like for five years because she doesn't like change. She's afraid to try new things and step out of her comfort zone. She expects the worst in every situation.

Like Jackie, Christine has low emotional intelligence. People with low emotional intelligence are often pessimistic and they invalidate other people's joy. They often need rules to feel secure. They are rigid, inflexible, and afraid to try something new. They carry grudges and they are unforgiving. They often present themselves as a victim.

Now, take a look at Ann's story. Ann was born to a poor family. Her parents didn't have enough money to send her to college. So, Ann had to work at McDonald's to send herself to college. It was difficult, but she was persistent. She wanted to get out of poverty so she worked hard. After graduating from college, she was hired as a junior manager in a software development company.

Ann was well-liked because she listened to her subordinates. She let her team have time to rest. She was good at reading cues and body language. She used these skills to motivate and influence her team. Because of this, her software development team consistently did well and Ann was eventually promoted to vice president in just three years with the company.

Ann has the ability to identify her emotions. She knows when she's stressed so she uses healthy ways to reduce her stress — she runs, plays instruments, and writes in a journal. She also uses humor to deal with challenges and difficult situations. She has a good balance of work and recreation. She doesn't hold grudges and she deals with conflict in a calm manner. She puts herself in other people's shoes.

Because of this, she's well-liked at work. Ann is confident enough to know that she's good at her work. But, she's humble enough to know that she can't do it all. She knows when to delegate, but she doesn't simply pass the responsibility to her subordinates. She constantly checks on her people to make sure that they are well taken cared of.

People with high emotional intelligence are aware of their emotions. They know what makes them happy, sad, frustrated, stressed, and tired. Because of this, they are able to manage their emotions and respond to them accordingly.

Emotions are neither good or bad. But, they are either appropriate or inappropriate. They are also either negative or positive. Anger, for example, is a negative emotion, but getting angry is not necessarily a bad thing. Anger helps you identify your personal boundaries. It helps you point out the things that you are not willing to tolerate. But, lashing out at someone who tripped over your shoes is a bit inappropriate, to say the least.

Let's look at another emotion — happiness. It's a positive emotion. In its purest form, it is neither good or bad. It's just an emotion. But, if you feel happy when someone else fails, your happiness is definitely inappropriate.

Emotionally intelligent people express emotions that are appropriate to the situation. They are able to interpret and respond appropriately to their own emotions. They also have the ability to recognize and respond appropriately to other people's emotions.

People with high emotional intelligence are compassionate, but they are also assertive. They do not allow other people to walk all over them or disrespect their time. They are humble, but they are also aware of their value. They express their feelings clearly and directly. They also have the ability to balance emotions with reality, logic, and reason. They do not sweat over the small stuff and they definitely do not shout at waiters for bringing the wrong order. Negative emotions such as fear or anxiety do not cripple them.

Emotionally competent people are often optimistic, but also realistic. They are interested in other people's emotions. They are resilient and they stay strong even when faced with challenges and adversity.

According to Daniel Coleman, there are five key areas of emotional intelligence – self-awareness, motivation, self-regulation, empathy, and social skills.

Self-Awareness

We are always told to cultivate self-awareness. Sadly, not all of us are aware of who we are.

According to wise Chinese philosophers, self-awareness is the strongest weapon that you can use to defend yourself from your enemies. When you have a strong sense of who you are, it's difficult for other people to manipulate you.

Self-awareness is also linked to humility. When you have an accurate assessment of who you are, you'll know that the world does not revolve around you. When you are aware of who you are, it is easier to become who you want to be.

Self-awareness helps you live up to your full potential. It helps you exercise compassion and self-care.

Empathy

Empathy is the ability to put other people's shoes. It is the ability to understand other people's feelings and experiences. It helps you understand people better and it improves your cultural competence. It improves your leadership skills as it's a tool that you can use to motivate others.

Empathy is probably the most important skill that you can develop. It allows you to treat people the way they want you to treat them. It is important because it allows you to build meaningful relationships. It helps you deal with interpersonal conflict and helps reduce tensions.

Social Skills

Do you avoid speaking to others? Do you talk only about yourself? Do you often talk down to others? Do you lack patience? Do you find it hard to listen to others? Do you find it hard to compromise? Do you overthink other people's responses when you are in a social gathering? Do you find it hard to find common ground with most people? Are you unpopular? Do you say the wrong things all the time? Do you hate being around many people? Do you find it hard to understand social norms? Do you look at your phone when you're talking to someone?

If you answered yes to most of these questions, chances are, you lack social skills. Having great social skills helps you build meaningful relationships. It increases your efficiency because you don't have to avoid people you don't like so much. It allows you to establish a flourishing career.

People with high EQ are social butterflies, so they are generally likeable. They are patient. They are also open to new ideas. They smile when speaking to others. They are generally friendly and accommodating. They also listen before they speak.

Emotional Management

Do you often experience a nervous breakdown when exposed to extreme stress? Do you have persistent feelings of guilt? Do you have unreasonable fears? Do you have a hard time controlling your anger? If you have a hard time controlling negative emotions such as guilt, stress, fear, and anger, you definitely have low EQ.

But, how important is it to control your emotions? To illustrate the importance of emotional management, let's look at Walter's story, an electronic engineer. He is generally a good guy. He loves his family and he's a hard worker, too. But, Walter is also emotionally unstable. He's moody. He also has a tendency to get violent when he loses his temper. He gets angry over little things.

One day, his wife, Fern, took out Walter's toolbox and borrowed his hammer to do simple woodwork. But, she forgot to return it. After a long day at work, Walter found his hammer lying on the floor. Now, an emotionally stable person would just pick up the hammer and let this pass. But, Walter is an emotional mess. He got so angry that his hammer was not in the right place that he hit his wife over it. Devastated, Fern left Walter and took their two kids with her.

The ability to manage your emotions will help you handle conflicts in a healthier way. It increases your logical reasoning and inner peace. It also allows you to resist emotional manipulation. It helps you stay cool even when someone is pushing your buttons.

Let's take a look at the life of a lovely and emotionally stable woman, named Kylie, who works at an advertising firm. Her work is really cool and exciting. She consistently performed well and was up for promotion. This angered her more senior colleagues. Her co-workers tried to provoke her to derail her focus. They tried to make her feel worthless and unworthy by talking down to her and spreading rumors about her.

Fortunately, Kylie has high EQ. She is aware of her emotional triggers so it's easy for her to control her emotions when provoked. When her co-workers say off-handed remarks, she takes a deep breath and tries to ignore. She doesn't take these statements personally. She understands that these remarks are just a result of her colleagues' jealousy and limiting beliefs. She tries to walk away from things and situations that make her feel uncomfortable.

Self-motivation

It's hard to wake up in the morning when you're not motivated, you'll feel tired and depressed all the time. You'll have a hard time finishing your tasks and achieving your goal.

Let's take a look at the life of Karen, a student of medicine. She's brilliant and she wanted to be a doctor since she was a kid. She was determined to turn that dream into reality. But, something happened during her second year in med school. Her brother was diagnosed with a rare disease. The doctor could not do anything to save him. After six months of struggle, her brother died. It crushed Karen's heart. She didn't know where to go or what to do. Everything seemed bleak. She quit med school and worked as a medical transcriptor.

She does not perform well at her work. She always makes mistakes. She's passive and she constantly procrastinates. Many of her colleagues think that she's lazy. But, the truth is, she just lacks motivation.

If you seem stuck in life, you may lack self-motivation – the inner fire that fuels your desire for achievement. So, in a sense, it helps you win at life. It increases your personal satisfaction and helps you fulfill your potential.

All facets of emotional intelligence (social skills, self-awareness, self-regulation, self-motivation, and empathy) are equally important. To thrive in life, you need to have the ability to recognize your emotions and regulate them. You also need to increase your motivation to reach your full potential. And most of all, you must have empathy and social skills to build deep and meaningful relationships.

Emotional intelligence is the most powerful tool that you can use to handle the most uncomfortable situations. If you're a customer service representative, emotional intelligence helps you deal with difficult customers. If you're a soldier, you can use your EI or EQ to increase your mental strength amidst the chaos and violence around you. If you're a leader, EI helps you build relationships with your subordinates and create a unified culture of tolerance and optimism.

Whoever you are and whatever you do, you need to have high emotional intelligence to thrive and succeed in life.

Tip #1: Develop A Strong Sense of Who You Are

There's one person that we spend most of our days with - ourselves. Yet, it's an irony that most of us don't know ourselves very well.

To effectively manage your emotions, you must have a strong sense of who you are. You should have a clear understanding of your strengths, weaknesses, traits, likes, and dislikes. You must know what makes you tick and what makes you snap.

To know more about yourself, practice writing down everything that you know about yourself so far:

What kind of a person are you?

What makes you sad?

What makes you happy?

Who makes you happy?

Are you a cheerful person?

What makes you leap out of bed?

Do you like helping others?

Knowing yourself does not only increase your emotional intelligence, it also allows you to make good life decisions. It keeps you from making bad decisions. It allows you to identify your passions and do the things that are important to you.

Self-awareness allows you to regulate your emotions. It

increases resiliency – an invisible trait that allows you to bounce back whenever you get knocked down by challenges.

Funny girl Amy Poehler said, *"You attract the right things when you have a sense of who you are"*. You cannot achieve great things unless you know who you really are. Self-knowledge is also the starting point of self-improvement.

To illustrate this point, let's study the story of Edward - a young lawyer. He's a brilliant man, but he does not know who he is. Until now, he has no sense of who he is. He does things just to fit in.

He engages with people pleasing behavior. He is not aware of his values and what's important to him. Thus, he is unable to resist flattery and other forms of manipulation.

When he graduated from law school, he was hired as an associate in a big law firm. At that time, he did not know what his priorities were. He built a career protecting criminals. When he turned 60, he was rich and successful, but he felt empty. He did not know what he stood for, he wasn't able to find his purpose in life, and at his deathbed, all he got were regrets.

Self-awareness is one of the most valuable assets that you can have. It helps you play with your strengths and adapt to any situation. It also allows you to identify your weakness.

There are five building blocks that make up who you are – your values, interests, temperament, life mission, and personal strengths.

Values are defined as general preferences of outcomes and appropriate actions. Your values reflect on what's right and wrong. Your values to influence your behavior and attitudes.

To know what your values are, look at the list below and check the box next to the values are important to you:

☒ Respect		☒ Credibility	
☒ Poise		☒ Devotion	
☒ Openness		☐ Elegance	
☒ Loyalty		☒ Empathy	
☐ Reputation		☒ Flexibility	
☒ Balance		☒ Honor	
☒ Beauty		☒ Independence	
☒ Boldness		☒ Intimacy	
☒ Creativity		☒ Keeness	
☐ Fame		☒ Leadership	
☒ Humor		☒ Knowledgeable	
☒ Honesty		☒ Maturity	
☒ Love		☒ Passion	
☐ Influence		☒ Persistence	
☐ Acceptance		☒ Playfulness	
☒ Ambition		☒ Precision	
☒ Calmness		☒ Prudence	
☒ Cheerfulness		☐ Restfulness	
☒ Clarity		☒ Dedication	

- ☒ Cooperation
- ☒ Forgiveness
- ☒ Tolerance
- ☒ Integrity
- ☒ Effort
- ☒ Self-control
- ☐ Sacrifice
- ☐ Simplicity
- ☒ Sophistication
- ☒ Tactfulness
- ☒ Gratitude
- ☒ Trustworthiness
- ☒ Variety
- ☒ Vigor
- ☒ Zeal

- ☐ Wisdom
- ☒ Wholesomeness
- ☒ Authenticity
- ☐ Zest
- ☐ Worthiness
- ☐ Victory
- ☒ Valor
- ☐ Traditionalism
- ☐ Thoroughness
- ☒ Temperance
- ☒ Success
- ☐ Strength
- ☒ Stability
- ☐ Spirituality
- ☐ Spontaneity

To live a fulfilling life, you must know what your values are. Do you cooperate with others? Is integrity important to you? Are you honest or do you lie a lot? Do you go to church? Do you say "thank you" when someone tries to do a nice thing for you?

Interest

Your interests include your hobbies and passions – activities that you like doing and things that you are curious about. To find out what your interests are, sit on a chair and take a deep breath. Then think about the things that concerns you. Are you concerned about the environment or fitness? Are you into farming? Do you like to spend your days in a gym? Do you like to write your thoughts and feelings? Do you like to create arts and crafts? What makes you forget about the time?

Temperament

Your temperament is your nature. It describes how you react and respond to the world. It is the foundation of your personality. Your temperament is not a passing mood or attitude. It remains constant throughout your life even when your personality changes.

There are four temperaments, namely:

1. Sanguine

Leona is a customer service representative at a designer store and she's good at her job. She takes care of her customers. She's friendly and accommodating. She's bold and brave. She once tried jumping off the plane (sky diving, of course) She also swam with the whale sharks when she was a teenager. Although Leona is intelligent, success is not that important to her. She just wants to have fun. Leona is a sanguine.

Sanguines are social butterflies. They like to be around people and they are generally easy to be around. They are optimistic, warm, people-oriented, and compassionate. They are flashy and bubbly. They have a good sense of humor and they are generally the life of the party.

Sanguines are pleasure-seekers. They crave for all good things in life. This could lead to credit card debts or becoming overweight. They are also unable to commit to anything as they prefer spontaneity over structure. They are more of a talker than a listener. They are expressive, dramatic, and they constantly love to be in the spotlight. They are naturally extroverted, so they flourish in the marketing, fashion, and entertainment industry. They also excel in team sports.

2. Melancholic

Melancholics are perfectionists. They are idealists and they have unrealistically high standards. They constantly criticize themselves and others. They are neurotic and they constantly overanalyze things and situations. They plan and think before they act. They also complain a lot and they are pessimistic. They always assume the worst.

They are naturally introverted and they prefer keeping an inner circle of a few trusted friends. They can be selfish, possessive, and intense. They are also very emotional – they are easily hurt and they can be moody. They are calm, but self-confident. They also pay attention to details.

Vincent Van Gough, Marie Curie, Albert Einstein, and Audrey Hepburn all have melancholic temperament. Accounting, management, and social work are perfect careers for people with melancholic temperament.

3. Choleric

Calista was born to a poor family in Queens. Her parents did not have enough money to send her to school, but she was persistent. When she was ten years old, she promised herself that she'll rise out of poverty. She worked on odd jobs to send herself to business school. Then, she built a manufacturing business from the ground up. She's driven and she would not let anyone stand in her way to success.

Calista became a millionaire before she turned 30. Although she's extremely attractive and wealthy, she's not likeable. She's bossy and she manipulates people to achieve her goals. She's extremely self-centered and she can be cruel. She has a low tolerance for bad performance. Calista has a choleric temperament.

Choleric people are irritable and short-tempered. They are goal-oriented, strong-willed, and decisive. They are well-organized and they are typically high achievers. They are persistent and they are great at handling emergency situations. They are also decisive and conceited.

People with choleric temperament are usually successful at whatever they do. But they can be arrogant and rude. They have the tendency to use other people to achieve their goals.

Vladimir Lenin, Alexander Hamilton, and Donald Trump all have choleric personality types.

4. Phlegmatic

Phlegmatic people are reserved, non-chalant, and relaxed. They are the walking definition of the word "chill". They have a good sense of humor and peaceful.

Phlegmatic leaders do not move as swiftly as choleric leaders, but they are more effective most of the time. They are great mediator. They are deliberate and it usually takes a while before they can make a decision. They are persistent and they are generally emotionally stable, empathetic, well-behaved, and trustworthy.

But, phlegmatic people tend to be indecisive and submissive. They find it hard to say no. They do not have the desire to win, they just want peace. They just want to lead a steady, calm, and quiet life. They do not stand out and they have the tendency to be self-righteous. They can be judgmental and passive-aggressive. They thrive industries like business management, programming, engineering, math, and technology.

Walt Disney, Bill Gates, Steve Wozniak, Abraham Lincoln, and Nikola Tesla are a few of the famous phlegmatic people.

Personal Strengths and Weakness

Your personal strengths consist of your talents, abilities, skills, and favorable personality traits. To get to know yourself better, you must be aware of your personal strengths. Are you intelligent, brave, or clever? Are you inspiring, logical, responsible, spontaneous, and persistent? What makes you lose track of time? What are the things that you can do effortlessly?

Doing an inventory of your personal strengths from time to time does not only increase your self-awareness. It also increases your self-confidence.

Nobody's perfect, so you must have a string of your personal weakness, too. Having a clear understanding of your weaknesses helps you grow. Are you reckless, messy, disorganized, or insensitive? Do you often procrastinate? Are you lazy and undisciplined?

Once, you have a clear understanding of your strengths and weaknesses, it's easier for you to focus on your areas of improvement. This understanding also allows you to keep doing what you're good at. If you're great at writing codes, it may be a good idea for you to become a computer programmer.

Life Mission

A life without purpose is an empty life. Everyone of us have a goal or a life mission. To live a happy life, you must be aware of what your life mission is and focus your energy in fulfilling that mission.

To identify your life mission, answer the following questions:

1. What do you want to achieve in five or ten years?

2. What areas of your life do you want to change?

3. What activities make you happy?

4. What makes you feel energized?

5. What activities make you lose track of time?

6. What makes you feel good about yourself?

7. What are you naturally good at?

8. What's your deepest desire?

9. What are your deepest values?

Sit on a chair and close your eyes. Then, visualize what your ideal life looks like. Just let your thoughts flow. Usually these visions reveal your desires, purpose, and mission.

Self-awareness is one of the best weapons that you can use against all the evils in the world. If you know who you are, it's easier for you to achieve your dreams and set boundaries. It's also easier for you to establish more meaningful relationships.

Tip #2: Reflect on Your Own Emotions

To increase your emotional intelligence, you must accurately identify your emotions. To do this, you need to go beyond the obvious to identify your feelings. Anger, for example, is an emotion that's characterized by antagonism. It is an intense emotion that increases your heart rate and elevates your blood pressure. We usually feel angry when someone crosses the line. But, we often mistake anger for other negative emotions such as frustration, impatience, annoyance, and irritation.

When you're feeling intense anger, ask yourself if you're really angry or you're simply grumpy, hungry, defensive, annoyed, irritated, or offended?

Like anger, sadness is also a general emotion. When you feel sad, you may be disillusioned, dismayed, paralyzed, disappointed, or regretful.

When you feel something, take time to think what that emotion really is. Are you hurt or jealous? Are you anxious or stressed? Are you happy or just simply thankful?

To improve your EQ, you must be able to precisely determine your feelings. You must also able to identify the intensity of your emotion and how you respond to certain situations.

How do you respond when:

- You get an angry email from your boss.
- When your spouse or lover blames you for something that's not your fault.
- When your co-worker cries unexpectedly.
- When you're tired after a long day at work.

- When another driver cuts you off on the road.
- When you move into a new home.
- When you get fired.
- When you don't have enough cash to pay your bills.
- When your kids get sick.
- When you are hungry.
- When you are reminded of a traumatic childhood memory.
- When you run into an ex-lover who hurt you deeply.

When you're aware of your emotions, you can easily manage them. So, take a few minutes every day to simply identify your emotions and analyze how you respond to them.

Tip #3: Pay Attention to Your Emotional Body Language

Your body is your temple. It is the most valuable possession you'll ever have. It is also your emotional compass. If you have a hard time identifying your emotions, you've got to listen to what your body is telling you. You have to pay attention to your emotional body language.

Here's a list of the common emotions and how your body reacts to them:

1. Anger

You normally clench your fist when you're angry. Your heart rate increases and you'll feel heat in your face and neck. You'd also clench your jaws and may feel headache and stomach ache.

2. Jealousy

That stomach pain that you've been experiencing lately may be caused by your inner green-eyed monster. Jealousy increases your blood pressure. It also causes pain in your gut by increasing the production of flight or fight hormones such as noradrenaline and adrenaline.

3. Sadness

Harry has gained weight in the last six months. He has been eating non-stop. He thought that he was just hungry. But, the truth is, Harry was depressed. He's struggling with emotional isolation and loneliness for a long time. He's in a rabbit hole and his only friend was food.

If you're sad, you'll feel a variety of negative symptoms. You'll feel headaches, back pains, muscle pain, exhaustion, and chest pains. You'll also experience weight gain.

4. Happiness

When you're happy, you feel giddy inside. It's like you're sliding on rainbows or floating in the air. Happiness is a positive emotion with positive physical symptoms. Studies show that happiness increases longevity. When you're happy, your muscles relax, and you have an open body language.

5. Fear

Fear is a powerful emotion that slowly kills your spirit and keeps you from living the life that you deserve.

When you're afraid, you do your best to stay in your comfort zone. This can keep you from growing and becoming the best that you could ever be. You say yes even when you mean no. You also procrastinate because you're afraid of rejection, judgment, uncertainty, criticism, and even success. You also get paralyzed and unable to make a decision.

When you're afraid, you'll experience different physical symptoms such as trembling, sweating, rapid heartbeat, dry mouth, nausea, clenched mouth, fidgeting, wide eyes, sweaty palms, dilated pupils, increase in blood pressure, and tensed muscles.

6. Shame

Shame is a strong negative emotion that can destroy your self-confidence and self-esteem. It is a dangerous emotion that can lead to inferiority complex. It also keeps you from living a free and happy life.

When you feel shame, your face is flushed and you are unable to maintain eye contact. You may also slouch.

7. Guilt

Are you often sleepless at night? Do you avoid the people you think you've wronged? Do you avoid eye contact? Are you often anxious and nervous? If you answered yes to most of these questions, you may be guilty of something.

Guilt increases your heart rate. It causes nausea and increases your body temperature. You may also have a bad posture.

Your body is your temple and your emotional compass. You should take care of it and you should listen to it.

Tip #4: Know When Enough is Enough

Vivian is a brilliant optometrist. She's kind and compassionate. But, she's also kind of a doormat. She has the intense need for approval. She's afraid to make mistakes and she does whatever she can to avoid conflict. She allows people to walk all over her. She feels that people only call her when they need her. She has no boundaries and so she ends up spreading herself too thin. Then, one day, she got fed up and had a nervous breakdown. She fell down the rabbit hole and unable to get out of it.

To thrive in life, you should know what you would and would not tolerate. You should draw the line.

People with high EQ know who they are. They know what they will and will not accept. To increase your emotional intelligence, you should know when enough is enough. You should be able to establish boundaries by following these steps:

1. **You should develop a healthy respect for yourself.**

Hey, you are important, too. Your needs are important, too. You should know that you're a valuable person. Take care of yourself and do not let other people define who you are. You should take responsibility and accountability for your life.

2. **You should name your limits.**

We all have limits. You can't set personal boundaries if you are not aware of what you can and cannot tolerate. Take time to identify your spiritual, physical, emotional, and mental limits.

How do you feel about lending money to your friends? Are you comfortable when someone touches you in a sexual way? Do you feel uncomfortable when someone shoves their spiritual beliefs down your throat?

3. Do not take responsibility for other people's emotions.

To live a happy and drama-free life, you should avoid taking responsibility for other people's emotions. You are not responsible for other people's drama and emotions. So, avoid giving unsolicited advice and do not feel guilty for other people's misfortunes.

4. Call out people who cross your personal boundaries.

If you feel that your co-worker or your spouse is not respecting your time, call him/her out. Communicate your boundaries with the people around you in a calm and dignified manner.

5. Stay away from people who do not respect your boundaries.

Some people would continuously cross your boundaries and if this happens, you've got to stay away. To increase your emotional intelligence and improve your mental health, you have to avoid people who don't respect your boundaries, time, and values.

Being aware of personal boundaries make it easier for you to manage your emotions. It also increases your self-esteem and self-respect.

Tip #5: Shift Your Focus Away From Yourself and Focus on Others

We all live inside an imaginary bubble. We all have our own world. We have the tendency to just focus on ourselves – our thoughts, needs, regrets, and sadness.

To increase your emotional intelligence, you should try to shift your focus away from yourself and focus on others.

1. Reduce your need for approval. You need to drop your "please validate and notice me" mentality.

2. Take time to observe the people around you – their posture, facial expressions, and tone of voice. This will help you identify what they're feeling.

3. In this modern world, we are all taught not to give a damn about other people. But, it is important to give a damn. To increase your emotional intelligence, it's important to try to understand other people.

4. Be there for others when you're needed. Take time to listen to the people you care about.

5. Pay attention to overall appearance. Take time to notice other people's appearance. Are they wearing casual clothes? Or are they wearing power suits? People who dress for success are usually ambitious while people who wear casual clothes are more spirited and laid back.

6. Check the posture. People who hold their head high are confident and are happier with their lives. But, in some

cases, these people may also have a big ego. People who slouch usually lack self-esteem or may be depressed.

7. Observe their movements for they say a lot about their emotions, beliefs, and perceptions. If a person leans towards you, it means he likes you. If a person is hiding his hands, it means that he is lying or hiding something. If you see someone biting his lips or nails, he might be anxious, worried, or under pressure.

8. To get to know other people better and connect to them, you have to habitually observe their movements and facial expressions. A happy person tends to smile or laugh while a sad person's mouth may be slightly turned down, like a pout.

Here's a list of common microexpressions and movements associated with emotions:

- Anger – aggressive body language, walking with exaggerated swinging of arms, disapproving frowns, clenching fist, sudden movements, snarling, flushed face.
- Anxiety – cold sweat, fidgeting, voice tremors, shaking, no eye contact, high pulse, crossed arms, damp eyes, trembling lips, and pale face.
- Shame – flushed face or false smile.
- Happiness – smiling, bright eyes, relaxation of muscles, and open body language.
- Surprise – open mouth, wide eyes, backward movement, and raised eyebrows.

People around you are fighting battles that you know nothing about. To empathize with other people and fully understand them, you have to be curious about other people's feelings.

Being curious about other people's feelings can help you build deeper connections and it allows you to empathize with them.

In your office, observe your co-workers – how they dress, their posture, the tone of their voice, and their disposition. Are they smiling? Do they have aggressive body language? How do they speak? Pay attention to verbal and non-verbal cues.

Tip #6: Stop Peddling Your Soul for A Pay Check

Stress is a silent killer. It can keep you from living the life that you want and deserve. It can destroy your health, too. Too much stress can take a toll on your emotional health and could significantly decrease your emotional intelligence.

So, to increase your emotional intelligence, you've got to stop selling your soul for a pay check.

If your work is slowly killing you inside, you just have to take a step back. Do you often feel lost? Do you think that you've stopped growing? Are you not happy with your work? If so, then it might be time to quit and get a job that feeds your spirit.

Remember that it's silly to lose your sanity over a job. If you feel that your work is sucking your soul and making you angrier by the minute, you should consider getting a new one. Find a job that excites you and gives you a strong sense of purpose. What do you really want to do? What makes you lose track of time? What do you want to be known for?

Tip #7: Identify Your Emotional Triggers

Emotional triggers are events, people, words, things, and situations that evoke certain emotions.

To effectively manage your emotions, you have to identify what triggers them. Knowing your emotional triggers allow you to balance your emotions and logic. Remember, you can't control other people, their thoughts, actions, and behaviors, but you can control how you react to them.

Not knowing your emotional triggers will make it hard for you to regulate your emotions. It helps you deal with painful emotions in a healthy and dignified manner.

Sit in a chair and take a deep breath. Close your eyes and imagine that you are in the workplace. Someone is asking you to do something that you do not want to do. How do you feel? Do you feel deep resentment? Do you feel anger? Do you feel like you are violated in some ways? Take time to identify and feel your emotions. If you feel an intense and pounding emotion in your chest, then being asked to do something you don't want to do can trigger anxiety and anger.

Take another deep breath. Now, imagine that someone is giving you a gift. Visualize yourself unwrapping the gift. Do you feel loved or appreciated? Do you feel intense gratitude? Do you feel shame, like you don't deserve the gift? Take a minute or two to examine your emotions. Feel those emotions.

Now, think about your pet dog, if you have one. Do you feel happy when you think about your dog? Do you feel guilty? Do you feel worried that you're not taking good care of your pet?

Shift your mind back to your workplace. How do you feel when your co-worker is disrespecting you. Do you feel intense anger? Do you feel like you're going to explode? Do you allow these disrespectful comments to get to you? Do you feel shame? Do you feel small?

Now, let's explore deeper emotional triggers. Imagine that your closest friend landed her dream job. She's now earning six figures a month. Do you feel jealous? Do you feel resentment? Do you feel like you deserve success more than her? Do you feel anxious that you're not where you're supposed to be in life?

Take time to listen to what you feel after you read each phrase. This will help you determine your deepest emotional triggers.

You can also identify your emotional triggers by answering the following questions:

1. *What makes you feel loved?*

2. *What makes you angry?*

3. *What makes you happy? What makes your heart leap with joy?*

4. *What annoys you?*

5. *What makes you afraid?*

6. *What makes you feel guilty? Do you have hidden feelings of guilt?*

7. *What makes you sad?*

8. *What drives you crazy?*

Identifying your emotional triggers gives you a strong sense of control. It allows you to respond appropriately to uncomfortable situations. It also helps you achieve emotional growth and maturity.

Do Not React To Your Emotional Triggers Right Away

To avoid becoming a slave to your emotions, you have to react in a healthy way. If you react to an emotional trigger right away, you may say something that you regret. Take Greg as an example. Greg is an emotionally available bachelor who never met his mother. So all his life, he's craving for a mother's love but he is unaware of this. He is also a successful businessman who has no plans of settling down anytime. He is at a time of his life where he wants to just date women and have fun. Then, he met a woman named Lola.

Lola is a lovely girl and she has a strong maternal instinct. She is kind but she had been heart broken far too many times. After sleeping together for the first time, Lola prepared a hot meal for Greg. He was surprised because no one ever did that before, he was used to eating microwaveable meals. He felt an intense feeling of joy that he cannot control, so he blurted the words "I love you". But, he did not mean those words. He was just caught up in the moment. That awkward moment was the turning point of their relationship. Greg began to pull away and Lola was heartbroken once more.

The best way to control your emotion is to delay your reaction. Delaying your reaction allows you to respond to emotional triggers in a calm and logical manner.

When you hear something that makes you angry, take a deep breath. Do not react right away. Count from one to ten and keep breathing. Think before you open your mouth so you would not say something that you would regret later on.

Tip #8: Learn to Manage Stress

As mentioned earlier in this book, stress decreases your ability to control your emotions. When you're stressed, you're more likely to feel anxious and depressed. You'll have mood swings.

Stress does not only decrease your emotional intelligence, it can also cause serious health problems such as neck pain, tension headaches, anxiety, gastrointestinal problems, obesity, insomnia, chronic fatigue, arthritis, diabetes, and high blood pressure.

To increase your emotional intelligence, you must learn to manage stress. Here's a list of 100 action items that you can do to reduce stress.

- Watch an inspirational movie. You can watch "Life is Beautiful (La Vita e Bella)" or a famous Indian movie called "Three Idiots". These movies give you hope and help you get through a bad day.
- Doodle on a paper using a paint or crayons.
- Get enough sleep. You'll have a problem controlling your emotions if you lack sleep.
- Say "no" more often to avoid spreading yourself too thin.
- Use your time wisely. Stay away from things that waste your time.
- Unclutter your life. Organize your bedroom and your workspace.
- Watch funny videos on YouTube.
- Read an inspirational book.
- Write down quotes from an inspirational book.

- Look at the stars.
- Sing a happy song.
- Whistle. Whistling reduces stress and it makes you happier.
- Make your own travel journal.
- Go to a place you've never been.
- Get to work early.
- Get up early so you have enough time.
- Listen to relaxing music and happy tunes.
- Kiss or hug someone you love.
- Go outside and feel the sun on your face.
- Dance like no one is watching.
- Try aromatherapy. Lavender scent helps reduce stress.
- Get a massage.
- Drink hot tea.
- Do yoga.
- Eat a small piece of dark chocolate.
- Do a digital detox and turn off your smart phone.
- Whenever you feel overwhelmed, take a nap.
- Go swimming as it is extremely relaxing.
- Look at some cat photos.
- Go for a walk.
- Do not trade your sleep for work. Your health is more important than your work.
- Do not create unnecessary drama in your life.
- Do not try to do everything by yourself. Try to get some help whenever needed and learn how to delegate.
- Stop worrying.
- Take a long bath.
- Do something that you're passionate about.
- Simplify your life.
- Always take your bathroom and lunch break.

- Stop smoking.
- Be patient.
- Learn to prioritize.
- Talk to a trusted friend.
- Play with your pet.
- Go to a museum.
- Drink more water.
- Exchange jokes with a friend.
- Grab a quick snack.
- Squeeze a stress ball.
- Drink a glass of orange juice daily.
- Go to a sauna.
- If you have a close relationship with your mom, call her. This helps release stress.
- Close your email. Do not check it for a few days.
- Drink black tea. It is extremely relaxing.
- If you have a toxic job, start looking for a new one.
- Walk to work.
- Eat a bowl of colorful and delicious fruits.
- Float in water.
- Take a trip to the nearest beach.
- Go to a quiet place.
- Just let it all out.
- Do not drink coffee. It makes you feel more agitated.
- Keep a journal and write about your daily experiences.
- Tickle your pet dog or cat.
- Stop a bad habit.
- Make copies of important documents. This will save you a lot of time.
- Buy new clothes. But, do this only once in a while. Shopping therapy is not a good solution to stress.
- Learn a new language or acquire a new skill.

- Buy some art.
- Get a haircut.
- Get some fresh air.
- Walk around the park.
- If you can afford it, go to Iceland. It is one of the most beautiful countries in the world.
- Set priorities. This will save you from stressful situations later on.
- Ask for help.
- Walk in the rain. It feels good.
- Hug a friend for no reason.
- Hum a popular jingle.
- Go on a picnic with a loved one.
- Watch a good movie and eat home-cooked popcorn.
- Praise other people.
- Remember that you always have a choice. You can always get out of a situation that you don't like.
- Stop trying to fix other people.
- Spray vanilla essential oil in your bedroom before you go to sleep.
- Connect with nature as often as you can.
- Move on from anything that no longer serve you.
- Get out of debt.
- Say less and listen more.
- Travel more.
- Laugh every day.
- Pay your credit card every month. This can save you a lot of stress.
- Spray fruity scents.
- Take a salsa class.
- Repaint your room.
- Grow a plant.

- Try surfing.
- Eat a lot of vegetables and fruits.
- Go skiing during the winter season.
- Try skating.
- Aim low. If you set your standards too high, you'll get disappointed too often.

It's easier for you to master and control your emotions when you're relaxed. After a long day at work, kick off your shoes and watch a good movie. It's good for your emotional health.

Tip #9: Learn How to Handle Difficult People

To save your sanity, stay away from toxic people or energy vampires. But, how do you spot these people? These are the most common characteristics of toxic people:

- They tend to be judgmental. They will criticize other people to make them feel bad about themselves.
- They don't apologize when they are wrong.
- They are manipulative.
- They make you work for their approval.
- They are always right.
- They complain constantly.
- They take up too much of your time.
- They create drama.
- They will lie to you constantly.
- They are self-absorbed.
- They play the victim.
- They can be temperamental.
- They lack compassion.
- They treat you poorly.
- They put you down.
- They blame you for their problems.
- They are defensive.
- They do not keep their promises.
- They have anger issues.
- They exploit you.
- They are bitter and vindictive.
- They rush you into doing things.

- They withhold affection.
- They are selfish and stingy.
- Use flattery or money to control you.
- They play games.

To protect your self-esteem, you have to stay away from toxic people and surround yourself with people who love you for who you are. Surround yourself with people who inspire you to become a better person.

It's hard to manipulate you if you have a positive self-image. Having self-confidence increases your power to regulate your emotions.

Tip #10: Bounce Back from Adversity

Resilience is a sign of high emotional intelligence. It is defined as the ability to bounce back from adversity.

Resilience helps you hold on to your dreams, even when faced with difficulties. It helps you move forward from a traumatic event and it keeps you in the driver seat of your life. It helps you take advantage of post-traumatic growth.

Resilience is an invisible muscle that you can develop over time by following these steps:

1. **Derive meaning from a difficult situation.**

This may sound like a cliché, but everything happens for a reason. If you let your emotions get the best of you, you'll never be able to rise up from a traumatic event. You just have to stop and give meaning to what's happening to you.

J.K. Rowling was jobless, depressed, and separated from her husband when she was in her early thirties. She was poor and her mental health was deteriorating. But, she had a big idea and a lot of talent. And so, she wrote the first Harry Potter book. Today, Harry Potter is considered as a literary gem that people of all ages love. If J.K. Rowling succeeded in her office job, she would not have the time to write Harry Potter.

Let's take a look at the story of Elizabeth, a PR executive. Three years ago, Elizabeth's sister died of breast cancer. It really broke her heart, but she chose to make the best out of the situation. She built a foundation for breast cancer patients who can't afford treatment. She met a great man named Harry in one of her fundraising events. They got married a year later.

Remember that there's always a reason why things happen. There's always a reason why we lose the people we love.

2. See your hardship as an opportunity.

Here's the truth, a challenge is an opportunity. It is an opportunity for you to grow and become stronger. It's an opportunity for you to make better decisions, learn from your mistakes, and become wiser.

3. Focus on what you can control.

You can't control everything that happens in your life. This is why it is important to focus on what you can control.

4. Imagine a positive outcome.

Visualization is a powerful tool that you can use to attract your desired outcome. It also gives you hope and it helps you relax during challenging times. So, when you're on the verge of an emotional breakdown, close your eyes and imagine a positive outcome. Imagine yourself rising above your current situation and achieving everything that you could ever hope for in life.

Life kicks our ass every once in a while. So, you've got to develop that invisible muscle called resilience so you would have the strength to fight back.

Tip #11: Control Your Temper

Mel Gibson is a charismatic actor. But, he has serious anger issues. He is a known racist and homophobic. When he got arrested for driving under the influence, he blurted out anti-Semitic remarks. He also has a long history of domestic abuse, calling his ex-wife a gold-digger and a whore.

Mel Gibson is good-looking and talented, but that's not enough to make it in the entertainment industry. You must have good people skills, too. The public had enough of Gibson's rants and temper. So, now, he virtually has no career.

If you want to succeed in life, you have to learn how to control your temper. You can do so by following these tips:

1. Think before you speak. This will keep you from saying things that you will regret later on. It's best to count one to ten before you respond to something that makes you angry.

2. If you think you're going to explode any minute, take a step back and go somewhere quiet. You can also put on a pair of earplugs and listen to good music.

3. Repeat relaxing words such as "take it easy".

4. When you're ready, express your anger in a healthy way. You can scream on a pillow or go for a run to release the negative energy. You can also vent out to a trusted friend. You can also release tension by doing creative activities like painting or dancing.

5. Stop talking about things that make you angry and stay away from things that trigger your anger. Learn to let go of your angry thoughts as they do not serve you.

If your temper is getting out of hand, it may be a good idea to get professional help.

Tip #12: Manage Your Impulses

Impulse control is a powerful emotional intelligence competency that you can use to solve problems and build a successful life. It reflects your ability to show restraint when faced with temptations. It also reflects your ability to control aggression and display irresponsible behavior.

Impulse management increases your credibility and trustworthiness. It also increases your conscientiousness, adaptability, and self-understanding. If you can't control your impulses, you may suffer from the following symptoms:

- Obesity
- Aggression
- Stealing
- Lying
- Depression
- Obsessive thoughts
- Lack of patience
- Anxiety
- Criminal behavior

If you don't have the ability to control your impulses, you have the tendency to jump to conclusions and send emotionally charged text messages or emails.

To control your impulses, you need to:

1. Practice self-discipline. Do not wait until you're in the mood to do things.
2. Eat healthy.

3. You must make a conscious decision to take small actions to bring you closer to your goals. Do you want to run? Run for 10 minutes. Do you have a report due? Write a few paragraphs. The key to self-discipline is to just get started.

4. If you struggle with ADHD, do interval training. Focus on your work for five minutes and then, give yourself five minutes to do something else. Then, increase your work time to ten minutes. Take another five minute break. After the break, focus on your work for 30 minutes. This strategy helps you get started and finish the task at hand.

5. Celebrate your success. Give yourself a cookie after writing a 10,000 word report. You deserve it!

Managing your impulses is not as hard as you think. So, control your impulses now before they control you.

Tip #13: Practice Humility

No one wants likes conceited people. To increase your emotional intelligence and likeability, you must practice humility.

According to studies, humble people exhibit higher self control. They have better work performance, higher grades, and better relationships. They are also less judgmental.

But, what is humility? True humility is not about thinking less of yourself. It is about thinking about yourself less. It is the exact opposite of narcissism and pride. Humble people do not have a problem admitting their mistakes.

If you're a naturally proud person, here's a list of tips that you can use to cultivate humility:

1. Have a clear assessment of your self-worth. Humble people are self-confident, too. They know their worth, so they do not see the need of putting other people down just to validate their importance.

2. Put other people first.

3. Do not speak about yourself too much.

4. Learn to accept feedback.

5. Do not seek admiration.

6. Help other people succeed.

7. Learn from other people.

Humility allows you to easily connect with others. It also increases the level of your happiness.

Tip #14: Find Out Why People Act The Way They Do

Christopher and Celine have been married for two years. They have a great house and they love each other so much. But, they have one problem. Christopher is a jealous man. He gets mad when Celine talks to other men.

Celine cannot understand why Chris is jealous all the time. One day, she had enough of Chris' jealousy so she left him.

But, here's the truth about Chris. When he was in high school, he fell in love with a woman named Taylor. They were together for three years until he caught her in bed with his best friend. It crushed him. He wanted to trust Celine, but the pain caused by Taylor's betrayal was too deep. If Celine took the time to get Chris to open up about Taylor, she could have saved her marriage.

Here's the harsh truth- the world does not revolve around you. You have to stop taking things personally and find out why people act the way that they do. This helps you understand other people at a deeper level. For example, your boss does not micromanage you because you're incompetent. She micromanages her staff because she's afraid of not being in control. Your daughter does not lie because she thinks that you are unworthy of her respect. She lies because she feels inadequate and she's afraid of disappointing you.

Observe other people's behavior and then, take time to identify the root cause behind their behaviors. This does not only increase your emotional intelligence, it also allows you to build deeper and more meaningful relationships.

Tip #15: Learn to Take Constructive Criticisms

Do you go on defensive mode when someone is giving you feedback? Do you have a hard time accepting your weaknesses? If so, you have low emotional intelligence.

Some people would criticize you to put you down and make you feel bad about yourself. But some people would criticize you to help you improve. You should shut out destructive criticisms. But, you must also learn to take constructive criticisms.

When, someone's giving you a feedback, you need to follow these tips:

1. Take a deep breath and listen to every word the other person is saying. Do not dismiss the feedback and try to listen for understanding.

2. Express gratitude and say thank you to the other person for giving you feedback. You can simply say, "I really appreciate that you're taking the time to discuss this matter with me. Thank you for your feedback". This does not mean that you agree with the other person's assessment. It just means that you are mature enough to handle feedback.

3. Do not take the criticism personally. A negative feedback is not an insult. It is just an observation.

4. Ask the person giving you feedback to help on how to improve your weak areas.

5. Create an action plan and present your progress. This way, the other person knows that you are truly working on your areas of improvement.

Remember that constructive criticism is good for you. So, you have to leave your ego at the door and take time to listen to feedback. This allows you to maximize your growth potential.

Tip #16: Practice Empathy

Empathy is a skill that allows you to connect with other people in a much deeper level. It motivates altruism and it allows you to truly care about other people. It builds trust and it helps you develop meaningful friendships.

Here's a list of tips that you can use to develop empathy:

1. Listen.

Listening does not only allow you to establish a profound connection with another person. It also increases your knowledge and it allows you to understand other people's perspective. Listening intensifies the conversation and it also saves money. If your job involves negotiating with other people or a group of people, listening is an important skill to learn because it allows you to overcome resistance. It also helps you make sound decisions.

When you talk to someone, look into his eyes and try to listen to every word he says. Nod while he his talking so he knows that you are really listening to him. If he's relaying an instruction, make sure to recap to ensure that you understood the instruction clearly. This habit increases your efficiency, especially if you're in a client partnership or customer service industry. This reduces misunderstanding and improves your relationships. It also helps you uncover opportunities.

If you're in a relationship with someone, never discourage your partner when he/she is airing his/her concerns. Listening may help you save your relationship.

2. Be tolerant.

People are raised in different environments. Everyone goes through different unique experiences every day. To increase your emotional intelligence, you have to be more tolerant of other people's views.

If someone is voicing out an opinion that's different from yours, learn to hear them out, without prejudice. Try to understand the other person's point of view and then, agree to disagree.

For instance, you despise President Donald Trump, but your friend is a die-hard Trump supporter. Before you engage in a heated argument with your friend try to listen to his views. He has his reasons for supporting the man, and you have your own reasons for not. After hearing him out, agree to disagree. You can say something like *"I understand where you are coming from, but I strongly disagree with that point of view. But, I understand you and it's okay to disagree from time to time. We can have different views and still remain friends."*

3. Show vulnerability.

To put yourself into other people's shoes, you also need to show your own vulnerability. You have to keep it real and openly communicate your needs.

If someone is sharing a difficult experience with you, listen intently and let him know that you understand. Then, show your vulnerability and share your own experiences. For example, if a coworker shares her difficult relationship with her parents, listen carefully and express your understanding. Then, share your own experience and how challenging your relationship with your mother is. This

115

does not only increases your empathy, it also allows you to deepen your relationship with the other person.

4. Try to understand other people's perspectives.

People have different upbringings and everyone grew up in different environments. So, it's normal that we have different perspectives. To increase your empathy and emotional intelligence, you have to try to understand other people's perspectives, even if they are different from yours. Once you see why other people believe what they believe in, validate it. Remember that validation is not the same as agreement. You can accept other people's beliefs without agreeing with them.

5. Encourage other people.

Do not walk on other people's dreams. Encourage the people you love to follow their dreams and pursue the things that they are passionate about.

For instance, your thirty year-old friend tells you that she wants to start a career as a singer. Instead of telling her that it's impossible for a newcomer her age to make it big in the music industry, simply encourage her. Give her the strength to take small steps towards her dreams. You can help her find a part time lounge singer job in hotels and casinos. You can also encourage her to take voice lessons to hone her talent.

6. Smile at other people.

A smile has a magical effect on people. It releases happy hormones and it makes you more likeable. It also makes you seem approachable.

7. Try another person's life for a minute.

For example, you're a successful accountant. You have a stable job and you like routines. You have a number of friends who are digital nomads. To understand your friends, try living their life once in a while. Work on freelance projects while you're travelling or on a vacation. This will help you understand them more.

8. Try mirroring other people.

Mirroring other people help you enter their spirits. It helps you persuade or influence them.

People are natural narcissists. For example, you probably like seeing yourself in other people. You are more likely to listen to people who look like you, talk like you, or share your point of view.

If you aspire to be a leader, you must have the ability to influence others. And you can do this by mirroring other people.

First, you have to maintain eye contact. This makes the other person feel like they have your complete attention. It makes them feel like they are the center of the universe at the moment.

Now, triple nod when you listen. Then, start mimicking the other person's actions. If the other person scratches his head, scratch yours. You can also mimic the other person's tone of voice and speech style.

Mirroring builds trust. You can use it to develop empathy and emotional intelligence. You can also use it to influence others. You can use this technique in various situations. You can use this when talking to your boss or when you're trying to convince your subordinates to see your point of view. You can also use this in handling a difficult situation.

When you're trying to influence other people, mirror their words, vocal tone, pace, body language, hand gesture, and even the way they dress. If your partner uses the word "awesome" too many times, try to use that word often, too.

9. Treat other people the way they want to be treated.

Remember the Golden Rule, *"treat other people the way you want to be treated"*. If you want to cultivate richer and deeper relationships, you have to treat other people the way you want to be treated.

Observe the people around you and pay attention to what they want deep in their hearts. Do they want respect? Do they want assurance or validation? Do they want to experience independence? Do they have the strong desire for inclusion? Do they want to increase their social status? Do they want peace?

If a subordinate asks for a little independence and self-reliance, stop micromanaging him. Do not breathe down on his neck. Give him enough freedom to exercise his creativity. Give him space.

10. Use empathy statements.

When you're talking to someone who is experiencing intense emotions, it's best to use empathy statements. These statements make the other person feel valued and understood.

Here's a list of phrases that you can use to express your empathy. But, only use these statements if you mean them:

- *"If I were you, I would feel the same way, too."*
- *"I understand you."*
- *"I get you. You are totally making sense."*
- *"You are right."*
- *"That sounds frustrating. If I were in your position right now, I'd feel frustrated, too."*
- *"You must be really hurt."*
- *"That sounds scary."*
- *"I agree with you."*
- *"You're doing great."*
- *"That's difficult, but I like how you handled it."*
- *"That must be really frightening."*
- *"That was not easy."*
- *"I hear you."*
- *"I feel you."*
- *"I am sorry that this happened."*
- *"That is so disappointing."*
- *"No wonder you feel that way."*
- *"Whatever you decide, I support you."*
- *"I know how that feels."*
- *"I know how frustrating that must be."*
- *"That's sad."*
- *"I've been through the same thing, so I understand you."*
- *"I would have done the same thing."*
- *"Yes, that's a difficult situation to be in."*
- *"I understand why you are angry."*
- *"If I were you, I'd be angry, too."*
- *"That's devastating!"*
- *"You have valid points."*
- *"I see why you feel that way."*
- *"That's totally frustrating."*

Empathy helps you build deeper relationships. It increases your influence on others. It also allows you to make new friends.

Tip #17: Use Humor to Relieve Your Tension

Use humor to relieve tension and gain control over your emotions. Humor relieves pain and it makes you more likeable, too.

Humor also makes you persuasive. It reduces hostility and it helps you deflect criticisms. It also distracts you from negative emotions. Most of all, it makes you feel good.

Try to find something funny in a difficult situation. Use humor to deflect tension. Let's say, you lost your luggage at the airport. To diffuse your anger and frustration, try to think about how silly you look when you found out that you lost your bags. If this does not work, try to think about something funny like a video you've seen on YouTube.

Also, try a new craze called laughter yoga. This yoga type increases your happiness and it also helps you cope with unpleasant circumstances. Laughter yoga relaxes your body and it helps you deal with painful emotions in a healthy way. It makes you more grounded and it helps you gain clarity.

To do this, sit on a chair. Then, start clapping or making faces. Be silly. Be childlike. Now, think about something funny. Then, start laughing from your stomach. Just laugh out loud. Laugh like you're crazy.

Then, chant the word "yay". After a few minutes, you'll feel more relaxed. You'll feel that joy surging from deep within you.

This exercise may seem silly, but it's a good emotion management technique. It helps relieve tension and pain. It makes you happier, too.

Tip #18: Go Oooommm

When you're stressed out, you'll lose a sense of who you are. When this happens, your emotional intelligence decreases.

Meditation helps you stay in tune with your spirit by decreasing stress. This practice increases your happiness and it increases self-acceptance. It also helps you manage your emotions by downplaying negative feelings such as loneliness, anger, depression, and fear. It helps you stay calm in stressful situations.

To practice meditation:

1. Find a private area where you can practice meditation. It's good to meditate near the beach or in the middle of the forest. But, you can practice meditation in the comfort of your home. You can build a meditation area inside your bedroom and decorate it with scented candles and cushions.

2. Wear comfortable clothing and turn off your gadgets.

3. Sit on a cushion or on a chair. Close your eyes and take deep breaths.

4. Then, listen to your breathing. Notice how your chest rises and falls as you inhale and exhale. Focus on your breathing. If your mind starts to wander, redirect your mind back to your breath.

5. Now, observe your thoughts. When you're alone, what do you think about? Do you worry about the future? Do you think about food? Do you think about what to wear?

6. Observe your emotions. Ask yourself, "how do I feel"? Are you sad or depressed? Is there a hole in your being that you cannot explain? Do you feel happy or blissful? Are you content with your life? Are you unhappy with how your life turned out?

7. Take time to feel these emotions. Don't just silence them. Feel them, acknowledge them, and then release them. Remember that all emotions are beautiful, even anger or sadness. So, take time to process these emotions. Take as much time as you need.

8. Keep taking deep breaths as you watch your thoughts closely. Do this for about five minutes.

9. Open your eyes.

Practicing meditation daily decreases your flight or fight response to stress. It increases your ability to control yourself and your emotions during challenging times. It also increases your optimism and it helps you resist destructive urges.

Meditation does not only increases your emotional intelligence, it also helps you achieve that one thing everyone wants – peace of mind. To reap the optimum benefits of meditation, practice meditation daily. You don't have to set aside a lot of time for meditation. You can simply meditate for five minutes daily.

Tip #19: Practice Social Responsibility

Practicing social responsibility does not only improve your personal karma. It also allows you to enjoy high levels of emotional experience. You can practice social responsibility in many ways, including:

1. Respect the rights of others. Do not step on other people's toes.

2. Be honest and trustworthy.

3. Volunteer in community projects. You can join a fund-raising project, plant trees, or simply pick up the trash in your neighborhood.

4. Be compassionate. Take time to listen to the people around you and try to reach out to them. Smile more and practice good manners. Remember that simple things can mean so much to the people around you.

5. Be a good neighbor. If you want to be seen as a mature and emotionally intelligent person, you must be good to your neighbors by considering their lifestyle. If your neighbors work in the night shift, do not play loud music during day time.

6. Respect other people's property and return things that you borrowed.

Little things can mean so much at the people around you. So, make sure that you practice social responsibility day in and day out.

Tip #20: Develop Grit

Grit is the ability to stay focused on a goal. It is a combination of courage, self-discipline, conscientiousness, endurance, resilience, self-confidence, optimism, creativity, passion, and perseverance. It is the ability to keep going even when faced with difficult circumstances. Grit is also known as mental strength.

According to psychologists, grit is the key to success. It is a quality that's more important than IQ.

To develop your grit, you can use these tips:

1. **Pursue things that you're truly passionate about.**

It's easy to stick to something that you're passionate about. To increase your mental strength, focus on things that you are passionate about. Get a job that excites you.

2. **Choose hope and optimism.**

Even when things are not going well, choose to stay hopeful. Believe that better days are coming. Always choose to look at the brighter side of things.

3. **Surround yourself with gritty people.**

To become more motivated, you have to surround yourself with people who have the ability to persevere.

4. **Practice conscientiousness.**

Do your best all the time. Be organized and practice self-

125

discipline. Do the things that you say you would do. Do not give up when things get hard.

5. Keep going.

A number of publishers thought that Harry Potter was not good enough. What would have happened if J.K. Rowling gave up? Bookworms would not have the opportunity to read one of the most precious modern literary gems.

You'll get rejected from time to time. You'll also experience failure at some point. But, if you want to achieve great success in life, you have to keep going. You must never give up.

6. Embrace change.

Change is sometimes uncomfortable. But, it is necessary. If you want to grow as a person, you have to learn to embrace change.

Change is sometimes unpleasant, but it is good for you. It allows you to step out of your comfort zone and expand your horizon.

7. Focus on the solution.

Instead of focusing on the problem, focus on the solution. Dig deeper and address the underlying causes of your problems.

8. Be brave.

To increase your self-motivation and grit, you have to be brave. You have to make bold decisions. Remember- no guts, no glory. You cannot achieve great success unless you're brave.

Self-motivation allows you to endure difficult circumstance. It empowers you to keep going even if you're faced with disappointments and failure.

People with low EQ easily give up on their dreams. But, people with high EQ choose to get going and wear their failures as battle scars.

Tip #21: Do Things Differently

One of the most effective techniques that you can use to increase your emotional intelligence is to try new experiences and step out of your comfort zone.

Stepping out of your comfort zone pushes you to use your untapped knowledge and resourcefulness. It helps you get to know yourself a little more intimately. It also helps you to grow.

Make a change in your daily routine. You can simply use another shampoo or take a different route to work. If you're comfortable with taking bigger risks, do it. You can travel to new places you have not been before. Travelling helps you discover things about yourself. It uncovers your inner joy.

Taking risks enhances your emotional intelligence by increasing your self-awareness. It also reduces the anxiety associated with risks. It helps you grow and increases your maturity.

Conclusion

Thank you again for the purchase of this book.

I hope that this book was able to increase your emotional intelligence. Now, let's do a quick review of what you've learned in this book:

- ✓ Emotional intelligence is an important trait. It is the key to success. Many psychologists think that EQ is even more important than IQ.
- ✓ To increase your emotional intelligence, you have to be aware of your emotions.
- ✓ Take time to feel your emotions. Remember that all emotions are beautiful.
- ✓ Make a list of your strengths and weaknesses.
- ✓ Set goals. Setting goals do not only increase your motivation. It also increases your ability to regulate your emotions.
- ✓ Do not react to your emotions right away. If you're feeling an intense negative emotion, count from one to ten before you react.
- ✓ Replace your negative emotions with positive ones.
- ✓ Empathize with the people around you. Empathy allows you to build more meaningful relationships. It also increases your influence and likability.
- ✓ Develop grit.

Emotional intelligence is something that you can develop over time. It helps you manage difficult situations. It helps you express yourself clearly and it helps you gain respect from others.

Cognitive Behavioral Therapy

The Complete Step-by-Step Guide on Retraining Your Brain and Overcoming Depression, Anxiety, and Phobias

Introduction

Cognitive Behavioral Therapy or (CBT) has had some amazing results in the treatment of depression, anxiety, and phobias. Psychotherapists who practice CBT take a thoughtful look at the unreasonable emotions and behaviors people exhibit resulting from mistaken feelings and beliefs. If left untreated, individuals who suffer depression, anxiety, and phobias often establish destructive and debilitating thinking patterns that prevent them from achieving their life's goals.

It's common for people to feel ashamed of their feelings of fear and depression, hiding their symptoms in hopes they will one day disappear. Unfortunately, over 15 million people each year suffer some level of depression, and two-thirds of them never seek proper treatment. Reported statistics from the National Network of Depression Centers (NNDC), show an overwhelming success rate of depressed people who do choose to get treatment, with as much as 80% who see positive results in as little as four to six weeks.

With help so readily available, why is it that we put such a stigma on these conditions that paralyze our ability to accomplish success in our personal and professional lives? We have been conditioned to believe that anxiety or depression is because of weakness, perhaps even an inability to function as "so-called" normal people. If we were smarter, had more courage, or weren't so weak-minded, we wouldn't be depressed, right? Wrong! Did you know that people with high IQs are almost three times more likely to suffer from depression or anxiety?

Some people also believe they're alone in their feelings of inadequacy and depression. Ah, but that is also a misnomer. If you suffer depression and anxiety, you're in good company. Famous people like Ellen DeGeneres and Jim Carrey face their fears and depression every day and perform before millions of individuals. Studies show that depression also plagues the workplace, ranking within the top three issues that cause dissatisfaction and nonproductivity. So if there is comfort in knowing that you're not suffering alone, rest assured many others feel just as you do.

The good news is, there is hope for you to learn to identify when you are under attack, and how to remedy your temporary troubles with depression and anxiety, and even phobias. In fact, that's the reason for this book. We believe it's time you stop being controlled by your negative self-talk, get off that couch you've been supporting for the better part of every day for weeks, and begin to make a real difference in your life.

Not only are we going to help you recognize your depression, but we're going to provide you with six practical steps to guide you through retraining your brain to overcome these maladies. Wouldn't it be great to kiss these issues goodbye, to learn to anticipate situations that could create a comeback of depression and anxiety and know you can handle it because you have past successes? Wouldn't it be wonderful to simply get out of your head for a while and relax in the company of friends and co-workers without feeling anxious or worried that you'll say or do something wrong?

If your depression, anxiety or phobias are slight, then these steps will help you to handle them successfully and move forward to more productive social and professional engagements. However, if your depression is long-lived and more rooted, it may take some psychotherapy to help you change your perceptions and behaviors. The most important thing to remember is that you don't have to continue suffering. Courage and confidence are right around the corner; all you need to do is be willing to discover and take the steps that will lead you there.

You won't have to go to any meetings and stand up in front of dozens of people introducing yourself and announcing the fact that you have depression, anxiety, and phobias. Chances are, you won't even have to take heavy drugs to diminish the mistaken feelings and behaviors. It might be that you can improve by just reading and following these six easy steps to recovery. If not, at least you'll learn to stop beating yourself up over the fact that you're somehow defective or unnatural. You're just having some issues that you can overcome when you stop protecting yourself and begin to practice the six steps offered in our book.

One way to encourage yourself to get help is to look at depression and anxiety differently; take a different perspective. Think of the way you feel as merely a discomfort, not a disease. Your mind is making you believe something that isn't true. Others are not ostracizing you, but rather you are holding yourself apart. You have built a wall of protection that 's hard to penetrate. The problem is, although nobody can get in, you cannot get out. Your depression, anxiety, and phobias are trapping you in a world of worry and fret.

If it helps, know that stress temporarily causes many forms of depression. Remove what is stressing you, and the depression will dissipate. There are some who suffer depression through no fault of their own, but because it runs in their family. They are predisposed to bouts of depression or anxiety.

It may also help you to know that some forms of stress can be good for you. It can enable you to recognize, react, and avoid real danger quicker than others who are not as aware. A little bit of anxiety can protect you if used as this small voice of warning or a shakedown that something dangerous is about to occur.

Our goal in this book is to give you understanding and encouragement. We want you to have tools that can be used to help change your perspective and override your fears and anxieties. We want you to know that if your suffering gets too severe, it's time to take your troubles to the next level of help— that of the professional psychotherapist. You don't have to hide your feelings, pretend you're happy and confident, or assume you're all alone in your depressed state. There are millions just like you who are functioning well in today's world. Before, you could be one of them!

Chapter 1: Step #1—Understanding Your Depression, Anxiety, or Phobias

There's a good reason why individuals have a certain amount of anxiety, and it goes back to our early days in the cave. When we were busy gathering food and battling dangerous predators, we needed our bodies to signal us when we were about to be eaten. By being hypervigilant, we lived longer and happier lives. Our bodies were well-tuned to warn us both physically and emotionally if something or someone threatened our way of life.

Today's society doesn't offer the same outlets for these physical and emotional alerts, and so we imagine people or events to be threats to our existence as an outlet for these reactions. We may not be worried about escaping a huge T-rex, but an outraged boss can play the part. We no longer worry about being traded to and enslaved by another tribe, but our behaviors can reflect the anxiety we feel because we're afraid of being isolated from friends or loved ones. The situations are different, but the feelings are the same.

To understand depression, anxiety, and phobias, let's first define them and identify some of their symptoms.

Understanding Depression

Depression is more than being sad or discouraged about something. It is much more intense and lasts significantly longer than a brief bout of sadness. Depression brings with it feelings of helplessness, hopelessness, and a belief that people you love would be better off without you. It is a relentless feeling of complete and total defeat. Many individuals who suffer depression frequently hear from friends and family: "Stop feeling sorry for yourself. Get off your butt and do something with your life."

They would if they could, but depression holds them captive, bound by ropes of unworthiness and rutted in pits of low self-esteem. Telling one suffering from depression to get over it is like telling a four-year-old to grow up. They would if they could, but without help and time, it's an impossibility. It's not like you just love being depressed and unproductive, but you don't know how to behave or feel any other way. That's where our six steps, therapy, or a combination of the two come into play. Knowing you don't have to live this way brings with it the freedom of discovery and choice.

Of course, some ways to temporarily escape depression is by abusing drugs, excessive sleeping, isolating yourself, or always busying yourself in mindless activities like obsessive television watching, streaming Facebook, or browsing the Internet. Doing these things might allow you to forget about those things that are causing depression, but they won't teach you methods to cope with and overcome your depression.

Why is it that some people who experience chronic illness and pain feel ongoing depression, while others rise above it all and still live a productive and active life? It's not because they aren't as sensitive as others, but because they have learned coping skills and strategies that change their focus, perspective, and behavior. One of the most important strategies is to recognize the depression before it has time to become a permanent fixture.

If you constantly feel tired, edgy or restless, have quick weight gain or loss, or are plagued with chronic stomach problems—be alerted to the fact that you could be suffering an attack of depression. Instead of accepting your saddened fate, or waiting for years to get help, move into action immediately to rid yourself of the negative feelings and behaviors. People who have already experienced the benefits of therapy are much more likely to get a little extra help when the need arises. After all, if therapy was able to pull you from a depressed state once, why not welcome a repeat performance?

Understanding the causes of depression is also helpful in overcoming its hold on your life. As we said previously, it could be a genetic issue that you're able to trace back from generation to generation in your family. Or, it could be due to adverse childhood experiences, such as abuse, abandonment, family issues, violence, and other deprivation. Depression can also have physiological causes, such as a chemical disorder like bipolar or a hormonal imbalance, which might explain why women experience depression more than men. It can also be caused by trauma or shock, evidenced by many returning veterans whose lives are disrupted by PTSD.

Whatever you do, doing nothing should not be an option. Why—because depression is one of the most prevalent causes of disability. Why not function at your highest level, work at optimal performance, achieve the most that you can? There's no need to let depression reduce you to a shadow of what you could have been had you decided on some CBT. If you are resistant to the idea of therapy, ask yourself if that could be another fear you need to overcome. Some people fear treatment, and some people fear the process of getting better.

Understanding Anxiety

Like depression, people experience stress at many different levels—from severe to a temporary feeling of discomfort. It is usually brought on by stress, or a buildup of unresolved fears. What feeds anxiety and fuels its fire, is negative self-talk. When you consistently expect the worst to happen, then your behaviors serve to help you fulfill your expectations and create the worst outcome. Consequently, the more you experience the worst outcome, the more you believe that's your fate.

For example, if you become anxious in a group of strangers, over-analyzing every conversation, over-thinking every word you say or don't say, you'll soon devise a way to alleviate your anxiety. The easiest thing to do is to avoid groups of strangers or to get quiet around people you don't know, hoping they'll just think you're a deep thinker. When you do these things, you temporarily alleviate the anxiety, and so the quiet isolation just perpetuates itself, and the depression returns when you are in another group of strangers. You haven't overcome or even learned to manage your anxiety, you've come to hide it. The more you hide, the less comfortable you feel in a crowd.

Everybody feels anxiety at one time or another, but it's the intense type of stress that robs you of a quality life. People whose anxiety is so high it causes them to have panic attacks have been known to isolate themselves in their homes for years. Others have such anxiety when their loved ones are late they picture them killed in a car accident or attacked by a thief. Others suffer so much anxiety over their health; they imagine their headache is a brain tumor or that a dry patch on their skin is cancerous.

Traumatic situations can also cause extreme anxiety. When fear causes you to change your normal way of behavior, or it causes you physical issues, you might have an anxiety disorder.

It could be temporary, which might be in the case of an event in your life, or it could be ongoing, like the kind that constant negative self-talk can create.

Some of the physical symptoms or behaviors that signal high anxiety are when you clench your teeth, ball your fist, your chest hurts, you have trouble sleeping or breathing, your neck or muscles spasm, you get frequent headaches, and your body feels tense. Sometimes anxiety surfaces as a sensitive stomach or bowel, which can bring about significant pain and discomfort. Many individuals live under such constant and extreme stress, that it has become their new normal. They don't remember what it's like to feel relaxed and calm.

Just as with depression, the six steps we discuss in this book will help you to identify and manage anxiety before it manages you.

Understanding Phobias

Phobias are uncontrollable fears of imagined dangers, which most likely will never harm us or threaten our lives. Not that some of our phobias couldn't hurt us, but we might never be near them or experience the situation we fear. Often, people who have phobias aren't afraid of the object; they're afraid of what might happen. For example, the fear of flying is not the phobia—it's the fear of crashing. The fear of heights is not the phobia; it's the fear of falling from that height. The fear of being closed in is not the phobia; it's the fear of never being released.

The mere thought of the object of your fear can bring a sweat to people who suffer phobias. They turn pale and become paralyzed when the object of their fear is within sight. Phobias render the mind useless, and it's only able to concentrate on the object of its fear. Early childhood or adolescent issues cause most phobias.

Although all phobias are fears, not all fears are phobias. Phobias occur when you begin to rearrange your life around the object, person, place, or thing that you intensely fear. For example, if your phobia is elevators, you'll climb ten flights of stairs to avoid standing in an elevator with strangers. If your phobia is flying, like the former football commentator, John Madden, you'd be terribly inconvenienced because you'd have to take a bus to every working event rather a plane. If your fear significantly disrupts your life, it's a phobia. Cognitive Behavioral Therapy has been particularly successful in the treatment of phobias. When you retrain your brain and body to think and react differently, your thoughts and behaviors become more rational and less disruptive.

Social phobias can be some of the most disruptive in our lives, and yet the most successful with a little professional help. Not that self-help doesn't work, but if you've tried to help yourself with social phobias and haven't accomplished much, it's time to see the professional. If you have refused to try anything and have, instead, hidden away, try the six steps offered in our book. It's a good first plan of action, and then, if necessary, move on to a more structured modification.

Whether it's through professional advice or self-help, trying a preventative measure once isn't going to do the trick. Many of these anxieties and fears have been with you for a long time, and it's going to take a while to overcome them. So, be patient with yourself. Give yourself lots of experience and practice in the steps presented in this book. If one method doesn't work, try another for a while. The important thing is that you don't give up and crawl back into your shell of avoidance. Keep believing that change is possible, that you can rid yourself of the fears that are holding you back from achieving your dreams.

Chapter 2: Step #2—Facing the Enemy

When you are suffering from depression or high anxiety, all you can think of is to escape the pain. Your greatest wish is just to run away, hide, and lick your wounds. Perhaps the reason many individuals feel this way is because of the way the public views these disorders, or any other mental illness for that matter. People have sympathy and empathy for those who have a cancerous tumor or a heart problem because they know it is through no fault of theirs that they are physically suffering. However, the treatment for those who are feeling the physical pains from depression and anxiety is not the same. Most people believe they need no empathy because they are feeling sorry enough for themselves. They think what causes depression or anxiety disorders are just individuals who want to get attention when nothing could be further from the truth.

The worst is when people who suffer depression or anxiety are told just to get up and get busy, and soon they'll pull out of it. When loved ones remind them of just how good they have it, somehow that's just not a comfort. Deep depression is usually not caused by outside pressures; it's a mental illness in which outside events or circumstances have little influence. You can be wealthy and famous and still have deep and ongoing depression. Depression is no respecter of persons; it can afflict anyone. Lots of people say they understand your depression, but unless you have been immobilized by its effects for weeks at a time, they can't know. It's impossible to know when you haven't suffered the kind of depression that takes your strength and leaves you wanting to curl up in a fetal position and hope against hope the pain subsides soon.

The thing that enables you to overcome depression and high anxiety is to face your illness, but that's the very thing you fear the most. You would rather feel trapped like a caged animal than to suffer additional pain, and you will experience more pain in the beginning as you attempt to manage the depression and anxiety. Most who suffer these mental illnesses believe they'd rather suffer a lifetime or even die before facing their fears.

Ignoring the Issues Doesn't Make Them Disappear

Not only does ignoring the problems of depression and anxiety not make them go away, but it exacerbates the issues. Here's how that can happen. When you feel dragged down by depression or anxiety, you reach into your toolbox of strategies that you've always used to help you get over the problem. You mistakenly believe that hiding or pretending helped you to overcome past depression. So, you continue to do the same thing again. In truth, hiding or ignoring the issues didn't make them go away, you just postponed the problem until the next time. Each time depression or anxiety rears its ugly head, it gets stronger and lasts longer until the cycle creates so much pain that it makes people take drastic action.

Hiding from the pain or pretending it doesn't exist creates more pain. Now, instead of facing the enemy and doing battle, you've run to protect yourself and allowed the enemy to feel as though it defeated you. You cannot rest because you know that in a short while it will march forward to finish the job. What you need to do is arm yourself first. Protect yourself with knowledge, courage, small successes, and positive and supportive people. Then get ready to do battle, knocking out one terrifying enemy at a time. Don't try to fight on all fronts at once; it will leave you weak and stretch your resources to the breaking point. Celebrate one small victory after another until you've conquered each battle and marched forward to win the war on your depression and anxiety.

Arming Yourself for Battling Depression and Anxiety

By reading this book and practicing the six steps given to help you overcome depression and anxiety, you've already taken a giant step toward success. You've admitted to having issues, and you're ready to tackle each one head on. Reading everything you can about depression and anxiety is an excellent way to gain knowledge that will help you to understand the depths of your troubles. It will also enable you to recognize whether you'll need some professional therapy to help you hurdle the significant obstacles.

Another way to gain knowledge is to talk about your depression and anxiety with a trusted loved one. What you need to know is that your perceptions, beliefs, and behaviors are flawed. You cannot trust yourself; how you feel about your depression or anxiety is faulty thinking. You cannot believe your self-talk when that voice inside your head tells you that people don't like you, or that you're stupid or not good enough. We'll teach you later how to silence the negative self-talk. Just know now that the voice inside your head cannot be trusted to speak the truth. That's why it's important to share your feelings with people who know you, perhaps better than you know yourself.

You don't want people who pay you lip service, either. You need to surround yourself with positive people who will honestly share their perceptions with you. They'll tell you when you have a reason to feel cautious and when your depression or anxiety is unfounded. If your feelings happened because of deeply rooted events that happened in your childhood, then you're going to need the help of a professional who knows how to help you manage your feelings. However, forcing yourself to talk about your feelings is a good way to begin facing the enemy.

Now that you have gained more knowledge and courage to share your feelings, you need to work on your mistaken beliefs. You are not stupid, not just having a pity party, and not being lazy when you sleep in until noon every day because you can't force yourself out of bed. No! Depression and anxiety disorders are mental illnesses that need focused treatment, and you deserve to be happy. You are a worthy person who has much to contribute, and you can do this. You don't need to protect yourself by hiding any longer when you have armed yourself with the strategies and tools to help you overcome your depression and anxiety.

Once you experience a few small successes in handling your thoughts, you'll be surprised at how empowered you'll become to march forward to the next battle. Successes, no matter how small, strengthen you. They change your beliefs and behaviors and allow you to see your situation as something besides hopeless. Every success is important, so celebrate each one. It takes a lot of courage and strength to delve into things that you've protected yourself from for so long. Having courage doesn't mean waiting until you no longer fear, it means you're willing to face the enemy and do what it takes to get better.

Partnering with Your Affliction

For most of you, making depression and anxiety your partner sounds rather insane, but there are ways to embrace these issues that will get them to work with you instead of against you. Turn your enemy into your ally, and let your depression and anxiety help you. It seems impossible for you to think of depression or anxiety as something good right now, but let's examine all the gifts that they can offer.

- When you have suffered depression and anxiety, you are more understanding and empathetic toward others who are in pain as well. You can speak to them from a real place of knowing.
- Depression and anxiety cause you to question the accuracy of your perceptions and beliefs. When you realize that your perceptions are inaccurate, it allows you to check other areas of your life where your thinking could be wrong as well.
- When you are in the process of healing, true friends stick by you and are there for you. So, depression and anxiety can let you know who your friends are.
- To work through deep depression and anxiety disorders, you must learn to trust yourself and to be decisive. Once you've learned to do this with yourself, you'll be able to apply these skills to other situations in the workplace or your personal relationships.
- To alleviate depression and anxiety, you must be open with your feelings and have the courage to make yourself vulnerable. This vulnerability can be an invitation for others to do the same. We are not admired for our perfections, but for how we deal with our flaws. It's so much easier for others to relate to us because they know we have issues just like they do.

Once you change your thinking about the depression and anxiety you suffer, you will be amazed at the freedom it provides. You won' t need to curl up and veg out any longer. Instead, you'll be able to use it to help yourself and others. There's no guarantee that your depression will disappear altogether, but you'll be able to see the signs coming a lot sooner than before, and you can begin changing your thinking and behavioral patterns much earlier. Your depression will then only be temporary visitors instead of unwanted, long-term houseguests that wear out their welcome.

Using your anxiety to give you a wake-up call and warn you of what could be a real danger is an excellent way to form a working partnership. The stress you were feeling before may not have been real, but the physiological responses to that fear are the same. So, when you recognize these feelings in your body, you'll know that you could be open to something dangerous and avoid the problem before it occurs.

Although you may tend to overthink everything that you were anxious about, when partnering with your anxiety, you can better appreciate your ability to think things through instead of just having a knee-jerk reaction to an important event in your life. Once you learn to control your self-talk, you can work with the voice in your head instead of just accepting every negative thought as gospel.

You Are Not Your Disorder

You have a lot to offer, and especially because of what you have learned and overcome regarding depression and anxiety. If you have always identified or labeled yourself as depressed or over anxious, understand this. You are more than your illness. There is a whole other dimension to your personality and behaviors. You are not a walking ball of depression. You are productive, educated, intelligent, funny, genuine, and an authentic person who is now more sensitive to the way others experience life.

It's incredible to think that people are so quick to label themselves with negative tags, but let the positive things about themselves remain hidden or taken for granted. For example, you might be a talented artist who suffers from depression. Instead of thinking of yourself as depressed, think of yourself as artistic. You might be a well-respected manager who suffers from anxiety. Instead of thinking of yourself as a mess of stress, why not consider yourself to be an understanding manager who encourages others to perform their best work? It's time you changed the perception you carry around in your head and stop obsessing about what others might think of you. Look around you! If your peeps have been with you for a long time, chances are they're enjoying the company.

Chapter 3: Step #3—Practicing a Step-by-Step Recovery

There are many things you can do to help you manage depression and anxiety. The following are seven steps to provide you with quicker recovery from depression and anxiety.

1. Exercise

You don't have to be a body builder to benefit from the effects of exercise on your depression and anxiety. Just a few minutes every day of regular exercise will give you more energy and confidence. When you exercise, your body releases endorphins, which are the body's natural painkillers. Heavy exercise or activity can make some individuals feel euphoric. The beautiful thing about endorphins, is they are all natural and non-addictive.

Along with endorphins, exercise also reduces the production of chemicals in the body that can weaken your immune system and increase depression. All these benefits don't happen with five minutes of exercise one day a week. Instead, the positives you experience come with "regular" daily exercise and activity. Once you've worked out during the day, you get a better night's sleep, which also helps to fight off depression and stress.

2. Get Some Sunshine

It doesn't take much time in the sun to give us a whole new lease on life. The sun's rays are most beneficial between the hours of 10:00 a.m. and 4:00 p.m., to avoid the damaging ultra-violet rays. It's not just that the sun warms our faces and arms and makes everything seem a little fuller and brighter, but getting the sun enables our bodies to release a mood-altering chemical known as serotonin. Serotonin helps you feel calm and collected, more focused and energetic. With brighter days come darker nights, which also encourages us to feel sleepy, and wake up more rested and relaxed.

Because serotonin also helps us produce more vitamin D, our bones feel better, and we experience fewer aches and pains in our joints.

3. Eat Healthy

Eating healthy can stimulate your brain and body to fight depression. Some of the foods most healthy for you are as follows.

- Avocados = They are full of the type of fat that is good for you and helps your brain operate smoothly and more efficiently.
- Greens = Kale, and Spinach reduce inflammation. Did you know that where there is brain inflammation you often see severe depression?
- Onions = Onions also help to reduce inflammation, and they have a positive effect on your gut. The gut contains over 80 percent of your body's serotonin, and from there it sends that calming chemical to all parts of the body and brain.
- Nuts & Seeds = They have lots of omega-3 fatty acids which are known to reduce the symptoms of depression. Walnuts, sunflower seeds, and flaxseeds are exceptionally healthy for one's mood.
- Tomatoes = Tomatoes contain folic and alpha-lipoic acids which help to fight against depression.

- Berries & Apples =Blueberries, blackberries, strawberries, and raspberries, as well as apples, have lots of antioxidants in them, which again reduces the symptoms of depression.

4. Get Plenty of Sleep

The number of people in the United States who suffer depression has grown to three times what it was in the sixty years previously. Some scientists believe that this may be due to our progressive sleep deprivation. It's like a vicious cycle, the less sleep you get, the more anxious and depressed you become. The more anxious and depressed you get, the more you suffer from insomnia. People today get an average of an hour and a half less sleep per night than our grandparents. Here are some things you can do to help you get more hours and higher quality sleep.

- Don't work in bed. Make your bed for sleeping only.
- Don't go to sleep with the television blaring. It is a proven fact that the light and sound from the television disrupt the time and quality of your sleep.
- Get in a sleeping routine by going to bed at the same time each night and waking up at the same time each morning. When you create a routine, your body will get tired about the time you usually call it a night and feel rested and ready to get up at your usual time.
- Don't be active just before going to bed. Calm yourself down. Read or watch television to prepare your mind to shut down.

It soon becomes very apparent when you are suffering from sleep deprivation. You aren't as decisive, and you compromise your ability to focus and remember. When you have no regular sleeping patterns, it also throws your appetite for a loop. You get hungry at weird times, and your digestive track is more easily irritated. When you're not getting enough sleep, your temper is more volatile, and your patience with others is limited. The next step from feeling tired and grumpy is to get anxious and fearful, which then leads right into depression.

5. Get off Caffeinated Beverages and Drink More Water

Since your brain's tissue consists of approximately 85 percent water, it makes sense that lacking hydration can create greater levels of anxiety and depression. Besides keeping you up all night, inordinate amounts of caffeine can cause anxiety. Water is like your bodies irrigation system, flowing through all your organs and passing along the proper nutrients and chemicals throughout every cell. Doctors recommend you drink at least 8 cups of water a day, but make sure it's filtered or bottled. Some city water is known to have many chemicals that can have adverse effects on the brain and body. There's one thing to remember, if you don't supply your body with enough pure water, it will get it one way or another—and that means robbing fluids from your brain, muscles, and bones.

6. Don't Abuse Drugs or Drink Alcohol

Although drugs and alcohol might help you to forget your anxiety or depression for a brief time, once they wear off the feelings will come back with a vengeance. Addiction is often a result of depression and anxiety, but it also acts as a champion of these devastating diseases. It's hard enough to change your thinking when you aren't under the influence of drugs or alcohol, but reasoning and perceptions are severely impaired when substances alter your brain chemistry.

If the drugs and alcohol aren't enough to depress you, just think of all the money you're throwing away in the process. That's sure to whip up some anxiety and depression. It's more affordable and practical to get professional help for the depression or anxiety without added drugs or alcohol to the equation.

Tune into Life Through Your Senses

If you suffer depression or anxiety, I'm sure you've had people tell you that you are just too sensitive—that you shouldn't take things so seriously, right? There is some truth to those statements. You probably are more sensitive than others who seem to just glide through life without a care. However, your hypersensitivity can also be used to help you manage your depression. Overly sensitive people see and feel things more intensely than others. You might see colors more vividly and feel someone's touch more acutely. Knowing this can help you to use your senses to help you cope with depression.

For example, when you feel depression hitting you like a ton of bricks, and you're feeling like a solid week in bed might be just the ticket, think again. Take a hike in the mountains. Enjoy wildlife on the trail. Get your dog to the park for a robust hour of playing ball. Ride your bike on a mountain path. Plant flowers or vegetables in your garden. Experiencing life through those hypersensitive senses of yours will help you to reward sensitivity rather than dread it. That's another way to partner with your depression or anxiety. Welcome their perceptions through your senses, and let your sight, sense of touch, smell, hearing, and taste encourage you to perceive the world differently. There is one other sense you possess that many other people do not. The amazing sense of imagination.

Think about it. You have already imagined all kinds of negative things that weren't true, so now it's time to use that incredible imagination to work toward the positive. Imagine a happier more satisfying outcome to the experiences that led to your depression or anxiety. Once you learn to control your self-talk, you can imagine all sorts of things that will help you remain confident and happy. You can also use your imagination to help you meditate and relax, which will serve to defuse some of your anxiety and depression.

Spoil Yourself

If you're used to doing for others but rarely leave time for yourself, make it a habit of taking time out to spoil yourself. Reward yourself! Give yourself something to look forward to doing that will help you when you are feeling anxious and depressed. It's okay to take time for yourself, even to spend some time alone, but not because you're trying to hide from your feelings. Make the time for yourself a real gift. Give yourself permission to enjoy your favorite hobby, to get a message, or to spend time with your best friend.

If you're into animals, that's a great stress reliever. Many returning vets have service dogs that help them with their anxiety and depression, and they also assist them to stay connected with people. While someone might hesitate to approach you, your dog is a whole different thing. Dogs encourage people to get more exercise, and they help us not to be so self-centered and lonely. We think we're taking care of them, but they're our guardian angels watching over us— always vigilant to our moods and stresses.

There's a reason why people began using service dogs to help alleviate depression and anxiety. They keep us calm and give us a reason to get out of bed in the morning. It's wonderful to see vets reunited with their dogs when they return from the frontlines. For a while, all is forgotten. The enthusiastic wag of that welcoming tail and the wet tongue across their cheek makes the rest of the world disappear. Dogs have a way of making you their focus every moment of the day, and they love you no matter what. Don't you wish that was true for everybody?

Whatever it is you like to do, treat yourself to pleasure. Don't be shy about celebrating your successful management of the depression and anxiety that once kept you in bed for days at a time. When you reward your soul for participating in your recovery, you're much more likely to get better quicker the next time you suffer depression and high anxiety. Celebrating success makes those moments memorable and remarkable, and it teaches you that good can come from bad and that depression and anxiety won't last forever.

head on instead of listening to her negative self-talk if the situation should arise where she turned on the waterworks.

She went into her new manager's office and shared with him the fact that when she thought another was criticizing her or displeased with her, her reaction might be to cry. She didn't want him to feel bad, but she also didn't want to spend an entire workweek trying to hold back the tears. Her manager thanked her for confiding in him and said he understood.

A few days later, the manager called my friend into his office. "I have come up with a solution, Susan. If you have displeased me, or I need to call you on the carpet for something, how about if I just hand you the box of tissue? That way, you'll know the conversation might be a little unpleasant for you, but we'll work through it together. You don't have to worry about whether I was upset. You can rest assured I am when I hand you the tissue."

For many years, my friend and her boss handled their "talks" this way. She didn't spend productive time having anxiety, and her boss knew what to expect when he had to deliver unpleasant information. She avoided all the negative self-talk by acting immediately, and she always knew the facts because of the passed box of tissue. Ingenious!

- O = Own Your Feelings

  Just as my friend did in the last story, you need to own your feelings to avoid all the random banter in your head. It took a lot of guts to approach her boss and be honest about her feelings, but by doing so, they worked through the issue with minimal fallout. Owning your feelings means you'll sometimes make yourself vulnerable, but it's much better to give your feelings five minutes of immediate attention than spending days and days worrying about the "what if."

Think about it; you cannot hide your feelings forever, so you may as well put yourself out there immediately and take charge. You'll respect yourself more and so will others when you own your feelings.

- I = Imagine the Alternatives

  Imagine for a moment that how you feel about a situation is inaccurate. Now you need to discover another way that situation could be perceived. How else could you have interpreted the situation that would make it more productive? Could it be that you were the only one who saw it this way? What if your perception is wrong, how would this effect the outcome? If you are right, and you made a mistake, is it going to be devastating or in the next day or two will anyone even remember? The voice in your head is the most powerful influence over your emotions. Things can't go any direction but up from there.

- D = Discuss Your Feelings

  Hidden feelings only give your negative self-talk power. The more you try to hide how you feel, the louder that voice becomes until the only way to shut it up is to sleep. That's why many depressed people sleep a lot. They sleep as a way of escape. To encourage yourself to share your feelings, keep in mind that people are not going to punish you for doing so. Once you change your perspective and think of sharing your feelings as a positive outcome, then it will get a bit easier.

Each time you bravely share your feelings, it gets a little easier to do so. The more you act immediate, the more sharing your feelings will become your automatic response to rectifying the situation. Be selective, though! Don't share with just anybody, and don't share with everybody. Speak to the person you trust. To give you courage, rehearse what you want to say to them.

Even If You Made a Mistake, Your Self-Talk Should Encourage

We've all made mistakes, and we could all benefit from some positive encouragement when we're down. Make it a habit never to say things to yourself that you wouldn't say to your spouse or best friend. If you believe your self-talk is too harsh to repeat, then don't. Never say things like that to anybody—especially yourself.

I once heard someone say they named the voice in their head Harry. It was so ridiculous that they couldn't be mad at themselves when they scolded Harry. "Now look Harry, what's all this about anyway?" Or, "Come on Harry, you don't mean that, do ya?" It became a silly game they played to minimize the negative self-talk. Whatever works, right?

Saying or doing something wrong shouldn't mean you need to beat yourself up about it. Admit you made a mistake and then say, NEXT to yourself. "I can't believe I said that. Oh well, NEXT!" It sounds easy, but for those who have made a habit of wallowing in their mistakes, they're saying—oh, but it can't be that easy. Believe me; it is that easy. Now, don't you feel silly for carrying around all that negative for years?

Not Everything Is Black or White

For many people who automatically accept the negative self-talk, their world is made up of issues that are clearly black or white. Either what they did was horrible or great; consequently, if what happened wasn't incredible it had to be horrible. However, most of the events or circumstances in our lives aren't polarized into good or bad. There's a whole lot of that gray area that is ignored by people who suffer depression and anxiety.

Examining that gray area closer, we know that it contains most of what we experience. For example, look back on your day. Can you pick out one thing that was unspeakably horrible or one thing that was incredibly wonderful?   Probably not! However, I bet you could list dozens of things that were a run-of-the-mill part of your day, right? Here's a test for you. Let's pretend you keep a daily "to do" list. There are ten items on your list for today, and you achieved nine of them. Do you congratulate yourself for getting so much done? Or, do you beat yourself up for missing that one item?

That's the difference between people with negative self-talk. That voice in their head would be scolding them about the missed item. It would be telling them they were lazy, not good enough to get the job done and get them to question their capabilities. If you suffer depression and anxiety, and I suspect you do or a loved one does because that's your motivation for reading this book, imagine this. Think about all the negative self-talk you experienced over the last week. Now, take that ongoing negative conversation in your head and pretend everything you said to yourself was positive. How much more do you think you could have accomplished? It's our bet, that "to do" list would contain 20 or more completed items.

Negative self-talk steals your time and energy; it robs you of being your best. Surprisingly, it doesn't take near as much effort to make it go away as it does to put up with it in your life. So, here's to saying goodbye to the "bull."

A Review of the Steps You've Learned So Far

Let's review the steps in our step-by-step guide that you've learned about so far that will help you minimize depression and anxiety.

Step #1:

Understand your depression, anxiety, and phobias. Read about them, and learn what triggers these types of feelings in you.

Step #2:

Face your enemy. Don't hide and hope your depression and anxiety will magically disappear.

Step #3:

Practice a step-by-step recovery. Have a plan. Ignoring depression or hiding from your fear isn't a plan, it's a symptom.

Step #4:

Control your negative self-talk. Don't let your negative self-talk be an automatic reaction to depression and anxiety.

Chapter 5: Step #5—Rewriting the Outcome

Have you ever wished your life was a movie script in which you could rewrite certain scenes? So, pretend with me for a moment that you can rewrite something you have experienced and it would change the outcome. Not only would it change the result for that one event or change your relationship with someone, but it would change your entire life. Yes, rewriting the outcomes of events, relationships, dialogues, and opportunities is so powerful it could change your thinking and behavior. It could even change your life.

Our minds are incredible machines, but like any machine, we are in control of it. We can shut it down, change its configuration, and we can tell it what to think and believe. We can also trick our mind into believing what we want it to feel. You see, our subconscious minds don't distinguish reality from pretense, and that's why you believe your negative self-talk. When you go into automatic mode as you are suffering anxiety and depression and accept the bad advice or false facts that you are feeding yourself. Your mind takes what you tell it as its new reality.

The same holds true when you decide to rewrite the scenarios and turn all the negatives into positives. When you rewrite the outcome, you are always the one in the right, the one who made the best decision, who did the right thing. When you recast yourself as the hero or the star of your movie script, your subconscious beliefs what you are writing and feeling. As far as your subconscious is concerned, if you say you're a star, you're a star. If you say you're a dirt bag, then that's what your mind accepts.

What a great tool you have. Rewriting your outcomes doesn't cost any money and doesn't take a whole lot of time. Let's look at the many ways you can choose to revise the events in your life.

Keep A Winner's Journal

First, there is only one rule for maintaining a winner's journal—never show it to anyone. Your journal will be one time that secrecy is encouraged, and that's because by keeping the rewrites a secret, you will have the freedom to write anything you like any way you like. Everything else is open season. You can write about any situation, event, conversation, or dialogue you like. It can be about work, relationships, and you can even do a rewrite with the little voice in your head.

For those of you who have kept a journal during your life, writing in one isn't going to be that much of a challenge. For those of you who haven't, you might sit down with pen in hand and not one word will come to mind. That's okay. Don't let writing in your journal be another stress. Just start writing. Here are some ways you can begin to put pencil to paper. Start by just writing down things about your day. What did you do? How did you feel about what you did? You can go back to an important event and describe what happened. You can write a letter to a loved one, a friend, an enemy, a tyrannical boss, a dead sibling, or even a confession to your priest. Whatever you want to write about is the perfect beginning.

If none of these subjects resonate with you, you can do a character sketch of yourself. Describe how you see yourself.

Now, explain how you wish you were. Chances are these two profiles are completely different, and there you have your first rewrite. You have now taken the first step in creating a whole new you. As you write, don't stop to judge your writing, just let the thoughts and words flow. Remember, nobody is going to see this except you.

Pretend People are Characters in a Movie and You're the Director

You're the director of a film. You get to choose the cast, the villain, the hero, the heroine, the supporting actors, and all the extras. Everybody that is in your movie is there because you chose them. Every scene, conversation, mood, and the outcome is written and directed by you. As well as being the director, you are also starring in the movie. You can play any role just how you like. The exception is that you base every scene or scenario on a feeling you have or something that happened in your life. It won't progress or end the same, but that's the whole point of the rewrite.

Now, set the stage by asking yourself these questions.

- Where does your movie take place?
- How old are you?
- Who's in the scene with you?
- What is the issue?
- How do you feel about what's happening?
- How will you make others feel about what is going on?
- What do you want to say to others?
- How do you want them to respond?
- How will this scenario end?

Once you have set up the scene, play it out on paper by describing the event and characters, including yourself. Write down your thoughts, movements, dialogue, and actions. Make the scene complete by doing the same with the other main characters. Then have the extras respond as you want. Write down what you want them to think, say, and do. Don't forget to involve your senses to make the scene come alive. Write about how things look, feel, sound, smell like, and if it takes place around a dining table, even describe how the food tastes. The more you involve your sense in your rewrites, the more your subconscious will accept it as reality.

When you are rewriting the scenario or scene, you don't have to write it as it happened. Instead, rewrite it how you might have wanted it to happen. Remember, you are the director of all the characters, including yourself. You can create such exaggerated characters that the scene is hilarious. Your movie can be a comedy, drama, science fiction, or suspense. It's not the scene or event that has to be believable, but rather the way you acted and the way you portray yourself and others' feelings that make it real. The following is a sample of how one of your rewrites might look.

Setting

I'm at the office working late with several of my co-workers. Our boss is an overbearing, demanding old wrinkled up man whom everybody fears. Before we see him come into our office pool, we smell the rankness of his body odor as he stomps into the room. He leans over my desk, his greasy hair combed over the top of his head, attempting to hide the evidence of his balding crown. When he looks around the room and smiles, the grin never touches his eyes but merely makes his yellowing teeth more prominent.

166

For the hundredth time, he has entered our area to embarrass me in front of my co-workers. This time, things will be different. This time he's not going to get away with blaming me for a mistake I didn't make. As he straightens himself to step out into the isle, he accidently trips over my garbage can and ends up sprawled on the floor. I cover my mouth as I gasp, but you can hear the giggles of my co-workers as they look up from their desks.

Now he's steaming and tells me he is keeping me late to make the changes. Everyone is upset with him because they know it was his mistake that created the problem. He moves to the door and then turns with orders for me to work until I get it right.

Dialogue

Me: (I've had it, and I now have saved enough money to fund my own business. "Oh, no you don't! There's no way you're blaming me again for your stupid mistake. You made the mess; now you get to clean it up." (I point to everybody else in the room) "Everybody else knows that you're to blame, and we're all getting sick of taking your crap."

Boss: "Maybe so, but you need your jobs—so, get to work. I don't care if it takes you all night." (Everybody else in the room gets up to walk over and stand behind my desk.)

Co-workers: "Not this time, Jack!"

Boss: (Turns to look at me.) "Really? We'll see about that." (Walks back to my desk and looks down at me.) "Pack up your things and get out. You're fired!"

Me: "You can't fire me, I quit! And, guess what? I'll be your new competitor."

Co-workers: "If she goes, we all go."

Boss: "You can't all leave. What will all of you do for work."

Me: "They're coming to work for my company. Now get to work—and, I don't care if it takes you all night." (I throw the words over my shoulder as I walk out with my co-workers. My co-workers and I are a huge success and end up running our old boss out of business.)

Rewrite your outcomes with passion and strength. Make them have the kind of endings that give you encouragement and hope. Make the words and actions bigger than life, and give yourself that over-the-top leadership quality that makes you a person everybody wants to follow. No matter what you rewrite, you be the winner, and you have the upper hand.

Once you get good at descriptions and dialogue, you'll be amazed at how good you feel when you complete your rewrite. After all, who doesn't want to script, direct, and star in a movie where they always win. You'll win the job, your love interest, the admiration and support of others, and you'll win against the villain's plot.

Most importantly, your subconscious will begin to think of you as a winner. Your self-talk will start to reflect the new you and portray you in your mind as a winner. Soon, you'll prove them all right and become a winner.

Chapter 6: Step #6—Creating Positive Associations

Studies show that people can break bad habits quicker if they replace the bad habit with a good one. For example, if you want to stop smoking, then every time you would have taken a smoke break, take a music break. Put on some easy-listening music and practice some deep breathing exercises to calm you. Or, play your favorite Motown and put on your dancing shoes. You'll learn to let the music and deep breathing relax you instead of the cigarettes. Or, you'll dance until you're downright happy. Who can be sad when they're dancing to Motown, right? Anyway you do it, you're replacing a bad habit with a good one.

You've allowed negative self-talk to become an automatic reaction to some event or situation that didn't go your way. Okay, so to break this bad habit, you'll need to create some positive associations that are strong enough to help you change your beliefs and behaviors. Once you have experienced some success with this step-by-step guide to assist you with your depression and anxiety, you'll be able to make positive associations between past experiences and present beliefs. These positive associations will help you to dispel the false talk that keeps you from moving forward and enjoying a future free of depression and anxiety.

What are Positive Associations?

Positive associations are when you take two or more objects or feelings and connect them together. For example, in Pavlov's experiment with the dog he would offer his dog a tasty treat, and as soon as the dog got the treat, he would ring a bell. After a period, the dog didn't need the food; he would merely hear the sound of the bell and begin to slobber in anticipation of the treat. He had made a positive association between the sound and his goodie.

Likewise, you can learn to make positive associations with your feelings and something positive. Without intending to, you have come to make negative associations with your sense of depression and sleep. You know that you can escape depression by sleeping. So, when you begin to feel depressed, you automatically want to curl up and sleep to get relief from the depression. Wouldn't it be wonderful if you could make some positive associations that would allow you to change your thinking? For instance, you also know that exercise helps to alleviate stress and anxiety. So, when you begin to feel depressed, it would be so much better if you automatically wanted to get active. It's an association that offers physical and emotional benefits.

At first, the positive association feels much like you are rewarding yourself for feeling depressed, but this isn't the case. You're creating an opportunity to link something positive to do that will occur automatically, taking the place of the automatic negative self-talk and need to isolate.

How Do You Create Positive Associations?

Creating strong positive associations doesn't happen right away. In fact, to make connections that can change your behaviors and perceptions requires lots of practice, repetition, and an intentional routine. The positive motivator also should be something you love, something that makes you feel incredible, free, and happy.

Many people think positive associations always deal with money, but it is the things that money can buy that create the connection. Having a lot of money sitting in the bank doesn't give most people a thrill, but enjoying an exotic vacation or buying a boat might be unbelievably powerful. Don't think that positive associations need to be expensive. Like Pavlov's dog, a routinely given treat might do the trick.

The longer you have suffered from depression and anxiety, the more frequently you will need to create positive associations to help you change your behavior and perceptions. Don't wait until you are in the middle of a deep depression to try to apply positive associations. Work on replacing the negative with positive when you're feeling good. If you are having an especially good day, use your journal to write down a description of the day. File in your mind how good it feels to be mentally strong and healthy. Enjoy the weather, and think to yourself how you're going to remember how warm and cozy it felt to enjoy the sunshine and be out in nature. Then, the next time you start feeling down, or you begin to hear negative self-talk, give your mental files a going through and search for those positive memories.

If your subconscious doesn't know the difference between imagined feelings and real emotions, then keep believing you're enjoying that incredible day. Think about how it felt to walk in the sunshine or lay in a hammock on the beach. Remember what it was like to take that dream vacation with your loved one. Smell the salt in the air, and feel the sand beneath your toes. Soon, your mind will focus on positive thoughts and associations rather than the negative ones. Your mind will focus on what you tell it to, so make your automatic "go to" thoughts be the positive ones.

Once you've got your ideas headed in the positive direction, you'll need to follow that up with immediate action. Don't just think about something positive, do something positive. Again, if Pavlov had not continued to follow the sound of the bell with treats, soon the conditioning would have disappeared, and the dog would have stopped slobbering when he heard the bell. The ringing of the bell created the physical response of slobbering, but the food was the reward. The thoughts encourage you to begin to change your thinking from negative to positive, but it's the repeated affirmative action that helps you to change your behavior.

Rewarding your positive thoughts with positive actions will keep the associations strong. Merely distinguishing the behavior cannot be the association or the reward. Sometimes the reward is not to change. When you've experienced depression and anxiety most of your life, you could just be too darn comfortable with your feelings. You have accepted that you are a rather sad and anxious person, and then you think about ways to justify your feelings.

"I'm supposed to be the thinker in the family, the serious one, the one who has their feet firmly planted." See, how you begin to talk yourself into your sad way of thinking so you won't have to go through the pain of change? Change brings with it newness, unfamiliar territory, and many people believe they are more uncomfortable with change than with their anxiety or depression.

Did you see what happened there? You made a connection between change and something negative. If you feel that change is hard and requires sacrifice, then you have created a negative connection. If you are depressed or highly anxious, you need to change your thinking. However, if change represents a negative experience for you, then you won't change that negative self-talk because change is negative. Getting caught in a negative cycle can be devastating for the depressed.

Passionate Memories Create Strong Associations

To create connections strong enough to change behavior you need to learn to live life passionately. Whatever you do, do it with heart—with emotion—with desire. When you're living life to the fullest, there's no time for depression and anxiety. If you're doing what you love, you will enjoy every day. If you're not doing what you love, you may be paying the price with depression and anxiety.

I know what you're asking yourself about right now: "But, what if I cannot support myself doing what I love?" Okay, I'll buy that. If you love horses, but you live in the city and only get to ride twice a year, how are you going to do what you love and support yourself? Residing in these circumstances doesn't mean you can't be passionate about what you love and find enjoyment from horses every day. It just requires you to be a bit more creative.

You could surround yourself with equine art so that you could enjoy the beauty of horses every day. You could visit the equestrian center outside of town once a month and smell the hay and groom the horses, and then take a pleasant ride in the country. You could put pictures of horses on your screen saver or your phone. You could volunteer with an equine rescue on the weekends. You could read about them and watch movies and documentaries about the magic of horses. All these things feed your passion.

Whatever you do, make every positive association remarkable. Build the positives in your life to be bigger and brighter than a full moon. It will take the wind out of your negative sails. If you can say "so what" to the negatives, then you take away their power. "Okay, so I did poorly on that test—so what? I have five more this semester to do my best. One bad grade isn't going to make me fail the course." Or, "I wrecked my car—so what? I walked away unscathed, and nobody else was hurt. It could have been so much worse." By minimizing the negative, you take away its influence over your thinking.

Thinking positive is like performing magic on your thought process. You may not know how it works, but you sure are enjoying the show!

Conclusion

Thank you again for purchasing this book!

I hope *Cognitive Behavioral Therapy: The Complete Step-by-Step Guide on Retraining Your Brain and Overcoming Depression, Anxiety and Phobias* will help you to understand better how to successfully manage your depression, anxiety, and any phobias from which you might be suffering. Our goal with these six steps is to give you the opportunity to learn strategies that will help you reduce the negative self-talk that holds you back from achieving your goals. Not only that, but we hope you will replace your depressed state and anxiety with the rewriting of a new YOU.

The next step is to begin applying these six steps to your life. By practicing the following measures, you can create new opportunities to work through the debilitating depression and anxiety that has plagued you for years and create hope for tomorrow that will close the doors on depression and open the windows to hope and happiness. To remind you of the steps, they are as follows.

Step #1—Understanding Your Depression, Anxiety or Phobias

Step #2—Facing the Enemy

Step #3—Practicing a Step-by-Step Recovery

Step #4—Controlling Your Negative Self-Talk

Step #5—Rewriting the Outcome

Step #6—Creating Positive Associations

We hope you refuse to wait one more day before fighting back, before challenging and changing your thinking to embrace the positive future that awaits you. Our hope is that you are encouraged by what you have read in the pages of this book—encouraged to find new solutions to your long-standing problems. To increase your knowledge and learn more about these topics, we'd like to invite you to read our other works. They are entitled *Cognitive Behavioral Therapy: The Definitive Guide to Understanding Your Brain, Depression, Anxiety and How to Overcome it* and *Cognitive Behavioral Therapy Mastery: How to Master Your Brain and Your Emotions to Overcome Depression, Anxiety and Phobias.*

The decisions are yours. It is your choice to face the challenges of change and do the work that will create greater opportunities to experience the positive. We hope we have inspired you to stop hiding from the discomfort and pain of depression and anxiety and begin to question your thinking and embrace a new perspective. Applying our step-by-step guide to retraining your brain will give you the practical tools you need to practice a whole new way of thinking. You'll learn to test your thoughts and verify the truth of your beliefs.

Once you experience some small successes in more positive and accurate thoughts of yourself, your performance and personality will begin to bloom. You will no longer be held down by the darkness of depression or the angst of anxiety. Our steps have given you knowledge, and knowledge brings with it the power to change.

Congratulations on all the positive changes you are about to experience. Thank you again, and good luck!

Cognitive Behavioral Therapy

21 Most Effective Tips and Tricks on Retraining Your Brain and Overcoming Depression, Anxiety, and Phobias

Introduction

I want to thank you and congratulate you for purchasing the book, "Cognitive Behavioral Therapy: 21 Most Effective Tips and Tricks on Retraining Your Brain and Overcoming Depression, Anxiety and Phobias".

This book contains proven steps and strategies on how to rewire or retrain your brain in order to change how you see and feel certain difficulties that happen in your life. In effect, it can also help treat different issues such as: phobias, anxiety, and even depression.

This book gives you a brief overview of cognitive behavioral therapy and how it can help you control your thoughts and actions. It also gives you useful information about rewiring or retraining your brain to unlearn unhealthy thought patterns.

Thank you and I hope you enjoy it!

Chapter 1: Cognitive Behavioral Therapy Overview

Has your life been robbed of beauty and fullness by fear? Are you tired of people telling you that the only way you can overcome your fears is to face them? While it is true that facing your fears is an effective way to overcome your fears, it is not the only way. In fact, there are other ways you can try to overcome your phobias, depression, and anxiety. One of these ways is rewiring your brain.

You see, your brain generally takes the easiest approach to deal with problems and that is fleeing. Fleeing is actually a learned response that is much easier than overcoming challenges and facing confrontations. Nevertheless, it is still possible to rewire the brain so that it responds differently to similar situations. Yes, it may require pain and dedication, but it is all worth it.

Throughout the years, your brain may have adopted certain ways such as fear, anxiety, panic, and worry; but all of these can be unlearned. You can rewire your brain to act the way you want it to so that it can successfully serve its purpose in your life.

For some people, the answer is COGNITIVE BEHAVIORAL THERAPY.

What is CBT?

Put in the simplest terms, CBT is a goal-oriented, short-term treatment that actually takes a more hands-on approach when it comes to dealing with the issues that people have. The primary goal here is to basically rewire the brain—that is, change a person's pattern of thinking, and in doing so, also changed the way they feel. It is used to treat a number of different issues; this treatment can help with relationship problems, sleeping difficulties, and even drug or alcohol abuse.

Alright, let's talk about rewiring the brain again. CBT is able to do this by focusing on thoughts, beliefs, attitudes, and images that are held by the individual's cognitive processes. Keep in mind that how these processes happen relates to how that individual behaves as well and how they cope with emotional problems.

Short-Term vs. Long Term

So, one of the more significant advantages that CBT has over other forms of treatment would be the fact that it is shorter in terms of duration. It usually lasts around five to ten months for most emotional issues that need to be treated.

A client would need to diligently attend one session every week, with each one lasting for about 50 minutes at a time. For the average individual, this is only a minimal chunk of time that they need to devote to it, but the results are worth every minute.

What happens during a session?

For the 50 minutes they spend in session, the client and therapist would work together in order to better understand what the real problems are. Once these have been properly identified, a new strategy for dealing with them is created—it is during this time that clients are usually introduced to a set of principles or philosophies which they can apply whenever needed. These are principles that is useful for any given situation and would last them a lifetime.

Cognitive Behavioral Therapy is a combination of **behavioral therapy** and **psychotherapy**. It takes psychotherapy's emphasis on the importance of the meaning we give certain things and the thinking patterns we form in childhood. From behavioral therapy, it derives the need to pay a closer attention to the relationship between the issues we have, our thoughts, and our overall behavior.

It must be noted that most psychotherapists who practice CBT will customize the treatment to the specific need of each individual client. Needless to say, there is no "one-size-fits-all" solution for everyone.

CBT Benefits:

People who have specific problems tend to be the most suitable for CBT as its techniques tend to focus on very specific goals. Most experts agree that it isn't as suitable for people who feel vaguely unfulfilled or have fleeting moments of unhappiness. The same goes for people who do not have specific areas of their lives they want to work on and improve.

It is also more likely to benefit people who related to the ideas behind CBT as many of them can be very different from other types of treatment. It is a very problem-solving approach, and is meant for people who want a more practical treatment as opposed to gaining further insight into the self.

It is most effective for:

- Anxiety and panic attacks
- Anger Management

- Chronic Fatigue Syndrome
- Chronic Pain
- Drug and Alcohol Addiction
- Depression
- Mood Swings
- Eating Problems
- General Health Problems
- Bad Habits and Facial Tics
- Phobias
- PTSD
- OCD
- Sleep Problems
- Sexual and Relationship Problems

Thoughts, Feelings and the Internal Dialogue

It was psychiatrist Aaron Beck who first realized the connection between an individual's thoughts and feelings, and that these two can significantly affect how a person behaves. The idea here is simple, imagine this scenario:

During a meeting with their bosses, an employee might think to themselves "My boss hasn't said much about my presentation. Are they displeased with it?" These thoughts can lead to the employee feeling anxious or distressed. In turn, they might continue thinking that, "Maybe they're simply distracted or perhaps, I haven't been providing enough interesting information to keep them focused." With that second thought, the employee's overall feelings might change.

These thoughts are what Beck refers to as "automatic thoughts", basically the ones that easily pop up in the mind when we're in situations that aren't comfortable. His studies show that most people are not aware of these thoughts, but they can learn how to identify and talk about them. Think about it for yourself; how many times have you found yourself upset and began thinking negative thoughts that were neither helpful nor realistic?

Negative thinking is automatic in these situations. Don't worry, it's totally normal. In fact, these could even be the key that would help you overcome your difficulties.

Cognitive Behavioral Therapy is meant to help you understand what is happening in your mind. It would enable you to view your automatic thoughts from a different perspective, basically giving you more insight into them. The thing is, negative and uncomfortable situations aren't things we can simply walk away from—but knowing how to deal with them properly is a good start.

Think of it as your first step towards breaking the pattern of you listening to your negative thoughts, and subsequently feeling discouraged because of it. Once you understand how it works, you would be able to separate yourself from these thoughts and figure out a solution to the dilemma you're currently facing. No, it won't be an easy road, but it certainly is doable.

So, where does one begin?

Chapter 2: Be Aware of Cognitive Distortions

These are your inaccurate thoughts that reinforce negative emotions and thoughts. Some people are quite prone to this, allowing the thoughts to convince them of a reality that is simply not true. For example:

"My officemate isn't replying to me. Maybe they're busy? Or is it because they don't like me and would rather not be bothered by my presence?"

If you aren't aware of cognitive distortions, you might easily believe the latter. However, it simply isn't true.

Here are some common distortions you must avoid:

1. Filtering.

This refers to a person's inability to see the good things that are also happening around them. Basically, they only dwell on the negative aspect of things, whether it be their own skill or the issue they're currently facing, and as such, they fail to see the other possibilities that may come from it. Many people are prone to this.

How do you overcome it? **Try making use of positive affirmations.**

Positive affirmations refer to the words that you tell yourself over and over until they become ingrained into your subconscious mind. They are practically messages that give you encouragement and motivation. They are also anti-negative self-talk. Hence, they can significantly improve your self-confidence and self-esteem.

The positive effects of positive affirmations are evident in a study featured in the Journal of American College Health. According to this study, female participants who applied cognitive behavioral techniques into their life, such as positive affirmations, were able to reduce negative thinking as well as alleviate symptoms of depression.

How to Create Positive Affirmations

The following are pointers that can help you create the most effective positive affirmations that will change your life:

1. Be mindful of the words, phrases, and sentences that you use. After all, you do not want to send out the wrong message to the universe and to yourself. Before you finalize your affirmations, see to it that you check the wordings and phrasings.

2. Keep in mind that your emotions are connected with your words. So, when you recite positive affirmations, your emotions follow suit. This is why you have to refrain from using words that can relate to negative emotions, such as 'hate'. You can replace these negative words with positive ones, such as 'love'.

3. Use the present tense. The subconscious mind is not able to differentiate positive and negative sentences because all it knows is the present. This is why you have to write and recite your positive affirmations in the present tense to get your desired effects.

4. Keep your mind calm, peaceful, and relaxed. If you want your positive affirmations to work, you have to recite them when your mind is clear so that it can easily absorb what you say. You must refrain from reciting affirmations if your mind is chaotic because this will send out the wrong messages to the universe and to yourself.

Remember to Look at the Bigger Picture

Experts say that in order for you to stay happy, you have to look at the big picture and not focus on the negatives. If you focus on the negatives, you will miss out on the positive aspects of things and you will not enjoy your life.

According to Paul Dubois, a Swiss psychiatrist, you have to get a piece of paper and draw a couple of columns on it. Then, you have to write down the things that trouble you as well as the things that make you happy. For everything that troubles you, you have to give it a happy counterpart. You have to do this exercise every night before you go to bed.

The main idea behind this exercise is to realize that you have positive things happening to you daily. For every bad experience you have, you will find a good experience. This will prevent you from merely focusing on the negatives and aggravating your depression or anxiety.

For example, if you arrive late for work, you may beat yourself up. You may think to yourself that you are going to get reprimanded by your boss and that you may have a bad record. However, something good can still come out of this. If you are religious, you can view it as God's way of sparing you from an accident or from an unpleasant situation.

If your fiancé left you at the altar, you may think that it is the end of the world; but it is not. You can either be depressed about this or view it as a blessing in disguise. You may have actually dodged a bullet by not marrying this person because you are meant to meet someone much better.

In doing this, you are training your mind to focus more on the positive and possibilities that may arise from difficulties. So each time you feel as if you're obsessing over the bad, make sure you do these exercises to remind yourself of the good as well.

2. Overgeneralization.

This is taking a single bad experience and using it as basis for how the others might turn out. Imagine this scenario: An individual is looking to get their art recognized. They have confidence in what they can do, but after a bad review, they began feeling discouraged and believe every negative criticism they were given. In the end, they refused to continue painting. Quite a waste, right? Don't let yourself fall into the same trap.

How do you overcome it? **Use the power of positive visualization**.

Visualization, which is also referred to as guided imagery, is another effective way to overcome any negative train of thought you might be having. In fact, it is also known to help people when it comes to dealing with their anxiety and depression—even phobias.

The idea here is rather simple. Every time you perform guided imagery or visualization, you imagine yourself in a place or time that relaxes you. If you are sick, you may also imagine yourself in a healthier state.

How does it work? Well, it replaces negative images in your mind with positive ones. Imagine the painter once more—this time, they're making use of visualization to help lessen the anxiety they feel over having to present their artworks. Through independent or guided visualization, they evoke images of an applauding crowd, even the biggest critics they have are wearing a smile and nodding their approval.

Their pieces are hung in some of the biggest galleries and in time, they get offers from people who wish to purchase them. All of that could be achieved if they simply took that important step of picking up their paintbrush again and looking past the negative review they were given.

It's such a simple practice, but it can be powerful enough to help restore an individual's confidence and replace the negative images they might have previously had in their minds.

Guided imagery or visualization is actually a form of meditative practice. It involves the use of words, visualizations, and/or music that encourages positive images to appear in the mind and create the desired effects on the body. It can energize or calm your body, as well as help eliminate your negative thoughts and emotions.

3. Personalization.

This is a kind of cognitive distortion that has individuals believing that everything they do actually impacts people and other external events. It doesn't matter how irrational the link may seem, the belief is stronger than logic. The person who suffers from this distortion would always feel as if they had a role in the bad events that happen around them.

For example, they may feel as if the company meeting was unsuccessful because they were late to it—despite the fact that their role in said meeting is particularly minor compared to other people's. This is also what happens in children who tend to blame themselves for the separation of their parents. They begin to believe that it is somewhat their fault and that, perhaps, if they were a better child, then it wouldn't have happened.

How do you overcome it? **Remind yourself that not everything is under your control**, and that sometimes, unless you were directly involved then the blame is not on you. Now, this would be difficult if the individual has gotten used to this pattern of thinking, but with practice it is certainly something that can be easily dealt with.

Take for example a friend of mine who experiences this ever so often. In order to avoid obsessing over the situation, what they do is take a 5 minute break to mentally list down possible solutions to the problem at hand. In doing this exercise, they are able to distract themselves and the feeling eventually passes. The productivity is a plus, and in some cases, they were able to come up with great suggestions for their entire team as well.

Remember, not everything is under your control, and despite your mistakes, you are not always to blame for things not going as they're supposed to.

4. Emotional Reasoning.

This distortion often leads people into thinking that if they feel it, then it must be true. For example, if you feel uninteresting or unappealing in a given moment, then it must be why people are not giving you any attention.

But does this line of thinking actually apply? Of course not. Our emotions will not always be an accurate indication of the truth. However, these feelings might be difficult to overlook for some. This is especially true if there are already underlying thoughts that further feed this emotion, insecurities that they may not have voiced out before, but have constantly been in their minds.

Again, we go back to: OUR THOUGHTS AFFECT OUR FEELINGS.

How do we overcome it? **Challenge your emotional reasoning**.

It will be a bit difficult at first, but it is the first step. Look at your situation and analyze how you're reacting to it. Perhaps the reason why no one's talking to you is because you're not putting in enough effort to connect with people. Say you're with a group, you'll easily feel left out if you don't participate in the ongoing conversation. Speak your thoughts every now and then or agree with an opinion that matches yours.

You cannot expect people to do all the work for you. If you remain hidden at a party, then the chances of you meeting new friends is very slim. The same goes if you maintain a stance that's a bit off putting—body posture speaks too. Try and be more open, you need not make a big splash or put on a show. Do what you're comfortable with when it comes to changing the situation; challenge your reasoning by testing your thoughts out.

5. Fallacy of Fairness.

More often than not, we are concerned with fairness and everyone getting the equal share. However, in this case, it is taken to the extremes. It is a fact of life that things do not always go our way—it will not always be fair. People who have this distortion tend to look for fairness in every experience they have, often ending up unhappy and resentful of the world, as well as the people around them.

For example, people tend to think that kindness will be rewarded with kindness. Say, you allowed someone to get ahead of you in a queue thinking that this would be reciprocated the next time you're in a rush. However, you are only met with rejection and judgment when you do give it a try.

Life is unfair! This will be your first thought—no, it would be most people's. It might leave you distressed and angry. Some people even become disillusioned the more it occurs, thinking that everyone is against them and that the world is simply unkind. Sounds dramatic? Not at all. There are people who think this way, and it is also one of the reasons why some of them end up becoming depressed.

How do you overcome it? Whilst you cannot change the world overnight, there are some changes that you can apply to yourself. The first of which would be reminding yourself that life will not always go your way EVEN if you put an effort into always doing things right. Do not expect to be rewarded for your deeds, and instead, simply do them because, well, the world needs more of it.

Each time you find yourself in an unfair situation, look at it and try to find the possibilities. There's always something positive in any negative situation, you just have practice changing how you look at them.

6. Fallacy of Change.

This refers to an individual's irrational expectation that other people would change according to what suits them. Basically, this means that our overall happiness becomes dependent on how other people act, and in their unwillingness to "cooperate" despite being pushed to or demanded to hinder us from feeling fulfilled. This is a truly damaging way to think and can cause depression and relationship issues, especially since no one else is responsible for our own happiness other than ourselves.

Ask yourself: Are the people around you providing you with positive encouragement? Are they focused on developing as individuals or are they simply hanging on to you because they gain some form of benefit?

The truth of the matter is this: There are cases wherein we find ourselves with a group of people purely out of convenience—because they're there. They do not contribute to our development as people nor do we influence them positively. In such scenarios, both parties might develop certain expectations that remain unfulfilled simply because their personalities, development as individuals, and overall path no longer match up.

It may also be that you're surrounding yourself with people who demand so much of you or whose expectations you keep trying to live up to, but feel as if you're unable to do so. This can cause feelings of inadequacy to take root and with that, lowered self-confidence, anxiety, and depression.

There's nothing wrong about outgrowing the company you keep. It happens to everyone and in some cases, it is much healthier to cut ties instead of hanging on to them. REMEMBER: You are responsible for your own happiness and as such, if you must take action, then YOU need to start now.

PRO TIP: Surround Yourself with Optimistic People

If you want to be free from depression and anxiety, you have to keep your circle happy. Negative people are toxic to your wellbeing because their negativity can wear off on you. Keep in mind that both positivity and negativity are contagious. Whoever you surround yourself with can have a great impact on your mindset and attitude. This is why successful people surround themselves with other successful people. Likewise, those who want to succeed in life find people who may influence them in a positive sense.

The same thing applies if you want to overcome depression, anxiety, and phobias. You have to choose your company wisely. If all you see all day are people who are sad, depressed, and blaming the world for their problems, you too will be like them pretty soon. Nevertheless, even though you cannot control the way they think and behave, you can still control the way you treat them. You can also control the way you react towards their negativity.

It would be nice to try to help these people change for the better. You can try to influence and encourage them to change their ways and be more positive. However, you just cannot force anyone to do something that they do not want to do. They have to be willing to help themselves. A lot of negative people are not even aware that they are toxic to others. So, if you want to save yourself and maintain your sanity, the best thing to do is simply walk away and stay away from them as much as possible.

People can only be helped if they really want to be helped. If they try to drag you into their drama, you must walk away. Rather than answer or fight back, you should just focus on your own thing. You must focus on yourself, your goals, and the things that can help you grow better as a person. You have to let go of the negative people in your life if you want to be happy and stress free.

You have to take care of yourself, which means that you have to take good care of your physical and mental health. Remember that your mind affects your body. So, if you do not have a healthy mind, you will have an unhealthy body as well. This is why you have to surround yourself with people who are beneficial to your mental wellness. You should only hang out with people who inspire, encourage, and support you.

Negative people are toxic to your sanity. If you have friends who are negative, you should cut them from your life, even if you have known them for a long time. If you have co-workers who do nothing but gossip and pick on other people, you should stay as far away from them as you can. Do not talk to them unless you really have to and it is solely about work. These people will only drag you down to their level and you do not want that.

7. Catastrophizing

This refers to the individual who is always expecting the worst possible thing that could happen even if the situation is minor or nowhere near the level of tragedy they're picturing. For example, you have a fear of water and despite the countless safety measures put in place, you still believe that something will go wrong. In your head, that waist-deep water can still drown you.

How to overcome it? Face up to your fears and expose yourself to them.

194

In doing so, you'll be able to see the reality of the situation instead of creating negative scenarios in your head. An effective way to get over your fears is to gradually face them until you become more aware of the fact that IT'S ALL IN YOUR HEAD. The more exposure you get the more familiar you become with the fear. This lessens its impact on you. So for example, if you want to be more comfortable with public speaking or negotiating, you can undergo exposure therapy.

Katherina Hauner, a neuroscientist from the Rehab Institute of Chicago, said that exposure therapy dramatically improves the way patients view their fears. This treatment method is typically performed in hierarchical steps. The series starts with a low level of engagement and increases with every step. For example, if you have a fear of water, try starting with shallow pools and gradually make your way to the deeper end.

The Right Amount of Exposure

In order for exposure therapy to work for you, you have to have just the right amount of exposure. You have to enter the situation with a clear goal to avoid making your anxiety worse.

Keep in mind that exposing yourself to a situation does not automatically mean having to walk into a room and standing idly. You have to ask yourself how you have to behave in this kind of situation. When you expose yourself to new situations and yet you still behave the way you did in the past, you will only end up feeling anxious again because you are just reconditioning yourself to do so.

This is why you have to act differently when you expose yourself to a different situation. If you are faced with a new situation and yet your actions are still the same, you expose yourself to the situation and avoid it at the same time. This prevents you from fully exposing yourself and allowing you to overcome anxiety.

Let's go back to our example. Instead of saying to getting in the water, try doing it bit by bit. If you feel more comfortable if you wear a life-vest then do so! The important thing here is to actually make the first step and changing your usual pattern of saying NO. This time, say YES to the experience. Sure, you may not overcome your fear after one try, but there is power in conquering that first level.

How to Expose Yourself to Challenges and Situations

Keep in mind that exposure requires proper planning and timing. You need to condition yourself and make a commitment to overcoming your depression, anxiety, and phobias.

You need to create a list of all the things that make you fearful, just as the one you have read previously in this book. You have to include everything, whether they are objects, situations, places, or people. You have to be as clear and specific as possible, writing down every detail that involves your fear.

Consider your environment. Some people feel more anxious about swimming in a lake while others feel more anxious about swimming in a pool. When you swim in a lake, you have less control of your environment. On the other hand, when you swim in a pool, there are lifeguards and you are also more aware of the water's depth.

The Fear Ladder

Then, you have to face your fears. You have also read about this earlier. You can start facing the fears that are at the bottom of your Fear Ladder or the ones that give you the least amount of anxiety. At first, you may spend only a few seconds or minutes facing your fears. As you become less anxious about it, you may spend more time facing such fears until you no longer fear them.

Every time you perform exposure exercise, you can track your level of fear. You can stay in the fearful situation until your fear level goes down by fifty percent. For example, if carrying a knife has a rating of 6/10 on your Fear Scale, you can continue carrying it until your level of fear drops down to just 3/10.

You also have to plan performing exposure exercises ahead of schedule so that you can have more control over your situations as well as easily determine what you have to do. Do not forget to keep track of your progress. Compare your situations before and after to see how far you have come as well as find out about the things you have learned along the way.

Regular practice is also necessary.

You also have to maintain your gains even if you have already gotten comfortable about doing something. You should not stop exposing yourself to your feared situation so that your fears do not return. For example, if you have successfully overcome your fear of the water, go swimming regularly. Do not let a long time pass by before you give it a try again as this might be detrimental to your progress.

Remember, the more familiar you make yourself with your fears the less you'll catastrophize the situation.

Chapter 3: Employ CBT Tools and Maximize Them

There are many simple tools that can help you understand your thoughts better, as well as what they might be rooted at. It is important that you use and maximize them in order to fully immerse yourself in the treatment. In this chapter, we present you with some of the most common CBT tools and how you can use them better.

8. *Journaling*

Think of journaling as a means of gathering data about your thoughts and your different moods. When writing in your journal, always try to expand on the mood or thought. Answer some of these questions:

1. *What was the source?*

2. *How intense was the thought or the mood?*

3. *How did you respond to it?*

This tool can help you better identify your emotional tendencies and thought patterns. Having a record enables you to look back as well, and look at everything from an outsider's perspective. A journal helps prevent you from being in your head too much as well—this can lead to negative thinking if you're not careful.

The Benefits of Starting a Journal

Journaling is a relaxing and effective way to express thoughts and emotions freely, without worrying about hurting others or being scrutinized. After all, you are the only one who gets to read your thoughts when you put it on paper. You can say everything you want without inhibitions on your journal. Hence, you can get things off your chest without making a fool of yourself in public.

You can keep your journal hidden to keep your entries secret or start an online journal that is available to the public. Do not worry because even if your virtual journal is available for all Internet users to see, you still get to keep your anonymity, just as long as you do not publish personal information such as your full name, address, and contact details. You may also want to change the names of the people involved so as to protect their identities.

Then again, this may be too much work for you, especially if you do not have time to edit names or use code names. An advantage of using a virtual journal is that you get to have unlimited space. You can write as many entries as you want, and you do not have to buy a new journal. In addition, you do not have to worry about misplacing your journal and having someone else find and read it. You can also write from anywhere, as long as you bring your computer with you.

Journaling lets you communicate with the areas of your psyche that have been frozen; thus, allowing you to tap into the deeper reserves of problem solving and creativity. When you write in a journal, you are able to gain a flash of awareness and knowing that you have not yet seen before. This enables you to gain clarity and reduce any feelings of depression or anxiety.

According to Dr. Michael Rank, co-director and associate professor at the International Traumatology Institute of the University of South Florida, journaling forces you to act and do something. Dr. Jessie Gruman, executive director at the Center for the Advancement of Health in Washington, agrees that journaling is an excellent way to cope with depression and anxiety.

What's more, journaling gives you a chance to see your feelings in black and white. More often than not, you judge your feeling and thoughts subjectively. This is not healthy because you may have the wrong interpretation. When you write down your thoughts, you can pause or reread them, allowing you to reflect and properly figure out how to deal with them.

9. Make Room for Pleasant Activity Scheduling.

The idea here is to indulge yourself in an activity that stimulates positive feelings in you. For some, this could be a good book and a good cup of coffee, for others it could be catching up with friends. What's important is that it must be an activity that's healthy for you—so, no binge eating or smoking. These things might stimulate the pleasure sensors in your brain, but they can actually worsen your overall state of mind.

Sugar can cause energy crashes. Smoking can cause addictions.

A good option to try here is creating a regular exercise routine for yourself. Regular, as in, something you do quite often if you cannot manage to do it everyday.

The Benefits of Exercising:

The physical and mental benefits of exercise have long been established. All experts agree that regular exercise can help fight against diseases and improve overall wellness. Exercise is not only good for your physical body, but for your mental health as well.

Numerous studies have shown that exercise can reduce fatigue, enhance overall cognitive function, improve concentration, and increase alertness. With this being said, regular exercise can help you focus better as well as increase your energy levels. More importantly, it can help you manage your stress and anxiety levels.

When stress affects the brain, along with its nerve connections, the body feels the same negative impact. This is why you need to condition both your mind and body when you are stressed or anxious. Since your body gets pumped up with adrenaline during moments of stress and anxiety, you need to put this adrenaline rush towards physical activity, such as aerobic exercises, to make you feel better.

Furthermore, scientists say that regular aerobic exercises can significantly reduce levels of tension, improve sleep, boost self-esteem, and increase and stabilize mood levels. So, even if you are too busy with work and you do not have time to go to the gym, you can still exercise. You can perform exercises in five minutes and still reap the same good benefits as you would when you spend half an hour to one hour at the gym.

What Exercise Does:

It is no secret that exercise is indeed effective in keeping yourself fit, healthy, and happy. The following are the immediate effects of exercise to your mind and body:

- It pumps up endorphins. When you engage in any physical activity, you encourage the production of endorphins. This enables your mood to quickly shift from angry, sad, or frustrated to happy, calm, and optimistic.

- It gives you the benefits of meditation, something that is also important when it comes to CBT as **it keeps you from ruminating**. Exercise can be regarded as meditation in motion. It requires mental focus just like meditation, but with the added body movement. When you exercise, you have to focus on your breathing, movement, and posture leaving no room for negative thinking.

- It serves as a positive distraction. If you are stressed or anxious, you can engage in active sports such as racquetball and swimming, or play any other fast-paced game. Afterwards, you will realize that you no longer feel as irritated and grumpy as before. This happens because exercise also serves as a positive distraction. So rather than stay consumed by worries, you become forced to focus on movement.

- It improves your mood. When you exercise on a regular basis, you improve your self-confidence levels. Physical activity can help achieve relaxation as well as reduce the symptoms related to anxiety and depression. Exercise can also help you sleep better at night so that you can rest and wake up feeling refreshed and rejuvenated.

If you want something a little less physically tasking or if something is preventing you from exercising, you can also opt for mindfulness meditation. It can provide you with the same mental benefits as exercising and can leave you feeling better, and much clearer.

10. Mindfulness Meditation.

There's a wide range of benefits to this, but it is one of the most effective CBT techniques when it comes to dealing with <u>AUTOMATIC THOUGHTS</u>. It enables you to disengage from obsessing and rumination, allowing you to stay grounded. In this manner, your feelings and behavior would not be swayed by any of the negativity that may go on in your mind.

The Benefits of Mindfulness Meditation

Numerous studies have shown that mindfulness meditation is effective in managing depression, pain, and anxiety. It is about training the brain to focus on the present moment instead of the regrets from the past or anxieties towards the future.

Whenever you worry, you focus more on what might happen in the future and what you have to do about it. This can make you anxious and stressed. Through mindfulness meditation, you can break free from these worries and bring your attention back to your present.

Mindfulness is about observing your thoughts and acknowledging them before finally letting them go. It refers to your ability to stay aware of your current feelings as well as moment-to-moment external and internal experiences.

When you practice mindfulness meditation, you are able to determine where your thinking causes problems. It also helps you get in touch better with your emotions. In essence, mindfulness is about acknowledging and observing your anxious feelings and thoughts, letting go of your worries, and staying focused on the present moment.

Mindfulness meditation can help you stay focused and calm in the present so that you are able to bring balance back to your nervous system. Mindfulness meditation has long been practiced in different parts of the world to reduce anxiety, stress, and depression among other mental health issues.

Getting Started

Before you can practice mindfulness meditation, you need to find a quiet environment first. Ideally, you must choose a place that is secluded, quiet, and peaceful. This can be anywhere – in your home, in the woods, or at a temple. Whatever place you choose, it has to be relaxing and free from any interruptions or distractions.

You also have to allot a specific time for your meditation practice. According to experts, the most ideal hours are early in the morning, particularly between 3 o'clock and five o'clock in the morning. The ancient teachers and practitioners of meditation said that it is during these hours that the mind is at its most refreshed state. They add that the mind is like a blank slate which you can easily fill with positive and helpful thoughts.

In addition, meditating in the morning helps you prepare for the long day ahead. In the evening, meditating allows you to clear your mind and get rid of the stressful things that happened throughout the day. It also prepares you for a good night's sleep so that you can wake up feeling refreshed and rejuvenated the next day.

Having specific schedules for practicing mindfulness meditation helps you form consistent habit. The more often you do it, the more automatic it becomes. You can set your timer or alarm clock at a specific hour. Pretty soon, you will no longer think or plan about practicing mindfulness meditation because your body will automatically go to your meditation room and you will start meditating.

You will feel the need to meditate upon waking up in the morning and before going to bed at night. Habits are hard to break, which is why you need to make meditating a solid habit.

1. Begin by finding a comfortable position. When you meditate, you should feel comfortable when you sit. If you are not comfortable, you will not be able to focus on meditating. Make sure that you wear comfortable clothes as well. Choose clothes that are loose, light, and breathable so you can move freely.

2. You can sit on the floor or in a chair, whichever feels more comfortable for you. There are different sitting positions you can choose from. For example, you can choose full lotus, half lotus, or quarter lotus.

3. If you are using an alarm clock to help you keep track of the time, you should place it near you but not too near that it might distract you. You also have to position its face away from you so that you will not be tempted to check the time every now and then. This can be distracting from your meditation session.

4. Do not forget your point of focus. This can be anything, whether real or imaginary. If you prefer to meditate with your eyes open, you can stare at an object as your point of focus. For example, you can stare at the flame of a candle or at a point on the wall.

5. If you prefer to meditate with your eyes closed, you can visualize your point of focus. For example, you can imagine seeing a ray of light. You can also select a mantra or a phrase or word with a special meaning. If you have a mantra, you have to repeat it throughout your meditation session.

It is important that you have a non-critical and observant attitude towards mindfulness meditation. You should not worry about harboring distracting thoughts because it is normal for beginners to have wandering minds. If distracting thoughts come across your mind, you should just let them be. You should not try to fight them, but rather gently bring your attention back to your point of focus.

11. *Cognitive Reframing*.

Cognitive reframing or restructuring is one of the core parts of CBT. It is also considered to be a very effective treatment when it comes to common issues that people face, including: anxiety disorders, binge eating, and depression.

How to do it? It's basically taking something that's making you feel bad, and turning it into something that's good. Let's take anxiety for example.

Reframing Anxiety as Excitement

When you reframe your anxiety as excitement, you are able to devote more resources and energy to the situation. According to Alison Wood, an assistant professor at Harvard Business School, the most ideal way to deal with anxiety is to get excited. This finding is in contrast to the belief of most people, which is to keep calm.

You see, your emotions occur at two levels: arousal and valence. Arousal refers to the physical sensation that occurs in the psych world while valence refers to the way you interpret this arousal mentally.

Whenever you become anxious, your heart rate soars. When this happens, you experience high arousal, and that is a negative valence. So, whenever you feel anxious, you have to reframe it as a feeling of excitement instead of dwelling upon it with feelings of dread. By reframing it, your heart rate soars, but with it comes positive feelings instead of restlessness.

Moreover, researchers have found that those who reframe their anxiety as excitement are able to become better when it comes to dealing with the subject of their problem. These people tend to have higher confidence levels, which are beneficial for success. They also tend to be more optimistic and friendly, traits that can get you far in life. So, the next time you feel anxious, you should find something to be excited about.

Recognize that You Are Doing Alright

Everyday, you have to recognize that you are doing alright. During random moments of your day, you have to take a pause and congratulate yourself for being fine.

Rick Hanson, a neuropsychologist who writes for Psychology Today, says that your instincts for survival make you constantly fearful and unsettled. While these instincts protect you by preventing you from letting your guard down completely, they also make you anxious.

Feeling anxious? Tell yourself that everything is alright, and that it is okay to be feeling this way. It's only natural—after all, you're doing something huge and EXCITING. Do not let the feeling dictate negativity into your mind. Use it instead as a fuel by reminding yourself that you're doing just fine.

12. *Write Down Self-Affirmations*.

This may seem similar to reciting positive affirmations, but there is one distinct difference and that is THE TOPIC OF YOUR AFFIRMATIONS. This exercise centers on you as an individual and on your core values—ones you may have formed during your childhood. These are the ones that have the strongest association to feelings of positivity, especially if they are somehow related to your family.

For example: If you're find yourself having a bout with anxiety before presenting an new idea to the company, tell yourself "My mother always taught me that there are no big challenges, only people who are not up to the task." Repeat that thought until the negative thought is gone and you're only filled with these encouraging words.

Always make sure that you affirm core values before any challenging situations, especially if you start feeling terrified or plagued by thoughts of failure, and rejection. By doing this, you can stay positive in any situation.

So, the next time you go to a job interview or face a difficult situation, you have to pause for a while and remember your core values. Take a deep breath and recall the values that you grew up with.

These core values may be about your family, relationships, creativity, or career success among others. You have to select one of these values and determine why it is important for you. Get a piece of paper and write down your reasons as to why they are important. You have to be as vivid as possible.

Psychologists and researchers both agree that it can help reduce stress and anxiety. In a study that involved eighty-five undergraduate students, it was found that writing about core values helps reduce stress levels.

The participants were told to give five-minute speeches as members of the audience yelled at them to speak faster. Before they gave their speeches, however, the participants selected the value that they thought to be most important as well as the value that they thought to be quite irrelevant. Then, they half-wrote about such values.

Sure enough, those who have written about their highest rated values were found to be less stressed out during their speech. They also had lower levels of cortisol than those who wrote about their lowest rated values.

13. *Imagery Based Exposure*.

This exercise would involve you recalling a recent memory that produced an intense feeling of negativity within you. Now, once you have it in mind, analyze the situation.

For example, you found yourself in a distressing situation at work where you ended up arguing with one of your officemates. They might have said something hurtful that left you reeling and completely out of it.

Yes, the exercise might bring back some of those feelings, but try focusing on the purpose at hand instead of those emotions. Remind yourself that the situation has passed and now, you're merely studying it to gain a better understanding of how you reacted.

Next, label the thoughts and emotions that you went through during the conflict. Identify and write them down.

How does this help? Well, by visualizing this situation, it can actually help you take away its power to trigger the same emotions in you. Exposing yourself again to those negative feelings and urges will take some of its ability to affect you once more.

14. Thought Recording.

For this exercise, you will be testing out the validity of your thoughts. Basically, this would involve having to gather and then analyzing any evidence for and against a thought you might have. What this enables you to see is a fact-based conclusion on whether said thought is valid or not.

For example, you might think that your boss thinks low of you and that they find you inadequate for the job. You would need to gather all the evidence that makes you believe this is true, such as "They weren't smiling as I was making my presentation and he asked many questions as if to embarrass me." Then think of evidence that is against this belief, such as "They did give me a pat on the back after the presentation" and "They also told me to keep it up. If they thought ill of me, then they wouldn't have encouraged me in that way."

The goal here is to create a more balanced picture in your mind, as well as get rid of the unreasonable negative thoughts that you have formed prior.

For example, "Perhaps my boss was listening intently to my presentation hence why they did not smile much and asked many questions. I should listen instead to their encouragement, and keep up what I'm doing to become a better employee."

yourself consciously has a direct effect on your subconscious mind.

If you engage in negative self-talk, your subconscious mind will receive the negative message and carry it out. On the other hand, if you engage in positive self-talk, you will have positive results.

Just like the crew of the ship in the above given example, your subconscious mind does not question the orders of your conscious mind. Whatever the conscious mind says, the subconscious mind receives without judgment.

The Science of Self Talk

David Sarwer, clinical director and psychologist at the Center for Wright and Eating Disorders at the University of Pennsylvania, uses a large mirror when dealing with his patients. He makes them stand in front of this mirror and tells them to use neutral and gentle language when evaluating their bodies.

For example, a patient who is overweight should opt to say that his abdomen is big, round, and bigger than he likes it to be, rather than his abdomen is grotesque and disgusting. According to Sarwer, his goal is to get rid of the pejorative and negative terms in the self-talk of his patients. He adds that it is not enough for his patients to lose or gain weight along. They also have to change the way they view their bodies so that they can maintain their ideal weight once they reach it.

In 2013, scientists from the Netherlands did a study that involved women with anorexia as participants. They observed these anorexic women walk through the doorways of the laboratory. They noticed that the women turned sideways and squeezed themselves into the doorways even though there is a lot of space available around them. These anorexic women apparently had a notion that their bodies are much bigger than they actually are.

In a similar study conducted in 1911, neurologists Dr. Gordon Morgan Holmes and Dr. Henry Head, published a series of studies discussing the connection of the brain and the body. They found that women who often wore huge hats with feathers on them ducked each time they walked through doorways. They did this even when they were not wearing the hats. In their mind, they were still wearing the hats.

According to Dr. Branch Coslett, a cognitive neuroscientist at the University of Pennsylvania, each person has an internal representation of their own body. You need this part of yourself so that you can understand and learn how much space you take up. This also helps you do and complete your tasks better and faster.

Researchers have also found that such internal sense is very powerful. Neurologists have done research on motor imagery, which shows that the same neurological networks are both used in imagining movement and actually moving. So, imagining a certain movement repeatedly can have a similar effect on your brain as actually doing it.

Why Self Talk Matters

People do not always get what they want in life because they get what they expect and attract. Your self-talk actually creates your self-concept. It is your self-concept that identifies your level of performance in the different aspects of your life.

You can have over a hundred different individual self-concepts. For example, you may have a high self-concept of yourself during social events and situations. You may tell yourself that you are an excellent conversationalist and that you make good jokes. On the contrary, you may also have a low self-concept. You may tell yourself that you are not going to be promoted at work or that there are a lot of people who are smarter than you.

You should know that your subconscious works hard to make sure that your performance stays consistent with your self-concept, whether it is negative or positive. This is why you have to opt for the positive instead of the negative if you want your life to get better.

15.   *Positive Self-Talk Counts.*

Positive self-talk is regarded as the physical manifestation of the psyche, which provides encouragement. However, the researchers have found that the thoughts of an average person consist of 80% negativity and only 20% positivity. You should practice self-talk more often because they come with a lot of benefits.

- **Positive self-talk can help reduce stress and anxiety levels.**

Whenever you feel like you are being overwhelmed or stressed out, you can practice positive self-talk to uplift your spirits and make your mood better instantly. The American Heart Association says that stress control is one of the greatest benefits of positive self-talk.

- **By reassuring yourself that things are going to be all right, you become less anxious and much calmer.**

Then again, you have to take note that positive self-talk is not the same as lying to yourself about the real state of things. When you give yourself positive self-talk, you still have to be consistent with the reality. Things will only get worse if you lie to yourself and believe such lies.

Imagine this scenario:

If your husband just divorced you, you cannot lie to yourself that your relationship will magically return to the way it was. You should not fool yourself into thinking that you did not have problems. If you get back together, you will realize that things have gotten worse. This is why you still have to stay realistic. You can tell yourself that you will eventually get through the pain and move on with your life. This self-talk is positive yet realistic. It allows you to deal with your situation effectively and prevents you from making foolish decisions.

- **Positive self-talk also protects the heart and heart muscles.**

Stress, as you know, is among the most common causes of heart diseases. Since positive self-talk can reduce stress, it can also reduce your risk of heart diseases. This is proven by a study done by Susanne Pedersen, researcher at Tillburg University in Netherlands. According to the study, the participants who maintained a positive outlook in life had lower risks of mortality for the next five years.

- **Positive self-talk prevents depression and anxiety.**

Oftentimes, the people who are depressed feel worthless, hopeless, and useless. This affects both their minds and bodies, which is why they tend to experience eating problems, lethargy, and lack of sleep. If you give yourself a positive pep talk every now and then, you will stay happy and stress-free.

- **Positive self-talk can also increase your confidence.**

Lack of self-efficacy and negativity are two great hindrances to fulfilling your tasks. When you start to doubt your abilities, you set limits on the things that you are capable of doing. For example, if you are afraid of failing your exam or messing up your presentation, then you already set yourself up for failure. Negative self-talk attracts negative and undesirable results.

- **Positive self-talk can solidify and strengthen your belief in your own self.**

For example, if you truly believe that you can win the debate or get perfect scores on your exams, then you already prepared yourself for the outcome; which is winning the debate or acing your exams.

It is worth noting that your relationship with yourself is not the only thing that benefits when you give yourself a positive self-talk. You are also able to form better relationships with other people. This is because you become a reflection of positivity. Eventually, your positivity starts to spread to the people you are with. You start to recognize the good traits of your family, friends, peers, and co-workers, and ignore their less attractive traits. You become a more approachable person who is fun to be around.

Furthermore, positive self-talk can help improve your performance in different areas of life. For example, it is a vital part of sports psychology. When athletes practice positive self-talk, they are able to lessen their performance anxiety and pre-race jitters. Positive self-talk enables them to prepare for their event better as well as improve their overall performance. Likewise, positive self-talk can help you get ready for anything that you are about to face or undertake.

Chapter 5: Situational CBT Exercises

16. Behavioral Experiments.

These are done in order to test the validity of certain negative thoughts that you might be having, as well as any underlying beliefs to them. For example, in school, you often find yourself having a difficult time when it comes to saying no to your friends. We've all been here, haven't we? There is always some degree of peer pressure that happens in which we all think that saying NO might cause us our friends and people won't like us anymore.

One underlying fear here would be that of exclusion. We were afraid to say no because we did not want to end up an outsider. Besides, what could go wrong if we said YES? Plenty—this is what your adult self would say.

Behavioral experiments are a lot like the typical experiment you would do in class. Through it, you will be testing out a hypothesis. Will your friends really think ill of you should you say NO to them?

Test this on someone close to you. Tell them NO and then observe what happens next. Gather information and study how they react to it. Ask yourself these questions:

- Did they really end up liking you much less?
- How are you able to tell?
- Are you certain that this isn't just a false assumption?

After this, you can try doing the experiment again, but this time, do it with one of your friends. Say NO to them and see what happens and what's different this time.

In doing this, you're able to present yourself with evidence that disproves your negative thinking and subsequently tackles the underlying belief that's associated with it as well. There would be no fear of rejection after you realize that you were worried for nothing.

17. *Nightmare Exposure and Rescripting.*

Here's the thing, anxieties and fears aren't always confined to when people are awake. Whilst sleep is comforting thought to some, there are people who dread having to close their eyes at night because of the nightmares that tend to accompany their slumber.

At its very core, this exercise is meant to help you face your fears and strip them of their ability to bring your grief. It is similar to other exposure exercises with some minor differences. This technique goes hand in hand with rescripting.

How to:

- Confront your nightmares. Remember that just like stories, these nightmares can have a number of different interpretations, too, and they are not always negative. Instead of avoiding sleep, remind yourself of this, and try to look at your nightmare from a new perspective. What do these monsters represent?

- It helps to write things down. Doing so may not be as easy since you have to recall things that have frightened you, but it would enable you to look at things clearly. Are there common themes between your nightmares?

- Analyze the details of your nightmare and focus on the experience.

- Once you've got all these things written, it's time to visualize a new story. This time, focus on the things you want to feel while dreaming. Change the frightening events into something better, let your imagination run wild. When it comes to dreams, you can do just about anything.

- TELL YOURSELF THAT YOU HAVE COMPLETE POWER OF THIS.

- It is important that you begin light. Never start with your worst nightmares. Instead work your way up, eventually you'll get to the point where even your worst nightmares no longer affect you and you can easily transform them into something else.

18. Play the Script Until the End.

Think of this technique as a rehearsal for when the worst case scenario does happen. Sounds terrifying, it sort of is meant to be—after all, it is mimicking one of your worst fears. That said, the point of this technique is to help you avoid becoming crippled by your phobias and your anxieties. Through it, you'll be able to examine what could happen in the worst possible scenario you can conjure up.

Alright, where to begin? Again, start small. Save the worst fears for later and make sure you work your way up slowly, but steadily.

For example, one of my worst fears is driving off the road and somehow ending into a deep body of water. In this scenario, I am so crippled by fear that all I can do is watch as my vehicle slowly sinks. Of course, this isn't what I want to happen.

To put this technique to use, I imagine myself seating in that car and remembering all the things I have learned while researching. There is a way out and as long as I follow what I know, it'll be okay. I have a few minutes to get everything done, all I need to do is stay calm and get moving.

The first time you do this, it would be quite jarring. However, the more you imagine the scenario and play it in your head, the better you will be at coping. Eventually you wouldn't even flinch when you think about it.

19. *Exposure and Response Prevention.*

This particular CBT technique is known to work great for people who have OCD. Put simply, it is a type of therapy that gets the client to face their fears—then try their best to keep from ritualizing. First off, note that this can be extremely anxiety provoking. This reaction is only normal, even expected during the initial stages of the therapy. Eventually, it lessens and with continued exposure, it even disappears.

For example, a friend of mine in high school had issues with germs. She would always wash or sanitize her hands, to the point where the skin on it becomes dry and flaky. When we got into college, she began taking steps to expose herself more to what she feared most.

How? We would often go on hikes where she would need to touch the ground or the plants with her bare hands. In some cases, we even walked barefoot. At first, it was very hard for her—to the point where we had to turn back because she began feeling sick. She was diligent with it, however, and today, she can do just about anything without ritualizing.

The thing with ERP, and I noticed this with my friend too, is that it does take a while and the process can be daunting. There is also some degree of stress associated with it, and I remember having to comfort her each time she felt as if she was failing at it. The important thing to keep in mind is that there's no such thing as failure—as long as you keep pushing forward in trying to break your thought pattern, you are succeeding.

20. Interoceptive Exposure.

This technique is commonly used to treat panic disorder. It involves carrying out exercises that trigger the physical sensations associated with panic attacks. This includes: hyperventilation and high muscle tension. The goal here is to eliminate the conditioned response that a person has; after all, most people who have the panic disorder believe that experiencing this sensations will eventually lead to an attack.

But is that really the case? Not always.

The idea here is that in removing the fear of the stimulus associated with panic attacks, it lessens the overall instances where they do experience attacks. It seeks to get rid of the "fear of the fear" because there are cases wherein panic attacks occur simply because the individual "felt" like it was about to happen. This leads to them hyperventilating which then triggers the disorder.

For example, an individual has a fear of public speaking. In an engagement or an event, they were requested to provide a speech. Now, because of the anxiety over this task, they might begin to hyperventilate and as this happens, they also believe that a panic attack is sure to follow. However, the reality is that they only need to practice breathing exercises in order to calm down their breathing.

Now, if they use this technique, they can effectively extinguish that "fear". The fear of their hyperventilation leading to something worse. It takes practice, much like the other techniques, and it can be equally as jarring as these sensations are never pleasant. However, as we've been emphasizing since chapter 1, the more you familiarize yourself with the feeling, the less power it has over you.

The same applies here.

21. Progressive Muscle Relaxation (PMR).

This is a technique that's not specific to CBT, but is often used for it nevertheless. PMR is basically an exercise wherein you relax one muscle group at a time as a means of relaxing the entire body. The most ideal way to accomplish this would be to follow a guided tutorial. There are plenty of PMR audio recordings available online, but there are also therapists who offer one on one sessions for this technique.

It is a bit similar to meditation in that you'll need to be relaxed and clear-minded, but the overall experience is plenty different.

Along with this exercise, it is also recommended that you try relaxed breathing. With regular practice, you can begin to learn how to slow down your breath. You may not think much of it, but this can have a significant effect on your body.

To close this, allow us to leave you with one very important advice if you're starting CBT. Always leave yourself room to make mistakes. It will teach you a lot and help you grow. Not everyone would get these techniques on the first try, not even on the second or third. For some, it might even take years.

Remember that speed shouldn't be your biggest concern. Always work at your own pace and think about what's best for you.

Conclusion

Thank you again for purchasing this book!

I hope this book was able to help you utilize effective techniques on how to overcome depression, anxiety, and phobias.

The next step is to apply what you have learned from this book and start living your life the way you want to.

Thank you and good luck!

How to Analyze People

*How to Read Anyone Instantly Using Body
Language, Personality Types and Human
Psychology*

Introduction

Nonverbal signals are a major part of the way we communicate with those around us. It's something that everyone is using in social situations, all of the time, whether they are conscious of it or not. However, the majority of people only have a basic, subconscious understanding of body language and the way it functions. Luckily, if this skill isn't something you can do naturally, or if you only want to improve your existing abilities, there is information you can study and internalize to become better in this area, starting today. There are many advantages to taking the time to do this.

- **Increased Confidence:** When you know how to read people accurately, there is far less confusion. You know what they're trying to say to you and thus know exactly how to respond. When you can accurately decipher what body language cues people are sending, or understand them on a deeper level due to personality type, you can also accurately adjust your nonverbal signals to be appropriate for the occasion, resulting in the best outcome possible.

- **Improved Relationships:** Relationships are tough, and this is because much of the time, we don't know how to accurately read each other. Not only will you be able to tell when someone is interested in you when it comes to dating, but you'll be able to understand your loved one on a deeper level if and when you get into a more serious relationship. All relationships require trust and open communication, and this becomes a whole lot easier when you can read each other in an accurate and reliable way, then respond in kind.

- **Increased Personal Safety:** Learning how to analyze people is not only beneficial for self-confidence, it can also mean the difference between protecting yourself from dangerous situations and being victimized. In chapter 4, we will explore the biases that hold people back from accurately reading people and spotting red flags that could save your life.

- **A Better Social Life:** People who are socially awkward or simply don't know how to react out of shyness, are usually this way because they haven't yet learned how to both send accurate nonverbal cues and read those of other people. Maybe you're the type who likes to keep a wide circle of various acquaintances, or maybe your interest lies more in forming fewer, but deeper, bonds with people. Whatever your intentions are, learning how to analyze people will help you achieve your social goals and send the right signals to other people.

- **More Professional Opportunities:** Something that goes hand in hand with learning how to analyze people is building rapport a lot more quickly, which opens up the door for better opportunities in terms of your job or career life. An interviewer is much likelier to choose the candidate who sends the right impression or who they feel good about, and you have a better chance of fitting this profile when you are educated in reading nonverbal cues and accurately judging or assessing the body language of others.

231

As you can see, there's nothing to lose and everything to gain with teaching yourself these valuable skills. In this book, you will learn which signals to watch for to tell you who a person really is on the inside, along with how to apply this information. Thank you for downloading this guide and I hope you learn something interesting from it!

Chapter 1: The Personality Types

In an attempt to understand people and better analyze them in an accurate way it helps to have a basic understanding of common personality traits. Have you ever wondered why certain people attract the same type of person over and over, or why certain types of people hold similar positions in the business world? The answer is quite simple, most of the things we or others do personally and professionally can be attributed to our unique personality type.

While there are many books out there that tackle this subject, delving into the multitude of personality types as well as their subtypes, we've taken this opportunity to narrow it down for you and make it easier for you to identify particular types and their characteristics. Following are four key personality types and how you can more quickly identify and relate to them.

The Leader

These are the people who love to be in charge. They don't usually have to search for the position of leadership because the task typically falls to them regardless of what group of people they might surround themselves with. Leaders have strong personalities and are rarely afraid to choose a challenging course for their teams. They have overpowering confidence that causes others to naturally follow their lead. Leaders are quick thinkers and tend to be energetic.

Leaders hold positions in business as presidents, executives, administrators, and supervisors. They tend to arm their vocabulary with strong words that convey power and authority.

While they smile you can still see tension in their facial expressions, as they always appear to be serious people. Their body language usually sends the same message. While talking to groups they usually use their hands and pace the room they're presenting to.

Money and prestige are highly important to these personality types. They often prefer high-priced vehicles, big homes, lavish vacation spots and the trophy spouse. Because they are serious people and driven, family and relationships usually take a backseat to their professional lives.

The Fraternizer

The Fraternizer rarely meets a stranger. They are the social butterflies of the world today. Fraternizers hold a commanding presence in a room full of people and attention seems to flow toward them effortlessly. Their out-going personalities convey optimism and enthusiasm and Fraternizers have little difficult saying what's on their mind as they enjoy engaging others in conversation.

Fraternizers enjoy looking their best and hold positions such event planners or venue coordinators, anything that deals with the public on a personal level. They like nothing more than fun in every aspect of their lives. They love to be around people and enjoy entertaining. You'll find that Fraternizers have a great sense of humor and are rarely seen without a smile and open arms that invite everyone to join the party.

This personality type favors fun above all else. Their drive and determination is fueled by excitement as well as adrenalin. Fraternizers are risk takers who seek adventure through travel, group gatherings and outdoor activities.

The Identifier

Providing a listening ear is what Identifiers do best. For them there is rarely anything more important than a relationship built on trust and in-depth discussions that promote nurturing and soul-searching. They tend to pose open questions instead of standard questions that can be answered with a simple "yes" or "no" response. Identifiers will think before they respond, evaluating feelings more than thoughts. While they are very likable, Identifiers tend to be socially timid so others will most likely need to initiate the conversation.

Because of their compassion and ability to empathize, Identifiers make great counselors, teachers, nurses and volunteers. Identifiers are known to use words that convey trust and comfort. They're always available to help and are great care-givers. The body language of the Identifier is usually relaxed and open allowing others to feel relaxed as well.

Identifiers value people and relationships above all else and have an innate ability to care for others, both emotionally and physically. They often put others first while their needs may go unmet due to lack of time or resources.

The Perceiver

Self-control and cautious behavior are the primary traits of Perceivers. Typically preferring analysis over emotion, they thrive on order and clarity in both conversation and relationships. It's not uncommon for this personality type to seem stand-offish to others, but once you get to know them you'll quickly realize how dependable they can be.

Perceivers primarily hold positions that encourage working in autonomous environments. Because they prefer analytical thinking their careers usually consist of engineering, technology, mathematics, and scientific fields. They often prefer conversations relating to educational topics focusing on theories and facts exploring various aspects of the subjects being discussed. Perceivers don't usually engage in topics associated with anything that is emotionally based. Perceivers usually appear serious or thoughtful and their body language is often viewed as closed, with folded arms and an a tense or stressed demeanor.

Because they prefer facts and numbers over personal relationships, Perceivers usually form relationships with like-minded individuals who understand their lack emotion and their need for stability and structure.

It is more common than not that people possess more than one of these four basic personality types. For instance it is not uncommon for Leaders to also carry traits of Fraternizers, Identifiers, or Perceivers. However, it is extremely rare to find a true Perceiver who holds personality traits of any type other than Leader, and it is equally as difficult to find true Fraternizers who hold personality traits of anyone other than Leaders. Following are some examples.

The Leader-Fraternizer

Leader-Fraternizers have incredible energy and can be highly successful. These personality types are what famous motivational speakers and entrepreneurs are made of. Imagine someone who can takes risks socially and physically while maintaining an open circle of friends and acquaintances. Leader-Fraternizers will have you fighting for their cause with them without hesitation, never questioning their vision or path.

They rarely see anything in the world as unobtainable and will go to great lengths to find success. With their ability to motivate those around them effortlessly, Leader-Fraternizers are able to delegate quickly and without much deliberation. They're tuned-in to the people they are surrounded by and utilize this to their advantage never forgetting to repay their efforts with praise and encouragement.

The Leader-Identifier

Leader-Identifiers are less common and more subdued. While they are still successful they are not as likely to standout as the Leader-Fraternizers do. Leader-Identifiers make fantastic mentors and friends. They are well equipped mentally and emotionally to help you succeed while fulfilling their own agenda. Many of the traits of the Leader follow the Leader-Identifier, but you'll find that the Identifier quality causes them to be more approachable and their reasoning better understood.

The Leader-Identifier will also pay closer attention to the people they lead on a professional as well as personal level. These individuals basically have the best of both worlds with regard to personality make-up. They can be highly successful individuals and are able to adapt quickly to just about any environment because of their ability to read people and situations quickly.

While they are less apt to take the same risks as other personality types, the Leader-Identifier is able to meet the professional terms of a business as well as adapting to the rapport building skills of the Identifier alone. Many businesses search for these individuals to take positions as HR directors or marketing reps.

The Leader-Perceiver

While Leader-Perceivers are successful they are more difficult to get to know on a personal level. They prefer to keep subjects on target and leave little room for building a rapport based on any type of emotional bond. Leader-Perceivers are strong business figures with a great capacity for maintaining a path to specific goals, making sure nothing interrupts or interferes with the overall outcome of their agenda.

Because of their preference for working autonomously they are better suited for careers in areas related to technology or science simply because these areas focus less on emotion and more on facts or data.

The personal relationships of Leader-Perceivers are much like those of the Perceiver; they gravitate toward like-minded individuals preferring to keep emotion out of the equation as much as possible. This is not to say that this personality is not capable of emotion, it's just not something that is natural or extremely comfortable to them.

You're less likely to experience confrontation with this personality type. They are very good at assessing and categorizing their thoughts and/or feelings prior to any professional encounter and rarely react to situations without careful consideration.

The Fraternizer-Identifier

While it is rare, this combination does exist and they can be the most accepting, inviting people you'll ever encounter. The Fraternizer-Identifier might have a decreased energy level as compared to the Leader-Fraternizer or the sole Fraternizer, but that is compensated by their ability to spread their positive outlook to others.

Fraternizer-Identifiers make an excellent youth counselor or life coach because of their ability to remain cheerful and emotionally grounded simultaneously. They are positive-thinkers and dislike conflict. It is likely that this personality type would be able to easily blend into most professional and social atmospheres with little difficulty.

While it may be hard to pin point the two personality traits at first, practice will enable you to identify them more quickly. Begin by looking first at the most obvious characteristics of the individual and go from there. Identifying key attributes such as the stress level in their facial expressions, body language, or how they speak with others, i.e. using "I" statements or inviting the other person into the conversation as a valuable participant can be important indicators of which defined personality they most likely adhere to. It will always be easier to identify the strongest characteristics first.

When all else fails trust your gut. We were all designed with an internal gauge that helps us to identify those around us and how we should relate to them. Look for that instinct and build upon it. Ask yourself how this person makes you feel; what it is about the person that makes you feel comfortable or uneasy depending on the circumstances? Would you feel comfortable with this person in a one-on-one conversation or are you more comfortable observing them from a distance. The better you know yourself the better you can identify and analyze others instantly.

Chapter 2: How Each Personality Type Communicates

As soon as you figure out which personality type someone fits into based on the information in the last chapter, you can figure out other aspects of their personality. Communication is the most important consideration in many respects, including relationships, social life, and more. You can use the following information to understand those around you based on this.

The first foundational quality of a person you should look for is whether they are emotionally-based or not. Fraternizers and Identifiers are typically emotionally based, while Leaders and Perceivers are not. The amount of emotion you can look for in a Leader or Perceiver depends on the other personality traits he or she maintains. We've provided examples below.

Leader-Fraternizer

You'll have a great time communicating with this personality type. They stay focused but are able to exert a great sense of humor and a fun while they're headed in the direction of their goal. Caution should be used in confusing this personality type with the solid Fraternizer type. Leader-Fraternizers are less "stuffy" as the typical Leader, but they are still quite goal oriented, so don't let that take a back seat to the humor and fun that can be experienced. Stay focused or they may quickly let you know your place. They don't like wasting time but they do enjoy a happy work-place.

Leader-Identifier

The Leader-Identifier is not as gregarious as the Leader-Fraternizer, but they are a calming influence if you're prone to anxiety or don't do well under pressure. These personalities, while extremely focused and professional will take the time necessary to incorporate emotional needs in your day-to-day interactions. It is important to remember that while they value you emotionally, your emotions should not get in the way of goal-oriented tasks. Leader-Identifiers are more likely to put themselves in your position, so to speak, before expecting more from you than you can provide. They understand where you're coming from. They want you to feel comfortable in your environment and usually maintain an open-door policy to help alleviate any miscommunication within the business setting.

Leader-Perceiver

The personality traits of the Leader-Perceiver closely match the traits of the Leader alone. They maintain a serious persona and you might find yourself wondering if you're able to maintain a strong working-relationship with this person. The key is to keep your communication on a business level, discussing things that pertain to achieving the tasks at hand. Your attempts to bring humor or emotion into your conversation or agenda will fall short of meeting their expectations. They prefer to remain on-task, and not waste precious time with such frivolity.

While this might make it simpler for some, chances are if you are an emotionally-based person, such as the Fraternizer or Identifier, it will be difficult for you to function effectively under the guide of the Leader-Perceiver. Generally speaking, emotion-based personalities require more communication than the Leader-Perceiver is able to give. But if you want something done efficiently and correctly with little interruption or interaction, these would be the people for the job.

Fraternizer-Identifier

The Fraternizer-Identifier communication style is probably the easiest and most rewarding. This person can be both fun and easy to build a strong rapport with. The Fraternizer-Identifier will take the time to communicate their feelings as well as encouraging and validating your feelings on a continuous basis. While they have a lot of energy they are more subdued than the person who carries only the traits of the Fraternizer.

Why is this information relevant and useful when it comes to analyzing or reading people? There are many different reasons why this is the case, but let's take the example of a professional situation. Before you enter a negotiation with someone else, knowing what type of personality traits they possess presents you with a distinct advantage. If you're a sales person, you will benefit more from noticing that your customer is a Perceiver and needs some time to reflect and think about the sale. Pressuring them will have a detrimental effect on their choice and lead them to say "no" when they might not have otherwise.

Successful relationships, both personal and professional, require effective communication. With a wide array of personalities we have a variance just as broad with communication types. The thing to remember, in all types of communication, is to think before you speak. How many times have you left a conversation wishing you had or had not said something in particular whether it was because it could be misconstrued or because it gave a false impression of who you truly are? If we're honest, we each have a story or two to share.

Even if you're a Perceiver by nature, there will be times that you will have to communicate. Each of us, regardless of our personality type, need to be familiar with how other prefer to communicate. It's not only a sign of respect it will leave a good impression if one of these types happens to be interviewing you for a position.

Now we'll take some time to go over each personality type and how they deal with personal communication.

Leader

Leaders are very direct and typically only use emotion when it will further their agenda or meet their goal. This is not to say that they are narcissistic in nature, it is simply not in their nature to incorporate emotion with their personal communication. Leaders have a difficult time separating business from pleasure. Leaders are often misconstrued as being cold or detached, when in fact they are trying to get things done in a constructive and productive manner. You can however teach a Leader to reach some level of feeling emotion by allowing them to take their time and learn from your ability to express your feelings. If you are truly an emotionally-based personality this relationship will take a lot of time and patience on your part.

Fraternizer

Fraternizers are a lot of fun but you might have a difficult time getting them to slow down and smell the roses. Because personal communication requires some degree of seriousness the Fraternizer may find it difficult to slow down long enough for something as mundane as serious chatter. It's not to say that the Fraternizer doesn't value personal relationships that might require more serious communication, it's that they are generally so free-spirited that they don't see the need to make everything so serious. The best plan of action is to incorporate your communication in a less serious tone. You can keep the communication style light and still convey the degree of intimacy that you may need.

Identifier

The Identifier will make personal communication easy, unless you're a Leader or Perceiver. Being emotionally-based people by nature they have no difficulty understanding what their ideas, feelings, and plans consist of and giving you ample opportunity to communicate your feelings as well. Identifiers are generally able to get along with just about anyone, because they are good at reading the body language and verbal cues of others. Their communication style is gentle in its approach and Identifiers are rarely confrontational. They generally think before they speak and are patient enough to allow you to do the same.

Perceiver

Personal communication with the Perceiver type personality can be tricky. Because they qualify information in an analytical frame of reference your communication skills will need to focus on that quality. You'll need to qualify the information you want to communicate in analytical terms before proceeding. For example, if you want to communicate to your Perceiver friend that you value your friendship, you'll need to phrase the information in this manner, "I feel as though I learn a great deal from you. I appreciate the time we spend discussing..." As long as you incorporate an analytical approach or an approach that can be measured in terms of growth, you'll be able to get your point across.

Leader-Fraternizer

The Leader-Fraternizer doesn't make personal communication very difficult, but you need to remember that they prefer direct statements presented in a light manner. It is best to stay away from communication techniques that incorporate vague feelings or a melancholy attitude. They take communication seriously and prefer presenting ideas instead of problems. Problems denote a need for immediate action while ideas allow them to weigh the outcome and calculate their approach from that aspect. The Fraternizer aspect of this personality allows the Leader to be more "in-tune" with their ability to communicate on a more personal level rather than dictating their expectations to the other party.

Leader-Identifier

Communicating with the Leader-Identifier is very easy to master. They don't shy away from in-depth discussion pertaining to personal relationships. They do, however, prefer to listen and act over listen and present. For example, if you tell a Leader-Identifier that you require more one-on-one attention, they will process the information and attempt to meet your need in their time frame. The results will not likely be instantaneous and they will probably ask for additional information to consider during the process, such as "why", "what" or "how".

Leader-Perceiver

The Leader-Perceiver communication style is factually based and doesn't leave room for emotionally charged discussions. Your personal communication with this individual is simple because there's little room for anything other than factual statements regarding expectation and how it will positively impact the relationship you share.

Fraternizer-Identifier

Communication on a personal level with a Fraternizer-Identifier type personality is light and easy. They prefer information of a personal nature to be presented in a light-hearted manner. They are open to hearing what you have to say and will respond likewise. While they typically don't prefer personal communication that includes long discussions that dwell on the emotional needs of the relationship, they do invite your opinions and thoughts openly.

Becoming more familiar with personal communication techniques is as easy as looking at your established relationships and how communication flows with regard to the other person and their particular type of personality. Remember to take into consideration your individual personality type because you in turn affect how others perceive and communicate with you. You may surprise yourself and hone the ability to expand on the positive attributes of your own personality and how you relate in both social and business situations.

Chapter 3: Techniques for Cold Reading People

Cold reading is an irreplaceable skill for anyone who wishes to master reading body language or analyzing people in general. This chapter will cover a few methods for doing that, but similar to any other skill, it does take plenty of practice to master it. Although it is typically associated with psychics, it's a logical process and works by selecting the language you use carefully and paying close attention to the responses of those you are attempting to read.

The our first method "Quick Statements", also referred to as "Shotgun Statements", is typically used by psychics or mediums generally always before other methods of cold reading are explored. This method uses as much information as possible with the idea that at least one thing you say should cause a reaction in the person. The purpose of this technique is being as vague as you can, allowing you to get a reaction from the individual or one of the individuals in the audience. This can't sound overly vague since most people would notice what you were doing, if it did. For example, if you're in a group of people you can mention slightly specific things such as "Very shy people usually do this," and see if it gets a reaction from anyone in the group.

When talking to someone on an individual level you can simply listen to what they say and try to make accurate guesses about the type of person they are. If they say, for instance, that they are usually very calm, you can use this information to make more accurate judgments about their current mood.

The Barnum Effect is the phenomenon where someone reads or hears something very general but believes that it applies to them. These statements appear to be very personal on the surface but in fact, they are true for many. Human psychology allows us to want to believe things that we can identify with on a personal level and even seek information where it doesn't necessarily exist, filling in the blanks with our imagination for the rest. This is the principle that horoscopes rely on, offering data that appears to be personal but probably makes sense to countless people. Since the people reading them want to believe the information so badly, they will search for meaning in their lives that make it true.

This provides you with a general area of information about someone that you can use to delve deeper and acquire more accurate, drilled-down answers from them. For example, you could say to someone, "It seems as though you've gone through a major change within the last year or so," and appear as though you know something specific about them, when this could apply to most people. They will often be surprised that you could tell this information and then proceed to fill in the blanks on their own.

You can give an accurate cold reading for someone by using information that was already given to or confirmed by you earlier in the conversation, this is referred to as reusing or recapping. Many therapists use this technique to begin building a quick rapport with their clients. As soon as you begin talking to them and using general Barnum statements, pay attention to how they respond. If they give specific details to you, save that information for later on in the conversation.

Although you won't always be in control of this aspect while trying to analyze or read people, it helps to find the right subject when possible. Choosing the correct person to observe makes a difference because some people are easier to read than others. When it comes to using cold reading to analyze people, you want someone who is open enough to finish your ideas and fill in the blanks with information about their self on a personal level. People who are very closed off or skeptical will make this much more difficult.

As soon as you have "warmed up" the person you are attempting to analyze or read by getting some predictions right, they are probably quite convinced at how perceptive you are by this point. This will lead them to loosen up or reveal more information with their nonverbal body signals, giving you another advantage that makes them easier to read. The idea is not to become a fortune teller or palm reader, but to draw off of those techniques to get better at analyzing people. This technique, in combination with the methods you will be given in the following chapters of this book, will make you a master at analyzing people.

Chapter 4: Using Profiling Techniques to Analyze People

What would you think of someone in your neighborhood that has children, goes out to work in a suit every day, has a clean house and great lawn, acts polite and friendly, seems to care about your day and life, and clears the snow from your driveway when you're away? The majority of people would assume that this person is great and genuine. So it might surprise you that someone who fit this description actually tortured people in his backyard. His name is David Parker Ray, a park ranger who appeared to admire and respect women but actually had been sadistically mistreating them for years. His neighbors were shocked and assumed that he was a regular guy, a nice guy.

This happens more than you realize, the assumption that people are okay just because they do the things that society expects of them. The problem is that even the most notorious criminals know how to appear as trustworthy or normal. If you watch or read the news, you rarely ever hear someone say, "Yeah, I thought he was up to no good." On the contrary, we hear over and over again how nice or normal or helpful someone was and how others can't believe that this same person could do such horrific things. Many times it's our own stereotypes that cause us not to delve deeper to see what's behind the curtain, or normal face.

We as society have grown complacent in accepting "nice" and "normal" appearances at face value and not looking any deeper thereby giving us a false interpretation of the individual we're looking at. If Mr. Ray's neighbors had looked more closely at him as opposed to his façade, they may have been able to identify key indicators that everything was not necessarily as it appeared. Because he is most likely narcissistic he would have given subtle clues to his true character. For example narcissists always have an ulterior motive for doing "nice" things. They don't do "nice" things when others aren't watching. They go out of their way to appear normal. Maybe if they had looked more closely to how Mr. Ray's family acted around him they would have seen another picture as well. Do others appear anxious around this individual or do they seem to go above and beyond to please the narcissist? Just because things appear okay on the outside does not mean that things are okay on the inside. The neighbors may not have seen Mrs. Ray out often or noticed the children out often. Narcissist's themselves are very good at controlling the individuals in their lives in hopes of controlling their overall appearance to others.

You might be asking yourself if it's possible to actually use profiling techniques to analyze anyone including the dangerous types of people as described above. The truth is a resounding "Yes!" It does, however, take practice and knowledge of what you should be looking for in terms of key factors used in this methodology. While there are many types of profiling techniques from a range of authorities such as law enforcement and the FBI, we are going to focus on those techniques most commonly used by professionals within behavioral medicine practices.

While someone could initially appear sincere or "normal", there are things you need to look at before making this conclusion too quickly:

Is their body language open or closed? People who are emotionally guarded tend to maintain a physical stance that suggests the same feeling. These types of people generally stand with their arms folded or their hands in their pockets. You can also tell quite a lot about a person when shaking their hand. If the hand is a firm grasp but pulls away quickly that could be a sign of being emotionally guarded or a lack of desire for truly opening up to the other individual. A firm handshake that lasts several seconds is adequate and should tell you that the person is open to knowing you. This feeling should be even further acknowledged if the person covers your shaking hand with their spare hand. Many people study handshakes and have the ability to convey a read that isn't necessarily accurate. For instance, sales people and politicians are keen at the hearty handshake, so it's very important to look at other indicators as well.

Do they have good eye contact? Those who are confident and typically honest will have appropriate eye contact. Eye contact is make-and-break over and over during an interaction. Someone who seems to stare right through you should not be trusted immediately. These types of individuals lack the ability to gauge natural eye contact and have most likely had to practice this to at least appear normal. They can also be very intimidating if they are doing this on purpose. On the opposite side, someone who is unable to maintain several seconds of direct eye contact without appearing uncomfortable could be either extremely shy or nervous.

What is their anxiety level portraying? People who are nervous or untrusting of their immediate surroundings are more apt to shift their weight back and forth and sometimes twist back and forth with their upper torso. Don't expect to see an obvious shift in body mechanics, this can be very subtle and the less the person desires to be seen for who they really are the more subtle the apparent anxiety will be to onlookers. You need to watch for several minutes before you can make your best assumption.

How do they look? This is a big one. And in today's society this can be a very touchy subject. We're not talking about judging someone based on their appearance, we are talking about how this person presents themselves to others. Let's look at couple of examples, because this can be complicated.

You are at a neighborhood barbeque and everyone is dressed in shorts, t-shirts, and tennis shoes. As you look around, you spot a male who is in slacks, a dress shirt and nicer shoes. This individual could have stopped in before going home to change or this could be someone who is unable to blend comfortably with others. If you're at a business-casual dinner party and someone is wearing a tie and dinner jacket or very expensive dinner dress, this person may be trying to appear more professional or more trustworthy. And then there is the offset that either of these people may take themselves too seriously.

Let's take a look at the above two scenarios and include body language and anxiety level. The nicely dressed individual at the pool party has their arms crossed and has their eyes darting back and forth between several people within the conversation. This person can be said to not only be uncomfortable with their environment but with themselves as well. If the person is perspiring, and the temperature isn't really a factor, you can be assured that this individual is ridden with anxiety and it's most likely not just shyness. Shy people are more able to blend in with their clothing choices and body mechanics. With the only identifying factors that separate anxiety from a threatening personality type being those of eye contact and anxiety level it is important to also view how others seem to respond to the individual's presence. Do others seem comfortable around this person? If so, the individual may very well be shy. But if others appear "put-off" or irritated by the individual you could be looking at a very different type of personality. Initially the practiced narcissist can appear as relaxed and inviting. But take a closer look. Try to observe them when others are not in their close proximity. Narcissists need "breaks" to refuel or reassess their environment. If you notice someone quite out-going who later steps back and begins searching the crowd, chances are that individual is reassessing their environment and fueling up for another go around.

When reviewing this information it's important to remember these things in using profiling techniques in analyzing people:

- What type of situation are you viewing the subject in?
- Is their personal appearance unkempt or is it activity appropriate?
- Does their body language suggest openness or the opposite?
- Are they using appropriate eye contact?
- What does their anxiety level suggest?
- How does this person seem to make those around them feel?

The more frequently you use these tools in analyzing others the easier it will be to formulate appropriate profiles of these individuals.

Chapter 5: Using Words to Read People

It is possible to get very accurate ideas about who someone is by closely listening to the words they choose to use in conversation. Listening to the clues a person gives while they speak presents you, the analyzer, with the perfect technique for reading them. Words are the way that we share and represent our thoughts, ideas, and moods. We can't ever be inside someone else's mind, but the closest we can ever be to understanding someone else is by listening to, or in some cases reading, their words.

Some words show behavioral traits in the person speaking or writing them, and provide us with clues to their personality. These clues increase the likelihood of predicting someone's behavior by thinking about which words they select when speaking or writing. They aren't enough, on their own, to determine someone's qualities or traits. However, they can give us valuable insights into how their thought processes typically function.

Begin by building your hypotheses. You can then extend your hypotheses based on additional clues and test them out by using further observations. You can then draw conclusions about that person based on credible information that you've gathered. Our brains are highly efficient machines, using nouns, verbs, adverbs, and adjectives to translate thoughts into language. We have choices that are practically endless in with regard to how we construct our sentences, and the words we do choose tell a lot about our thoughts and who we are as people.

An average sentence will contain a main subject along with a verb. The sentence, for instance, "I drove" contains the subject,

"I" and the verb, "drove" which explains the action of the subject. When you add any extra information onto this simple sentence, you are shifting or modifying the meaning of the sentence. Looking at these modifications can give us clues as to the person behind the words. Paying attention to this can help you to develop a theory or hypothesis about the speaker and figure out who they are on a deeper level.

For example, if you are talking to another person and they dominate the conversation with the word "I" or "my" you can easily assume that they are self-absorbed. This assumption is based on their need to "own" the conversation. Typically the only instances this person will use an alternative word choice is when they are assigning unwanted responsibility to another person. There are varying degrees of self-absorption that can indicate what level of sociopathy they might carry. Those with a high level of sociopathy or narcissism will have firm, strong language skills that are quite capable of steering a complete conversation with another person. The narcissist has had years of practice in speaking in a way that others will respond to in a manner that is acceptable and predictable by the narcissist.

Someone else who uses the "I" or "my" quite often but isn't very high on the level of sociopathy is someone who has a lower self-esteem but want to present themselves in a different light. They desire and need to be seen as strong and competent but don't usually have the necessary social skills to adequately portray this mindset. Another easy way to differentiate between these two types is how they present themselves. The first individual uses firm, strong language while the second individual will seem almost as if they are asking you to validate their statements. They are looking for reassurance from you. If you ever feel that your validation is being sought, you can be reasonably assured that it isn't from a higher level narcissist.

People who continuously divert attention from themselves by their attempts to keep you talking about yourself are usually uncomfortable with any type of attention, especially positive. They will exhibit discomfort with compliments or an increased interest by another person. These are indications of a low self-esteem or low self-worth. This is not to say that these individuals are insincere or manipulative, they are merely attempting to keep the conversation at a comfortable level for themselves. They don't often understand how to appropriately respond to compliments or genuine interest by another person therefore they can grow quite good at steering the conversation toward the other participant.

Using the words people use to read them can become somewhat difficult at times, but as in the other methods of analyzation they can become quite useful when practiced. You need to "read between the lines" so to speak. When people use boastful language it can mean that they either need affirmation or they need you to understand how powerful they are. When people steer the conversation from themselves to you it can mean that they have a low self-esteem or it could mean that they are not ready for you to know them for the type of person they truly are. They may be trying to gain your confidence as an ally in another situation.

It's important to listen carefully to tone and inference when using words to read others. Firm tones are usually associated with demands while softer tones are associated with a desire for trust. There is your answer right there in that one sentence. Do a person's words denote a demand or a desire? Demands are absolute and unforgiving. Desires are easier to respond to as their delivery is less toxic by nature. When words instantly provoke a particular feeling within you, you need to look at both the word and the tone. This will allow you to easily identify the motive of the speaker.

Which of these sentences are you less likely to feel comfortable with?

- I need you to understand how I got the ball on my side of the court!
- The ball was on my side of the court.

Now these two sentences:

- My daughter is an excellent gymnast!
- My daughter enjoys gymnastics.

The first sentence is a demand or proclamation leaving little room for your point of view, whatever it might be. The second sentences are merely informational and tend to invite participation in the conversation. If your goal is to win the acceptance of the self-absorbed it will require that you give them what they crave or demand, and that is constant attention to them and their own importance. On the other hand, if your goal is to shut down the sociopathy associated with this type of individual, it can be a little bit more difficult. You will mainly need to strengthen your end of the conversation. Offering insights as to how others might compare to them in a positive light is less tolerable to them as well. Those who are self-absorbed will usually find another party who is willing to allow their boasting and feel more comfortable interacting with these individuals. They will rarely waste their time with someone who can offer a conversation that demands equal time and consideration.

How we respond to others is based on their words and tone. If you listen carefully to a person you can instantly understand their motives and desires all in how they present the words they speak. But don't forget that while you're learning to use words to read a person, someone else is most likely doing the same to you; quite often without even realizing it.

Chapter 6: Reading Body Language Cues and Changing your State of Mind

One major reason why people are interested in learning how to read body language and analyze people is to learn how to detect when someone is lying. This is a very understandable motivation for learning about this subject. However, it isn't as simple as being able to look at a tiny expression on someone's face or the way they move their hands and know immediately that they are lying about something. It's a bit more complicated than that, but definitely worth thinking about!

The best way to gauge a person's emotions or thoughts in the most accurate way possible is to look at how comfortable or uncomfortable they are in the moment. This spectrum of comfort and discomfort is much more reliable and important than just trying to read one expression and assume that it means something specific for every person you come across. Experts claim that people who lie (and therefore, likely feel guilty) have to walk around knowing that they are not being honest, and that this can make it hard to feel comfortable. In fact, oftentimes they are walking around with distress and tension that is visible to those who know how to spot it.

Trying to hide the fact that you're being deceptive puts a lot of stress on the brain as you struggle to come up with answers for questions that would have been easy to answer truthfully. When people are really comfortable talking to us, it's easy to tell when they are displaying signs of discomfort, which can indicate that they are not being truthful.

This means that your goal should be to get the person as comfortable as you can through building a rapport. Then you will be able to figure out how that person normally acts, or what their "baseline" of behavior and mood is. When you can familiarize yourself with the way a person appears and behaves when they aren't threatened or nervous, you can more accurately recognize when they are.

Although looking at things such as context and the situation is helpful and relevant in detecting lies, it can be used to approach every aspect of reading body language. For example, if you visit a social gathering and everyone there is chatting and having a great time, but there is one person in the corner with their head down, that person is going to stand out to you. They will probably come across as uncomfortable which will lead you to think that there is something going on with them. You may ask that person if there is something wrong with them. However, observing this exact same demeanor in a person at a hospital, for example, wouldn't raise any flags because people are often uncomfortable at hospitals.

Paying attention to someone's comfort level in a specific context offers you clues for the way they are feeling at that moment. When you're on a date with someone new and the person appears to be comfortable, you can probably assume that they like to be with you. If you are giving someone an interview for a job and the applicant looks confident and comfortable until you ask a question about their history with stealing, this is something to take note of. Although body language isn't a concrete or precise science, using some acquired knowledge in combination with your own common sense and observations about context and environment, can lead you to be pretty good at it. Then you can accurately assess what the people with you are thinking.

Most parts of our body are sending signals about what we desire or the way we feel, on a subconscious level that we often are not aware of. There are specific cues that can signal certain thoughts or ideas, but you must also keep in mind the spectrum of comfort or discomfort and remember that an isolated signal you pick up is far from the entire picture. Now let's look into some specific body parts and what signals they may be sending.

A lot of people assume that facial expressions are the most reliable or obvious indication of someone's thoughts or moods. But you should first realize, when thinking about reading someone's face, is that their facial expressions are not the most reliable gauge of their thoughts or feelings. There are a few body parts that are more honest than this, which you'll find out about soon, but let's focus on this one first. Most of us are taught starting at childhood that certain actions and facial expressions are meant for specific events or occasions, even if they are not genuine or what we really feel. This means that people give fake expressions all the time. But there are a few cues that you can still read from the face or head.

One simple body language cue to teach yourself about which isn't always easy to recognize, is a person's fake smile. A fake smile, such as one we give in social events because we "want" to be polite or because we "have" to be polite, is only visible on the mouth. Everyone knows how to do a fake smile, but not many of us realize that fake smiles do not reach our eyes. When we smile for real, our eyelids, eyebrows, and sometimes even the entire head is involved and moves upward.

Another method for recognizing when someone is growing uncomfortable is looking for pursed or tight lips on them. This can be seen in old videos of politicians admitting to something shameful, where their lips almost disappear as they give their confessions. This shows that they don't like to be saying what they are saying, and oftentimes, pursed lips show that someone is telling you only part of the truth.

These are only two simple techniques for recognizing what some facial expressions may mean, and they can reveal quite a bit about someone's true or false feelings. However, so many different variations exist that it can be more complicated than this, and as already mentioned, faces are not always reliable when it comes to body language. That's why you must pay just as much attention to the whole body, if not even more. What other body parts can you look at to tell how someone is thinking or feeling?

Although this isn't a body part that people often think about when it comes to reading people and analyzing body language, our arms are a huge part of expressing feelings and thoughts. A lot of gestures and expressions are trained or taught to us throughout life, like the fact that it's rude to point. Apart from these obvious social norms, there are some other considerations to make about arms when trying to read someone's moods. Look at how much room or space they are taking up with their arms, and also how high their arms are reaching.

Gestures that seem to defy gravity, no matter what body part it happens in, are typically positive. As soon as someone becomes interested, excited, or happy, their arms rise, their chins and heads go up, and even their feet or legs might start to bounce or point upward. A person's arms are especially versatile when it comes to reading this behavior. When we're happy or excited our arm movements are unrestricted and we may raise them over our heads. A happy and energized person makes motions that go against gravity with their arms. This is easy to remember since someone feeling "up" means they are happy, while the opposite means that they feel the opposite. When someone is in a confident mood, they affirmatively swing their arms as they walk, while an insecure person will keep their arms restrained as if gravity is pulling them downward.

If you tell a co-worker about a costly and drastic mistake they made while working, their arms and shoulders will visibly droop and sink. Negative emotions cause all of our body parts to experience gravity more, which is why we call them "sinking" feelings. These responses are automatic, subconscious, and happen immediately. For instance, right when our team scores a goal, we punch our hands into the air. These behaviors accurately show our feelings at the exact moment that we feel them. In addition to this, these signals might affect those around us and become contagious. Smaller hand gestures can help show specific, conscious concepts, such as the "thumbs up" sign, or a wave, but if you want to look deeper and get to the comfort level or subconscious moods of someone, pay attention to the gravity of their arms and body in general.

The middle of our body or torso (made up of the belly, chest, and shoulders) is absolutely vital for our wellness and general survival. This is where most of our important organs are, and so we have a subconscious need to protect this area at all times, instinctively. But this isn't only apparent in body language when we are in physically threatening or safe situations. This applies even in more relaxed social environments. To put it plainly, we leave our torsos free and open when we feel comfortable with the situation or person.

Our torsos show our limbic brain's desire to avoid and distance ourselves when we are feeling threatened. For example, if someone feels as though there is something wrong in their relationship, they are probably picking up on this degree of distance from their loved one and reacting to it, even if they aren't consciously aware that this is what is actually happening.

263

This distancing might also mean that they are showing ventral (or front) denial. The fronts of our bodies are sensitive to our likes and dislikes. When something is going well, we will turn these parts to what we like, including situations or people. If something is going wrong, on the other hand, we turn away or shift in the opposite direction.

The front side of our bodies is by far the most vulnerable, so our subconscious and limbic brain feels a need to automatically protect it from threat. This is why we start to turn our sides a bit when we get approached by someone we don't want to talk to at a social gathering, for example. When you are observing people in situations involving dating or courtship, this is a highly reliable indicator of whether the relationship is going well or not. Either denying or sharing the front of your body with others is most obviously observed when it comes to romantic or dating situations. When a couple is new, they usually angle their torsos toward each other, rather than away from each other. This happens when they're sitting down, standing, or one of them walks into a room.

This happens because they are comfortable with each other, have a favorable standing, and so their bodies don't have to protect their limbic systems. When we deny or protect access to the center of our bodies is when we encounter unpleasant or threatening situations or people. When we leave our abdomen and chest open, or point them to someone, we feel safe and happy with the situation.

You might be surprised to find out that you can actually tell a lot about someone's internal state by what their legs are doing. But this is actually where the most honesty can be found. While some may believe that the face is a good indicator, this is the part of our bodies that we have been trained and conditioned to lie about our emotions with. We grew up being told to smile, look friendly, or quit making silly faces. But countless years of human evolution have ingrained within us that our legs must be ready, at a moment's notice, to escape danger.

The simplest, and most reliable, method for figuring out someone's feelings or intentions by looking at their legs to see which direction the feet are pointing in. Just like the way we angle our torsos away from or toward people, our lower bodies usually point or lean toward the way we want to go, or the direction we're interested in. When people are having a conversation, they are usually talking with their toes pointed toward each other. But if one of them starts to turn their feet away or points one foot outward, this is a sign that they want to walk away or go somewhere else. This behavior of the feet is a sign or a signal of intention. Someone's torso might point in the direction of someone they don't like out of feeling consciously obligated, but a person's feet are honestly reflecting the brain's desire to stay or escape the situation or person.

On the other hand, if someone has their legs crossed, especially as they are standing up, this is a strong signal that they want to stay put. Again, this comes from our basic subconscious need to survive and protect our best interests. Even if we are pretending that we're having fun in a situation, crossed feet or legs means that it would take us a lot longer to escape from a threatening or dangerous situation. Even if someone is consciously aware that they aren't in actual physical danger, our brains will still react as if there's a physical threat when we want to leave a social situation.

One aspect of reading body language cues that you can't escape or ignore is first establishing a person's baseline. This is the most crucial aspect of analyzing people. All individuals have their personal habits and quirks. Someone who is shy, for example, might normally hold their arms close to themselves and keep their heads down, even in normal situations. A "leader", on the other hand, will do the opposite. While people who don't know them well may take these signals to assume that they are going through a unique emotional state, it's actually just showing their default body language. A single isolated behavior doesn't necessarily show that there has been a change in someone's mood.

As you become more familiar with someone, however, and the way they act in typical situations, unusual behavior can serve as a far more reliable indication of the way they feel at that moment. Don't only keep an eye out for someone with their head up or their legs crossed, as this may be default behavior that just signals what their personality or usual demeanor is like. Instead, pay attention to something they do that is outside of the way they usually behave.

Many times, you don't have to look very deep to find out what someone is reacting to or figure out what they're thinking. If they seem calm and happy one moment, and then make a pained face when a certain person walks up, you can safely assume that the person caused this reaction. You should rely on your own instincts, context, and feelings, in addition to these body language signals, which can mean many different things. The only way to get a full picture is to use a combination of methods.

Body language is important not only for deciphering what the people around you are feeling and thinking, but for changing your own state of mind or sending the right signals to the people around you. Part of becoming a master of analyzing others is learning how to improve the body language cues you are using on a daily basis. Using body language effectively can determine whether your interactions with people go well or fall flat. Here are some useful tips and tricks for sending strong signals in nonverbal communication.

Research has proven that when you hold yourself in a "powerful" or expansive pose (such as standing with your arms open or leaning on a desk with your feet apart) for a couple of minutes, your body will begin to create more testosterone. This means that you instantly start to feel more in control, dominant, and powerful. When you are feeling doubtful or nervous about your confidence but want to either seem self-assured or make yourself feel better, assume poses like this. People will respond more to their personal feelings about you than the words you choose to use, another reason why body language matters a lot.

In order to encourage others to participate and speak up more, make sure that you are not multitasking when they talk, which can be seen as very discouraging, to some. Although it can be tempting to look at the clock or check your email, you need to show that you're listening to get people to open up. You can do this by making sure you are facing them with your whole body and looking them in the eye. Tilting your face, nodding, and leaning forward are also good signals to send that show you're listening and paying close attention to what they're saying. While listening and hearing are important, showing that you are doing these things is equally important.

Obstructions can be a huge detriment to collaborating with people. If you are talking to someone and you want them to collaborate or work together with you on something, remove anything that may be forming a barrier or blocking your view of them. Even on breaks at work or in meetings, be aware that holding something in front of you can be subconsciously interpreted as you trying to distance yourself from someone or block your view of them. People who feel comfortable in social environments hold their hands at a lower level, than those who feel insecure or threatened.

Physical touch is a powerful and primitive body language cue to use. If you touch someone on the shoulder, hand or arm, it can create a warmer bond, but only if they are comfortable with it. Of course, you should use your best judgment for when this would be well received or not. In a professional environment, warmth and touch are typically established using handshaking, and even this small amount of contact can create a positive, lasting impression on the other person. When you shake someone's hand, you are twice as likely to remember them, and see them as friendly and open people.

A real genuine smile can not only heighten your feelings of happiness, but it can send the right messages to the people around you. A smile indicates that you are trustworthy, cooperative, and approachable. A true smile will light up your face, crinkle your eyes, come on slow and leave slowly. Smiling influences the way those near you will respond to you. When we give someone else a smile, they almost always give one back, and since body language or expressions affect mental states, this can leave them with a positive impression or mood.

When businesspeople or clients imitate your nonverbal cues subconsciously, they are sending signals that they either agree with you or like you on a personal level. When you consciously and purposely "mirror" those around you, it can cause them to feel a strong rapport with you. Paying attention to someone's body language and expressions, mirroring them subtly and naturally will help them feel accepted and understood by you. Be careful, however, not to go overboard on this, as this will cause the opposite effect you're hoping for.

Gesturing is linked with speaking, and using more gestures as we talk can add fuel to our thinking and articulation. Try this out and you will notice that when you use your hands as you talk, you have a clearer mind and can find the words you're searching for more easily. Many people do this without even being aware of it, but consciously using it to your advantage will get you far.

If you hope to come across as authoritative or respectable to those you speak with, you should be conscious of the pitch of your voice. When we're nervous, we might talk too loud, too quietly, too high or too low. This is a habit you should work on for maximizing good impressions. Before you are making a phone call or going into an interview, practice keeping your voice at an even pitch. Don't talk too loud, too fast, or too unevenly, and you will send the message that you are confident and capable of whatever you're about to do.

If you are hoping to be more effective at storing important memories, try uncrossing your legs and arms as you listen. This can also be used to help people interact more in a meeting or conference. If you notice a lot of people are sitting with crossed legs or arms, encourage them to stand up, move around, and interact with the environment. This will automatically cause them to feel more engaged and involved, and all around more positive about the experience.

Now that you have a better understanding of body language and how it affects communication, as well as its ability to change your frame of mind, you'll need to use it in practice yourself and try to identify it in others as they interact. While there are many different facets involved with body language and interpreting its meaning it is a knowledge base that can be easy to learn if you continue to practice.

Don't get so caught up in the terminology that you forget how much of this is already planted in your subconscious. Many of us have this so ingrained that we take it for granted and forget that it is actually imbedded in our minds. We commonly watch people interact during most phases of our day, and if you think about it you are usually assessing or analyzing these people without even thinking about it. It's usually when force the issue that we over complicate the ability to do this naturally.

Conclusion

Thanks again for purchasing this book. I hope that you were able to gain valuable insights as to how to recognize certain personality types and what this can help you realize about individuals. In addition to this, hopefully you understood the benefits that can become apparent to you by mastering the art of reading body language. You can now start enjoying these benefits:

- **Controlling your Body Language for the Best Results:** Most of us know the way we want to come across and seem to others, but not how to do it. Now that you've read this book, you're equipped with the knowledge you need to effectively send the signals you want to send. Whether it's a job interview you want to master, showing your boss that you're capable of taking on more responsibility, or getting someone to accept a date with you, now you can do it.

- **Understanding Others:** One of life's most confusing and mysterious subjects is trying to read other people. Now that you have the information given to you in this guide, you can look deeper than someone's smile or frown and get to know what they are really feeling deep inside. You can use this information to deepen relationships, make new friends, or score more professional opportunities in the workplace.

- **Impressing People with your Knowledge:** Many people aren't good at listening, paying attention to others, or reading them accurately. If you are one of the few who can master this subject, you will impress people by how much you notice and see. Since impressions go a long way in all areas of life, this is a valuable skill to have.

As with any other skill, reading nonverbal cues and body language is something that you need to test out as often as possible in order to get better with it. The more you practice at this, the easier it will get.

How to Analyze People

How to Master Reading Anyone Instantly Using Body Language, Human Psychology, and Personality Types

Introduction: The Importance of Analyzing Others Instantly

When communicating with others, we have become extraordinarily dependent upon just what we see and hear on the surface. However, just below the shallows is a whole other world of motivations that direct behaviors and determine the effectiveness of our perceptions. Often others' surface expressions, words, and actions are not congruent to what is happening on that deeper level. To be dynamic communicators, we need to have "deep see" vision to analyze others real motives and reason behind what they say and do. Not only will analyzing others give us a more accurate perception of them, but it will also give us greater insight into ourselves.

Have you ever felt an almost uncanny creepiness about a person or an immediate kinship with someone, but you have no clear explanation as to why? That's because you were sensitive to other non-verbal signals, behaviors, and traits that the other person was so desperately wanting to hide to gain your trust. Once you train yourself to be mindful of others' covert messages, you'll have much more confidence in your perceptions and ability to handle almost any situation before it becomes threatening to your well-being. So, let's look at what learning to analyze others can do for us.

Accurately Analyzing Others Can Keep Us Physically Safe

Linda is an excellent example of how carefully analyzing others can protect you. As a Realtor® for over ten years, Linda attributed much of her success on her strong communication skills. She had been told on numerous occasions that she was a good judge of character, and it had paid off in spades. When she was with clients, it was as if she knew what her prospects were going to say or do before they knew. One afternoon, these skills served a far greater purpose than merely winning her the contract.

Each morning she had coffee on her way to work. It was a great way to socialize and pass out her business cards. As Linda waited in line for her coffee, she struck up a conversation with the gentleman behind her. As usual, she gave him her business card, and he immediately shared his need to sell his home and move into something larger. He had just been promoted at work and wanted his lifestyle to reflect his new position, and Linda was eager to help him search for the perfect home. He gave her his address, and they arranged to meet the next day at his home with a current market analysis to determine its value.

Never suspecting danger, Linda went by herself to his home, knocked at the front door with her usual confidence, and waited for his invitation to enter. He welcomed her into the home and stepped behind her to lock the front door. She immediately felt this was a bit odd but dispelled the feeling in hopes that it was out of habit rather than a need to trap her inside his home. As she looked around, she noticed no sign of a feminine touch, with the minimal furnishings showing nothing but masculine appeal.

Unable to rid herself of the creep factor, Linda began to ask questions. "I'm ashamed of myself, but I didn't even get your name yesterday." She held out her hand to introduce herself— "Hi, I'm Linda, and, you are?"

"Oh—Jeff. My name's, Umm, Jeff," he replied, as he looked down at his feet. As if remembering he should behave differently, Jeff then looked up and smiled and offered his hand. That's when Linda noticed something else that was odd. His hand was clammy as if his nerves were getting the better of him. Upon closer inspection, she also noticed that although Jeff offered a smile in response, it was tight and didn't reach all the way to his eyes.

"Hello, Jeff," she smiled back, trying not to show her nervousness. "Do you mind if I look around so I can get an idea of the value of your house?"

"Oh, right—right," he said, walking behind her in a herding manner, and moving closely behind her toward the hallway.

"Well, let's start out here in the living area and kitchen, shall we?" As she passed the hall, her neck hairs began to stand to attention, and she went on full alert. The first room to the right of the hallway was entirely black, and she caught a glimpse of the corner of a daybed with a pink boa draped across its sidearm. It was difficult for Linda to hide her dismay at the sight of this little island of femininity in Jeff's otherwise overly masculine house.

Linda continued to take notes as she walked around the kitchen, asking light questions to try to keep the conversation casual. The quieter the two of them became, the louder Linda's little voice in her head shouted for her to get out of there. "You know, it got chilly this morning. I have such allergies in changing weather like this. Would you have some tissue?"

"Oh, yeah, he moved once again to position himself at her back awkwardly. Come on back," he said, as he then moved around her to walk down the hallway.

"Why don't you get some, and I'll get my jacket in the car?" The moment Jeff began walking down the hall, Linda made her getaway. Thankfully, she maneuvered herself between Jeff and the locked front door but opened the deadbolt quickly. She quickly grabbed her briefcase and car keys from the side table, ran to her car, and pulled out of Jeff's driveway as if the devil himself were after her.

Upset and shaken, Linda immediately reported her fear and behavior to her broker, warning other females not to go to that address alone. She wanted to call the police, but there was nothing to report, so she shook off her feeling of foreboding and took off the rest of the afternoon. Three nights later, Linda realized how close she had come to the horrific realization of her feelings that all was not as it should be at Jeff's house. As she watched the 10:00 news, she saw police leading Jeff out of his house in handcuffs, and the anchor people sadly reported his connection to two murdered women on the west side of the city.

Linda called the police and shared her story, and as she told them what happened, she realized that her analysis of Jeff had been spot on, but it was not what he said that had tipped her off to his possible deviant plans. It was how he behaved, what she observed, and her overall perceptions that signaled the alarm. Linda knew that she had always been able to read others well, but this time her intuitive perceptions had done more than fund her life—they had saved her life!

Analyzing Others Can Bring Us Professional Prosperity

James had never considered himself a natural born leader, but he had been asked to act as company vice president after the unexpected departure of his boss. He dreaded the first office meeting when he would have to share with the team that he was now the new vice president. James just knew that everybody had loved Eddie. He had a quick wit and a welcoming smile, always inviting others to participate and share their feelings about any new ideas or required changes. He gave the salespeople full reign to do their thing, and the team seemed to enjoy the freedom.

James, on the other hand, was a quiet contemplator. He knew that his discomfort with public speaking and quick decision making had negatively impacted several potential promotions for him throughout the years. Now that James finally had the opportunity to lead, he couldn't help but feel out of his comfort zone. James was shocked that he had been chosen for the position, and second to his disbelief was his feelings of inadequacy and unpreparedness. Just two months previously, James had attended a communications seminar where the speaker talked about the effects of misunderstandings in the workplace. Now James wondered if others would mistake his quiet demeanor and reticent manner as a lack of leadership skills.

James welcomed the opportunity to promote his assistant to become the new executive assistant to the vice president, knowing her strengths were his weaknesses. She was confident, outgoing, and easily trusted when James tended to hang back. Yes, Susan would be the perfect complement to him in this new position, and he looked forward to having her input. As it turned out, James fears were put to rest when the team began to flourish under his gentle guidance and Susan's nurturing nature.

Together, they created stability in the sales team and encouraged even greater participation and higher-level contributions from all parties. It seemed the wrong perceptions were on James part. What he believed everybody thought was real leadership had been a gathering of the "good ole boys" club, where little was expected and even less achieved.

In record time, the salespeople thrived under James leadership and his assistant's support. James' confidence and performance were surprisingly successful in creating peak performance for the entire team, and he and Susan worked together to build the highest selling team in the company.

There are many other ways analyzing people can benefit you. Learn and apply the strategies in our book, and you'll gain a new perspective on yourself and others. When you begin reading others and yourself with an open mind and willing spirit, your new skills will lead you to even greater successes in your personal and professional lives. Your relationships will improve, your confidence will increase, and your analytical knowledge will open doors for you that you never dreamed possible.

Analyzing Others Can Give Insight in Your Personal Relationships

For the longest time, the HOA board meetings had consisted of Ally and her husband. Until Theresa came along, nobody had been interested in the need to keep the greenbelts clean and the streetlights were working. Ally was a contradiction of feelings; although it was great to have another's opinion, she felt somewhat uncomfortable around Theresa. After the board meeting one evening, Theresa was on her way home when Ally's husband offered her a ride.

Nothing seemed out of the ordinary on the surface, but Ally felt wary of Theresa around her husband, Eddie. When she voiced her feelings to Eddie, he brushed her off and said something sarcastic about seeing her claws come out whenever Theresa was in the room. The more Ally tried not to let things bother her, the more the thoughts rolled around in her head. Perhaps it was because Eddie had worked so much overtime the last

279

two weeks, and his boss was so selfish in his overtime pay that created such suspicious thoughts in Ally.

The next morning, Ally was checking the sprinklers out front when her neighbor walked over and told her something that confirmed her fears. The friend told Ally she had asked Eddie to say hello the other night when he was standing outside Theresa's house. "Oh, what night was that?" Ally asked.

"I went by the night before last, and he was standing outside Theresa's with a big box in his hands. I wondered if she was moving."

"I don't know." Ally was so upset that she excused herself and went into the house quickly before her neighbor could see her tears. The rest of the day was spent wondering what she was going to do. She wasn't going to put up with a cheating husband, but she just couldn't imagine herself without Eddie. It was her birthday, no less, and Eddie hadn't even wished her a happy birthday before going to work that morning. She just could face the heartache of telling him she knew, so she left before he could get home. As Ally passed Theresa's street, she noticed Eddie's car parked in front. Too hurt to stop and too mad not to, Ally decided she would put an end to this behavior and stop Eddie in his tracks.

She quickly ran to the front door, not realizing what a mess she looked with her makeup smeared and her hair still wet at the temples for trying to clean her face up before leaving the house. Nobody answered, so she rang the doorbell once again, and this time Eddie came to the door. "What are you doing here, honey?" Eddie took one look at her and knew she must be having an emergency. "What's wrong? Are you hurt?"

"You might say that, Eddie." Ally waved her arms in the air and continued with "I'm hurt about all this. How could you do this?" she asked, before bursting into tears.

Eddie grabbed her by the arm and pulled her into Theresa's house. "Okay, okay, what's all this about? What do you think I'm doing?"

"I've seen how you two look at each other as if you've got a secret you don't want anybody else to know about."

Theresa came out from the other room and walked over to Ally, "We do. We've been planning your surprise birthday party for the past two weeks."

Ally's misunderstanding had caused her pain and hurt, and it could have been the end of her marriage. Relationships are made and broken by poor communications and false perceptions. We would probably be shocked at how many couples had split because of mistaken beliefs caused by unfounded suspicions, as well as how many others were able to mislead their significant other and hold a shaky relationship together through deceit and negative manipulation.

These are the reasons we've written this book on how to analyze others. You'll learn to be more decisive, and rely on your perceptions to give you clarity in your personal and professional life. It won't take long before the benefits of that "deeper see" vision pays off in longer-lasting, more rewarding relationships and more profitable business associations. So, let's get started, shall we?

Chapter 1: Identifying Personality Types

Even though there are four main personality types, most people are a combination of two or more types. You might be primarily one type with a few traits of another, or you could be middle of the road between two different types. There are also some people who have a few traits of every type. Several things determine your personality types, but the strongest influences are typically one's upbringing, hormones, and chemical makeup.

If you read my other book *How to Analyze People: How to Read Anyone Instantly Using Body Language, Personality Types and Human Psychology,* then you might already be familiar with these four personality types. In this chapter, we'll review the different personality types and go into greater detail about the positive and negative traits of each types, and their identifying behaviors and language.

Knowing others personality types and identifying behaviors and language that are characteristic of these types of people will help you know how best to relate to them in your personal and professional endeavors. After you have studied the personality types, take the time to do a personal inventory to discover your personality type. Knowing how you prefer to relate to others and how they want you to relate to them is paramount in making the necessary adjustments to the way you communicate with people of all different personality types and traits.

The Leader Personality Type

Leader Personality Types make great presidents and executives, administrators and wall street moguls, or managers and supervisors. Many politicians are Leader Personalities as well.

Positive Traits of a Leader Personality Type

Confident	Direct	Strategic	Problem-Solver
Decisive	Driven	Courageous	Bold
Independent	Goal-Oriented	Money-Oriented	Proud
Energetic	Focused	Competitive	Hard-Working
Powerful	Tough	Determined	Take Charge

Negative Traits of a Leader Personality Type

Tense	Workaholic	Opinionated	Temperamental
Stressed	Too Controlling	Power Hungry	Too Authoritative
Unforgiving	Rude	Aggressive	Judging
Distrusting	Unavailable	Detached	Unsocial
Impatient	Self-Centered	Overly Competitive	Stubborn

Identifying Behaviors of a Leader Personality Type

- They don't take a lot of time for family and friends.
- Most of their conversations center around work and money-making ventures.
- They respect strength and competitiveness, so they will usually be sports-minded and fit.
- They have a strong, confident handshake.
- Since they are money-motivated, they will usually drive an expensive car, live in a luxurious estate, and wear designer watches.
- They don't have much patience with people who don't display appreciation for the finer things in life.
- They are attracted to intelligent people and usually will not associate with others whom they feel are not on their level.
- Their body language is often a wide stance with arms folded in front of them or braced at the waist.
- It will be difficult for them to focus on conversations that don't center around work or intellectual matters.

Identifying Language of a Leader Personality Type

I My Intellect Ambition Challenge

The Identifier Personality Type

Identifier Personality Types are especially caring and nurturing people. They love nothing more than to educate, help, or heal others. These personality types make outstanding teachers, nurses, and counselors.

Positive Traits of an Identifier Personality Type

Nurturing	Encouraging	Sympathetic	Cooperative
Understanding	Relational	Expressive	Unassuming
Considerate	Charitable	Soul Searching	Trusting
Good Listeners	Compassionate	Agreeable	Empathetic
Emotional	Imaginative	Idealistic	Contributors

Negative Traits of an Identifier Personality Type

Over-Thinkers	Drama Queens	Sacrificial	Imbalanced Lifestyle
Appear Needy	Too Agreeable	Indecisive	Demand Reassurance
Unfocused	Too Accepting	Take on Problems of the Universe	

Identifying Behaviors of an Identifier Personality Type

- Because Identifier Personality Types don't want to offend others, they are often too agreeable.
- They are most susceptible to suffering depression or moodiness.
- They do not take criticism well; they become too easily offended.

- If they are in a managing position, they prefer an open-door policy.
- Their managing style is more open and relaxed.
- If they fear confrontation or rejection in social situations, they can appear shy and timid.
- Their body language is usually open arms and trusting mannerisms.
- They can be a bit touch-feely for other's taste.
- They are comfortable talking about emotions and their warm and fuzzy conversations often center around feelings and charitable events.

Identifying Language of an Identifier Personality Type

Passion Sensitive Sweet Understand Sorry

The Fraternizer Personality Type

Fraternizer Personality Types enjoy high adventure and challenging themselves with almost everything. They are real sensation seekers whose hunger for the unconventional adventure is their ultimate enjoyment. You will usually find Fraternizer Personality Types working as comedians, entertainers, event planners, venue coordinators, or even travel guides.

Positive Traits of a Fraternizer Personality Type

Friendly	Storytellers	Energetic	Charming
Spontaneous	Curious	Engaging	Outspoken
Social Butterfly	Outgoing	Optimistic	Adaptable
Conversationalist	Athletic	Humorous	Fun-loving
Enthusiastic	Knowledgeable	Creative	Unconventional

Negative Traits of a Fraternizer Personality Type

Too Talkative	Doesn't Listen	Self-Centered	Unfocused
Easily Bored	Impulsive	Restless	Self-Absorbed
Procrastinator	Low Tolerance	Scattered	Uncalculated Risk Taker

Identifying Behaviors of a Fraternizer Personality Type

- They love to travel and talk about their adventures.
- Fraternizers enjoy outdoor adventures, and they're always up for something out-of-the-norm.
- They are not afraid to speak their minds, even if they hold the unpopular opinion. Usually, they get others to agree with them just because they are so likable.
- They are big spenders. Fraternizers will usually pick up the tab for dinner or drinks.

- Because they are so impulsive and social, they are often more susceptible to drug and alcohol abuse.
- It can be challenging getting them to settle down to find a solution to a pressing problem.
- Most Fraternizers have bigger-than-life gestures and expressions.

Identifying Language of a Fraternizer Personality Type

Adventure	Energy	New	Fun	Wealthy
Pleasure	Happiness	Travel	Active	Why Not?

The Perceiver Personality Type

Perceiver Personality Types are your more serious-minded of the four main personality types. Because they are so fact-driven, they are quite often engineers, mathematicians, scientists, and technology experts.

Positive Traits of a Perceiver Personality Type

Organized	Purpose-Driven	Concentrated	Logical
Analytical	Task-Oriented	Factual	Orderly
Predictable	Detail-Oriented	Structured	Dependable

| Deep Thinker | Investigative | Patient | Persistent |
| Sentimental | Respectful | Reliable | Planner |

Negative Traits of a Perceiver Personality Type

Unemotional	Too One-minded	Loner	Too Serious
Unsocial	Cold	Predictable	Anxious
Dogmatic	Hard to Please	Obsessive	Stubborn

Identifying Behaviors of a Perceiver Personality Type

- Since they value being thoughtful and self-controlled, they express themselves using very precise language.
- They don't work well with demanding deadlines, and they are challenged with high-pressure tasks.
- They can be obsessive/compulsive in their behaviors.
- They can often be judging and critical of others.
- They are uncomfortable being the center of attention, so you will usually find them standing in the back of the group or crowd.
- They don't know how to take compliments and show embarrassment when given one.
- Since they are such deep thinkers, they don't usually make quick decisions or act quickly in an urgent situation.

- Perceivers will be the ones who hold you up in the grocery line to count out the exact change.
- Their body language is closed, and you will often notice that they avoid making eye contact.

Identifying Language of a Perceiver Personality Type

Respect   Moral   Loyalty   Careful   Count on Me

Taking a Personal Inventory of Your Personality Type

Answer the following questions to discover your personality type or types. Circle the letter that best describes your feelings, thoughts, or behaviors in the given situations. When you have completed the personal inventory, tally up your points to see your most likely personality type(s).

1. When you're in a meeting, you usually...

   a. Try to get everybody to participate
   b. Be quiet and let others do the talking
   c. Act like I agree even if I don't so I won't be confrontational
   d. Offer my feelings on the subject and encourage others to as well

2. If your significant other is angry or frustrated, you ...

   a. Suggest an evening out on the town to relieve the stress

290

b. Go to my office for a while until he or she cools down

c. Feel bad and wonder what I did wrong

d. Let them think it out and then ask some pointed questions to seek closure

3. If your computer is acting up, you most likely would...

a. Search the manual or the Internet for the problem, carefully weigh the suggested remedies, and then try the most likely solution

b. Call a friend to come over for a drink and see what they can do to help me fix it

c. I get the IT guy at work to come over and fix it

d. I chat online and see if others are having the same issues and then try some of the things that helped them overcome the problem

4. If you get stood up for an evening out, what do you do?

a. Call another friend and go somewhere with them instead.

b. I enjoy the evening by myself at home.

c. I ask them if there is anything I can do to help them with whatever it was that kept them from enjoying an evening with me.

d. I do some work at home and get a head start on the next day's tasks.

5. When you lose a bet or a competition of some kind, you might...

a. Double down—I hate to lose

b. Wonder if they somehow cheated

c. Be happy for my competitor

d. Laugh it off and get ready for the next bet

6. If someone tries to tell you what to do, you usually ...

    a. Listen to what they say, and then figure it out for myself anyway
    b. Understand they have experienced this before and try to do what they suggest
    c. I think they've got their nerve and do what I want
    d. Make a joke about it and then wait until they leave and ask someone else to do it for me

7. If you told your significant other you didn't want a dog and he or she got one anyway, you would most likely...

    a. Smile and start playing with the dog.
    b. Try to be sensitive to their need for a dog and think of how I can help take care of it
    c. Remember what happened the last time he or she got a dog and then remind them of what a disaster it was
    d. Make them take the dog back from whence it came

8. If you paid to have your car detailed and they didn't do a good job, you would most likely...

    a. Realize that they usually did a good job and just live with it
    b. Be upset with them and make them do the whole thing over
    c. Kid around with them and ask them to touch it up in spots

d. I would give myself time to think about what I wanted to say and then take it back the next day and ask them to make it right

9. If you were dressed for and on your way to work and saw that your car had a flat tire in the driveway, you would...

a. Call a company to fix the tire and work from home until it was repaired
b. Call a friend or my significant other and ask what I should do
c. Call into work and let them know, call a repair company, and then go for a run until it was fixed
d. Look at the tire to see if it was tampered with, and then have it fixed, but I would be watching the street to see if anyone else was having a similar problem

10. If your child got a poor grade on his or her report card, AGAIN, you would most likely...

a. Sit down with them and listen to their explanation and then figure out with them how they could do better next time
b. Depend on my significant other to handle the situation
c. Offer them some money to do better
d. Probably blow up and let them know who's boss

Scoring—Discover Your Personality Type(s)

Give yourself a point under each appropriate personality type and then tally your points to see what personality type is dominant and which ones are secondary.

293

Question	Leader	Identifier	Fraternizer	Perceiver
#1	a	b	d	c
#2	b	c	a	d
#3	c	d	b	a
#4	d	c	a	b
#5	a	c	d	b
#6	c	b	d	a
#7	d	b	a	c
#8	b	a	c	d
#9	a	b	c	d
#10	d	a	c	b
Total	2	3	2	3

Under which personality type(s) did you have the most circles? The personality type with the most circles is probably your dominant personality type, and those with just a few circles have some influence in your behaviors and beliefs.

Now comes the big surprise. Even though you took this Personal Inventory and you "think" you are predominantly one personality type, you might find out differently when it comes to what you'll discover in the next chapter. It's all about perception. How you perceived yourself might be much different than how others see you. So, let's explore the principles of perception and see what influence these perceptions have on the way we analyze ourselves and others.

Chapter 2: The Principles of Perceptions

As you analyze others and yourself, you begin to form temporary and long-lasting perceptions. These truths are invaluable to get an accurate read of others and examine what motivates others' behaviors and beliefs. However, there are some universal truths about perceptions, and we call these the Principles of Perceptions. As you read others' body language and analyze their behaviors, keep the following Five Principles of Perceptions in mind. Knowing them will help your analysis to be more accurate.

Principle #1: Perceptions Are Deceptive

There is much information that goes into your analysis of yourself and others. However, it's not good practice to blindly accept the information that filters through your mind to create your perceptions. Why? To form your opinions of others while you analyze their behaviors and beliefs, you are working with a limited amount of knowledge and awareness. The following strategies will offer a more accurate analysis and verify or replace your initial perceptions.

- Spending more time with the people you are analyzing to form your impressions gives you a more precise read on their behaviors and beliefs. When you jump to conclusions about what motivates people to say or do things, you are playing off old tapes of past experiences. Your judgments can be tainted because of previous experiences you had when another person said or did similar things.

- Observing how others react to the people you are reading helps you to know whether you are too critical or judging of them. You need to ask yourself if your opinions of this person are based on personal likes or dislikes, or are your perceptions based on unbiased observations and effective listening skills.

- Have you rushed to judgment? When you are analyzing others, give them time to prove or disprove your perceptions of them. Avoid forming your analysis on just one or two encounters. If you must analyze another's behavior quickly, realize that there's a good chance your perceptions will not be entirely accurate.

Principle #2: Background Brings Accuracy

There are times when you must analyze others' behaviors quickly, but when you do your perceptions might be off the mark. After all, you have no background on this person and no history with which to form your impressions. For example, if you are in a group and someone moves away from you to stand on the other side of the group, what do you think? If you rush to judgment, you might believe that they are giving you the cold shoulder. Or, if you have experienced recent rejection, you might begin to wonder what is wrong with you. What you don't know when analyzing others can and will hurt your ability to form accurate perceptions.

Let's say this situation goes a little further and the person you are examining turns her head away from you. It's easy to convince yourself she is avoiding you—until you find out later in the evening that your subject suffered a severe hearing loss and needed to move closer to the speaker and tilt her head to hear better from her functioning ear. Suddenly, your perceptions of that person have drastically changed. Why? You have more background information.

Principle #3: Awareness & Accuracy Go Hand-in-Hand

The reason you need to be familiar with the four personality types, observe others' body language, and listen to the words they frequently use is because awareness gives you a broader and more accurate picture of what motivates them to act and say what they do. There is greater awareness when you gain more knowledge and apply that knowledge to what you see and hear. While you can observe behaviors, if you don't know the cause of the behavior, it's just empty information.

You can be aware of how others stand, sit, walk, and communicate, but if you don't know what these signals mean, the information is no use to you. Your perceptions of people continue to form based on nothing more than your past experiences, which give you a limited, one-dimensional picture. When you can combine your past experiences and motivations to a greater knowledge of what's behind these behaviors and words, then your relationships will magically improve, and your actions and beliefs will change as well.

If you want to increase your awareness and apply it to your analysis of others, you've come to the right place. Educating yourself on reading body language and recognizing personality types will enable you to achieve more efficient communications with people much different from yourself. Most people tend to form relationships with individuals who are like them, so learning to monitor and adjust your behaviors and words to match another will draw others to you.

Principle #4: Position Alters Perception

All of us would like to believe that our perceptions and analysis are not unduly influenced by another's position, but the truth of the matter is that we are all impressed or turned off by others based on many different criteria. Much of what impacts our analysis has nothing to do with how they behave or what they say.   Many perceptions are the results of the other person's position in life. Being influenced by another's position in life doesn't mean that every person who has a big title is automatically respected because some people resent others' success. The following are some things that alter perceptions.

- Career Choice
- Company
- Job Title
- Your Bosses' Favored-Peer
- Other Friends or Acquaintances Who Page Homage to Their Authority

If your perception of another is that they are above or below your status, then your analysis of that person will be impacted by your perception. If you review the personality types, you'll notice that Leader and Perceiver Personalities can be more judging than Fraternizers and Identifiers. Knowing you are a Leader Personality Type can help you to understand that you often allow others' positions to get in the way of your analysis and influence your beliefs about them. Gaining this knowledge about your personality type makes you more aware of how you respond to others' behaviors and beliefs, thereby creating better relationships.

Principle #5: We See What We Want to See

Have you ever noticed how what you expect to happen almost always happens? Well, this is no coincidence. Expectations influence our analysis of others' behaviors and words. In other words, we see what we want to see, especially if our emotions are involved. If we are in a highly emotional state, it's difficult to see past the anger, love, or fear.

Analysis based on emotion is not just slightly inaccurate, but those perceptions are often so slanted that when you share your thoughts with others, they think you've lost touch with reality. I'm sure you have heard of all the romance scams happening online these days. Men and women are being swindled out of hundreds of thousands of dollars because they are in a vulnerable state and allow another person to take advantage of them. There are now scammers who have developed "so-called" services that say they can help reveal a possible scammer. That's the web emotions can weave when it comes to analyzing the behaviors and motives of those we think we know.

Some people with a terminal illness believe they can be cured by a concoction provided through someone who claims to be a doctor. Unfortunately, this is what happened to Carl. Carl's specialist diagnosed him with third-stage cancer. His prognosis wasn't promising, but when Carl could not accept the hopelessness of his situation, he contacted a doctor he heard of who had experienced incredible results with his treatment of cancer. Carl spent thousands of dollars traveling to India, and thousands more staying at the doctor's treatment center. The treatments were uncomfortable, and they kept Carl away from his family for weeks at a time, but at the end of each treatment, Carl felt better for a while.

The doctor told Carl that it would take several treatments before he would experience lasting results, and each time Carl would see what he wanted to see. Although his family saw him getting weaker, thinner, and less energetic, Carl saw himself as more fit and in a calmer state of mind. Just days after his last treatment, Carl died of cancer, and his family felt cheated out of the time they could have spent with him during his final year of life. How could an otherwise intelligent, professional man have been so fooled? It's easy; he allowed his highly emotional state to override his better judgment. He wanted the treatments to work so badly, that he was victim to the fifth principle of perceptions—we see what we want to see.

The Importance of Knowing the Five Principles of Perception

To read and analyze others accurately, you must first understand how perceptions influence behaviors and beliefs and then judge the accuracy of your feelings. It just doesn't help to read one's body language if you don't realize your interpretation of your observations is skewed. All the while you are questioning others' motives, you also need to be examining yours.

Combining personality types, body language, the spoken word, and the way you form perceptions of yourself and others will give you the bigger picture—a more well-rounded view of our intentional and unintentional communications. Knowing what you know now, you can analyze others with confidence and assurance that the things observed and heard are indicative of the meanings you have attributed to them.

As you learn about how to read one's body language and listen for the verbal clues that identify one's true motives, you can attach your perceptions of the person or situation without the concerns that you have misjudged or misread their meaning. Now it's time to look at the incredible signals and signs we send out every day without being conscious of how they help others to form their perceptions of us.

Chapter 3: Body Language Speaks Volumes

Some people are naturals at reading others, but they couldn't tell you how they know what they know. That's because they are intuitively reading others' body language, but they don't have the knowledge to define why they are such good communicators. More than 70 percent of the messages we send and receive are through non-verbal language. Not only are the greatest percent of our messages non-verbal, but that non-verbal language is more honest and genuine than the words we speak. Our bodies don't sugar coat the message; we just respond and react without being conscious of doing so.

If people are saying one thing but their body language is delivering a different message, put more stock in what you see than what you hear. However, to make sure you are reading the person correctly, let's discuss all the different nonverbal messages we send. We'll cover the nonverbal signals and what they might mean, but keep in mind that different cultures and countries might attach a different meaning to your body language. When you're confused about the nonverbal message that another is sending, then listen to the words and take the signals in context with the phrases they use.

Another way to determine the message is through the tone, pitch, and volume of another's voice. It gives truth to that saying, "It's not what you said but how you said it." When all these things are examined during your analysis of others, you'll find clarity in the message. While we're at it, there is one more thing—pay attention to the other person's required personal space. If you are questioning whether the message they are sending is positive, negative, or benevolent, step inside their personal space and be aware of their reaction. Their feelings will then be quite pronounced. If the message was meant to be off-putting, they will immediately step back or adopt a space-claiming stance that will let you know their feelings in no uncertain terms.

Facial Expressions, Features, and Head Movement

- **Playing with Hair and Moving the Head**

  If someone slides their fingers through their hair at the temples and tosses their head back, this is an indication they might be flirting with you. On the other hand, if they are running their fingers through their hair from their forehead through the top of their crown, that is a sign they are confused or frustrated. Tilting the head and twirling the hair is also a flirtatious mannerism, indicating interest combined with a little nervous tension.

  When people nod their heads, it matters how many times they do so before stopping. For example, public speakers who are attentive to their audiences know that three nods mean interest and attentiveness. However, if you observe a group of people conversing, you'll notice the person who nods their head only once is eager to leave and will probably be the next one to make a quick exit.

  If someone is interested in what you're saying, they will often tilt their head in your direction. They could be showing curiosity or questioning what you are saying when they bring one ear closer to make sure they are getting every detail of the conversation.

- **Eye Movement**

  People usually blink six or seven times a minute, but those who are stressed blink quite a bit more. If someone covers their eyes with their hands, excessively rubs their eyes, or closes their eyes, they could be hiding something or feel threatened. When the eyes are shifty or rapidly moving from one person to another, it reflects some scattered thoughts that are going on in their heads. If there is a flickering interest between two people when this is happening, then it can also be a way for people to prevent detection as they were checking out the other.

  If someone has a habit of not making eye contact or looking down as they speak, it can show shyness or can also be a cry for empathy. They are waiting for you to ask what's wrong and open the way for them to share their feelings. Investigators have come to realize that a sustained glance from a person who denies involvement in a crime, may mean they are lying and trying to over-compensate by looking them straight in the eyes for a long time to show they're telling the truth.

  If you have posed a question and the person you asked looks upward, they are most likely trying to picture something they saw. On the other hand, if they look to the side toward their ear, they could be trying to recall a message they heard. If they look downward after your question, they are connecting your question with something negative and trying to find a way to avoid answering or revealing their feelings about the matter.

- **Eyebrow Movement**

  If individuals raise their eyebrows, it usually means the person is curious about or interested in your conversation. A quick popup of one eyebrow could be a flirtation, and if the eyebrow is raised a bit longer, it often means that the other person doesn't quite buy into what you say.

If the brows furrow, you can almost bet that person is having second thoughts about what is being done or said. It most likely indicates a negative emotion like fear or confusion, so it might be time for you to back off a bit.

- **Lips**

Of course, a smile sends a universal message, if it is truly a smile. We've all been at the other end of a fake smile, which is one that doesn't travel all the way to the eyes and make them wrinkle in agreement. We call those "Red Carpet" smiles. They are Hollywood smiles given by people who are trying to be friendly to their fans but just want to get inside, sit down, and make it through the night.

Individuals who plaster a smile on their face almost all the time, are usually nervous. If it's in the workplace, they could feel out-of-their-depth or incompetent. There's a good chance that foreigners who smile a lot don't understand a blasted thing, so they just smile and nod.

Another thing people do with their lips is to suck on them and bite them. Sucking or biting the lip is a reaction by those who need to settle themselves down. Like a newborn, the action soothes them and offers a bit of comfort in a stressful situation. If one clamps down on their lips or purses them, it can mean frustration or anger.

Body and Limb Movements

- **Body Positions**

  If there is a group of people standing and talking and one or more people open their bodies to you, that is an invitation to join the conversation. If they just turn their head, you might want to choose another group. You will know if you have captured the attentions of a love interest because he or she will turn slightly toward you and point their feet in your direction, to indicate they are interested in finding out what makes you tick. If you step into the group and the person beside you touches your shoulder or arm, this is a direct ploy to show you they are interested in exploring the relationship a bit further.

  When you step into the group, if the person beside you leans into you, they genuinely like you. If their head retracts backward, perhaps something you said surprised or offended them. If they physically lean away from you, they've already made up their mind that they're not going to listen to or like you. If they turn their head in the opposite direction and follow it with their shoulder, you just got the cold shoulder. So, forget about it!

- **Standing Positions**

  If someone is standing with legs about shoulder width apart, it often is a sign of dominance and determination, as if they needed to stand their ground against something or prove a point. If they stand with legs together, front forward, they will hear you out, but you need to make your point quickly. When the person you are speaking with is standing and shifting their weight from side-to-side or front-to-back, it might indicate several things. They could be bored, or they are anxious and need to sooth themselves with this rocking sort of movement. To determine their feelings, it is necessary to look further at what they are doing with their arms as well.

- **Arm Positions**

Don't assume that crossed arms always mean that the other person is upset. Not so! Some people will stand or sit with their arms crossed because it is just a comfortable position. You can distinguish the other's emotions by looking further at their facial expression. If they have furrowed eyebrows, their mouth pursed, and their arms crossed, chances are they are angry or upset about something. Crossed arms can also be a sign of protection or a closed attitude to the ideas you are presenting.

If someone is talking with their arms flopping around, it can mean they are excited and agreeable, or it can say that they are out of control. Again, you'll need to couple your observations with other nonverbal messages to be sure. Typically, people who are overly animated are less believable and have less control over their emotions, as well as having a lack of power. They flail their arms to gain attention as if to say "I'm talking now, so would somebody please listen to me?"

- **Leg and Foot Positions**

People whose toes turn inward could be closing themselves off to your comments, or they could just be pigeon-toed. To determine if there is a physiological issue that causes their toes to point it, you might need more background information. Don't rush to judgment, just wait, observe more body language, and listen to their words. Some people who began turning in their toes because they were insecure or awkward, might have created a habit that they find difficult to break. The only message they are sending is one that says; I have a physical issue that is impacting my body language.

- **Sitting Positions**

If a person is spread out all over your couch, they have a feeling of self-importance. On the other hand, they probably have a good deal of confidence as well. Legs open, leaning forward with elbows on knees shows an in-charge attitude that is still open to hearing what you have to say.

If a person is sitting next to you and crosses their legs at the knee, pointing their foot toward you, they are giving you permission to approach them. If, however, they are sitting next to you and angle their body in the opposite direction, you're probably not going to engage or connect with him or her. If that same person is fidgeting, quickly moving their ankle or foot, they are looking for a way out. Excuse yourself; both of you will probably feel more comfortable.

- **Hands**

When people sit on their hands, and the temperatures aren't below freezing, it could be an indication that they are deceitful—trying to hide something from you. If they walk with their hands in their pockets or behind their back, they might be relaying information, but you're not getting the full picture because they are withholding information. When you look at one's fingers and see bitten nails or chewed cuticles, you can bet that is a nervous person with low self-esteem. Or else they have put themselves in a situation that they find extremely uncomfortable.

When someone holds their hands like a church steeple and presses them to their lips, they have something important to add to the conversation but are trying to decide how to present their information. They are self-assured and will contribute when the time is right. These are the thinkers, the analytical types.

If the person is rubbing their legs with open palms pressed down, they are feeling vulnerable or uncomfortable with your nearness or your conversation. If nothing is said, don't think you are not sending a message that is perhaps louder than any words. Examine your body language and see what message you are sending to them that could be creating this reaction.

- **Walking**

  People who advance with rather large strides are purposeful and perceived as important and competent. People think those who walk with a little bounce in their step most likely have a positive nature. And those who walk hunched over with shoulders down—well, that kind of speaks for itself, doesn't it? They are probably prone to depression and wrapped a bit too tight.

What Does One's Voice Say About Them?

There are four indicators of the quality of one's voice. They are one's intonation, volume, pitch, and rate of speech. If the voice is monotone and rather flat, they are probably bored or boring. The lack of animation in the voice could also indicate the speaker is tired. If the person's voice sounds clear and concise, they most usually are confident and powerful, more like the

Leader Personality Type. If the volume is quiet or soft, the person is thought to be shy, or it could even mean they have a secret they don't want to share.

The rate of speech is also quite important when analyzing others, especially if you are attempting to mirror them to increase the chances of connectivity. For example, Leader Personality Types will usually speak fast and loud, and you need to match their volume and rate. Identifiers often speak slower than Leaders, and their pitch is more soothing than the dominant personality type. The voice can be a strong descriptive element of the individual's personality type.

By now, you have probably caught on that every movement has a message. Verify the meaning of some of the nonverbal languages by other things, such as one's words, voice, facial expressions, and gestures. To discover one's real message, you must become a student of human behavior, studying the other's movements, speech pattern, attitude, words, gestures, and expressions to analyze people successfully.

You've been introduced to the nonverbal language and the four main personality types, and to how you form accurate perceptions, but all these things are not separate from one another. They all blend to create effective communications. In the next chapter, you'll be asked to read some scenarios and identify the personality types, nonverbal indicators, and interpret the intended message.

Chapter 4: Interpreting and Responding to the Message

You've already learned how to analyze nonverbal language, but the key to excellent communications is knowing how to interpret and respond to the messages others send so that you can connect with them on a much more effective level. Wouldn't it be wonderful not to wonder what a person is thinking? Instead of questioning whether people are agreeable or accepting of your suggestions or opinions, you can use all the strategies you have learned in this book to look beyond the spoken word and read the hidden feelings people might be entertaining.

Some personality types are naturally more suited to one another, while others trigger feelings of annoyance and impatience, depending upon their key traits and character preferences. By examining each personality type a bit further, you'll gain some insight into why you instantly hit it off with some people and others just rub you the wrong way.

Leaders with Other Leaders

Partnering two Leader Personality Types is like putting two alpha dogs together in the same arena. Each one fights to lead, with nobody left to follow through and complete the task. With such competitive natures, Leaders struggle with one another to manipulate and control their environment. They are both sure their strategies and methodologies are the best, and compromise is not one of their strengths. For these reasons, placing two Leaders on a project can create unnecessary power plays, unless one's secondary personality type is a Fraternizer or Identifier.

When the relationship is personal, a coupling of two Leaders can be all work and no fun. If each is career-minded individuals, your lives will most likely not revolve around each other, but be centered on work-related events and projects. It is common when two career professionals hook up, for a while they will be quite intrigued by one another's focus and business acumen. However, as the relationship matures, the Leaders will tend to be more attentive to work-related issues, and their personal relationships suffer. If you are a Leader involved with another Leader Personality Type, you'll need to challenge one another on a personal level to keep the fires burning. Compete in a mutually enjoyed sport, or find a thrill-seeking, competitive hobby that interest both of you. It's necessary to be involved in one another's home life as well as your business endeavors.

Leaders with Perceivers

Leaders usually work well with Perceiver Personality Types because they are organizers and analytical thinkers, and their quiet, unemotional demeanor typically satisfies the Leader's goal-driven manner. The Perceiver doesn't challenge the Leader for "top dog" position because he or she doesn't enjoy being the center of attention. The downside to partnering a Leader with a Perceiver is that the professional or personal relationship can be cold and rather unexciting unless there are some Fraternizer traits in one or the other's personality.

Leaders with Fraternizers or Identifiers

If the Fraternizers or Identifiers have some secondary Perceiver or Leader traits, they will do well when relating to people who are almost all Leader types. However, if the Fraternizer or Identifier is strong in their personality traits, their empathetic and emotional behaviors will often grate on the Leader's last nerve. What Fraternizers and Identifiers need to do when communicating with a Leader or Perceiver Types is to learn to curb their feelings and reign in their emotions when interacting with these strong personalities.

The two personality types that are usually not good to put together are Leader to Leader and Fraternizer to Fraternizer, and here's why. As we said before, two Leaders will fight for the controlling position. Examining the Fraternizers, they too are competitive, and they will experience a struggle unique to their type. Fraternizers will almost always try to one-up each other, challenging one another to a more dangerous sport or a project that requires greater and greater risks. Or, Fraternizers will turn everything into such fun that there will be no work accomplished. So, let's examine how to respond best to each personality type.

Communicating with an Identifier

Avoid getting too emotional when talking with an Identifier Personality Type. Since they are rather indecisive, you'll need to continually pull them back to the task at hand and discuss the decision to make and its' probably outcome. Identifiers enjoy talking about feelings, and they will be sensitive to yours. While this is good in a personal relationship, in the office it can be distracting.

313

If the Identifier is your direct report, their open-door policy will enable others to frequently interrupt your time with them, creating difficulties when trying to get them to stay on task. So, be patient; your frustration will not change their policies; it will only serve to make you look grumpy and cynical. After their interruptions, they'll be tempted to discuss the other person's problems with you, which will take you further down the rabbit hole. So, count on your meetings with Identifiers taking longer and achieving less.

There is almost always delays in projects as well. The Identifier will want you to check with other team members to see how they feel about any new ideas or changes, no matter how seemingly insignificant. Or, they will insist on discussing this issue in another meeting with more managers and team members. If you aren't careful, beginning a project can take a month of meetings.

In your personal relationships, Identifiers can be a bit moody and overly sensitive. If you are a Leader personality involved with a significant other who is an Identifier, you need to get comfortable with a relationship that is emotionally demanding. Also, your need to stay focused and move forward may make them feel as though they are not being heard or valued. As a Leader, you will need to slow down and allow the Identifier to fulfill his or her need to nurture and comfort. You won't be allowed to hide away when you're sick, and too many evenings spent working at the office is going to create some emotional outbursts.

Communicating with a Perceiver

Being in a personal relationship with a Perceiver Personality Type can be a guessing game. They don't like to share their feelings, and they can be a bit stand-offish, so if you are an Identifier that needs more reassurance, just know that you're not going to get it from the Perceiver. They might have deep feelings for you, but sharing those feelings is a challenge for them.

On the other hand, if you show too many emotions in the relationship, they'll be confused and draw further back into their comfortable, quiet shell of self-protection. Perceivers can also be rather stubborn and set in their ways, so getting them to change is like pulling teeth. If you do expect change, make sure you give them plenty of time to think things through and avoid popping any surprises on them, no matter how pleasant you think it will be for them to experience the change.

For example, Laurie decided it would be a great birthday present to replace her husband, Al's football chair. It was embarrassingly worn, and the springs were giving way, so she felt he would be much more comfortable watching his favorite programs in a nice, cushy, new recliner. As a surprise, Laurie had the new chair delivered while Al was at work, and they took the tattered one away. She didn't quite get the reaction she was hoping for when Al returned from work. Although he has never complained much about his old chair, Al has merely changed his favorite seating area to a corner of the couch.

Al might have liked the idea of having a new chair had Laurie not surprised him with the idea and had his old one hauled away before he was ready for the change. He needed time to adjust to the idea that another chair could be just as comfortable, and he could have gone to the store, sat in a gazillion chairs, then slowly made his mind up to purchase the first one in which he plopped. However, without having the opportunity to think it over, look at the chairs to decide which one best suited him, and then compare prices and warranties, Al was not thrilled with Laurie's birthday present.

Communicating with a Fraternizer

Fraternizer Personality Types can get along with almost anyone, but some personality types will eventually grow weary of their tired jokes and constant need for entertainment. Also, a Perceiver will not appreciate the spontaneous spending that many Fraternizers practice. A died-in-the-wool Fraternizer with few secondary personality traits that are more grounded is often too immature and impulsive for a Leader of Perceiver in their personal relationships.

In the workplace, Fraternizers are often perceived as party people and not taken seriously. No matter how intelligent, many Fraternizers are not promoted to their potential because they allow their fun-loving spirit too much free reign in the workplace. Fraternizers usually don't make good quarterly budget planners because they spend too freely and are too rash when it comes to decision-making. If you work with a Fraternizer, you will need to keep them focused and grounded to achieve success with projects in which you are both involved.

Examining Some Personal Scenarios

Think of a co-working with whom you are currently experiencing some challenges when communicating with him or her. Now review the following questions to determine the other person's personality type and what you can do to create a more positive working relationship.

- What is your subject's dominant personality type? How do you know this?
- What is your dominant personality type?
- What does this person do that annoys you? Analyze these behaviors to see if this is a trait of their personality type?
- What do you think you are doing that annoys him or her?
- Is this your imagination, or are you reading their non-verbal language?
- What was the last challenge you experienced with him or her?
- Based on his or her personality type, how could you have responded better to create a more positive outcome?
- Knowing what you know now, how will you communicate with this person in the future to create a better relationship?

Now, think of a personal relationship you would like to improve and ask yourself the same questions. When you determine the other's personality type, make sure you verify your beliefs by observing their behaviors, listening to their words, and analyzing the body language they are displaying around you. Ask yourself if you are too sensitive because of your personality type, or if you really are having serious communication issues with this person.

If you cannot answer the questions about people who challenge you, then keep reading. The next chapter will deal with Three Key Elements to Connectivity, which will give you some useful tools to help you to analyze others accurately.

Chapter 5: Three Key Elements to Connectivity

There are three critical key elements to one's ability to successfully connect with others: mindful observation, listening with intent, and effective feedback.

Connecting with Others Through Mindful Observation

So, what is meant by mindful observation? Like most of us, you observe people and your surroundings all the time, but what do you take away from the things you see? How do you apply what you see to help you monitor and adjust your behaviors and beliefs? The reality is, most people use very little of what they see to improve their communications. If they are more aware than most, they might see that what they are saying is not being well received by their audience. Consequently, they just stop communicating. Most people make very few adjustments to improve their communications. Instead, they only pass the baton to the next person in the conversation who is eager to participate.

In most instances, there is no monitoring and adjusting of verbal and non-verbal language because many individuals have never learned how to analyze people and adjust their communication style to be more accommodating to that person's personality type. The powers of observation can only help when people put what they see to work and create a more active exchange of information.

To improve your observation skills, you need to work like a dog! You heard—just like a dog. Dogs have amazing observation skills. In fact, trainers say that the best way to teach a dog to do the trick is by letting them see another dog perform it and receive a reward. A dog's observation skills are so keen that they learn better by watching than by verbal commands. Who's to say the same thing isn't so for humans?

Marsha's dog is so observant, Hannah knows what she'll be doing that day based on the things she observes her owner doing. For example, if Marsha pulls out her running shoes, Hannah knows they are going for a run. If Marsha pulls her hair back into a ponytail, Hannah suspects they are going herding and runs into the garage to wait at the car door because Marsha always wears her hair in a ponytail when she takes Hannah herding.

The problem comes when Marsha decides to pull her hair into a ponytail, and she's not taking Hannah herding. Hannah is so sure she's going herding that she begins to scratch and pester Marsha as if to ask why she pulled the switch. Hannah is relentless in her attempts to get Marsha to do as she wants, confident they'll be leaving soon. Hannah's so sure of her ability to read her owner that she will stand at the garage door for almost an hour waiting for Marsha's approach. The problem is, although Hannah read all the signs, she didn't know that the same sign could have several meanings.

The reason I tell this story is to warn you that sometimes you can have excellent observation skills and yet with this one person this one time, they don't work. What you observe and attach meaning to isn't want was intended. You keep doing the same thing, and yet you aren't getting the results you want. Your communication isn't improving, and neither is your relationship. When this happens, change things. Don't assume the same thing works for all people. Try something different to get to better communications. The most important aspect to remember is that giving up gets you nowhere.

Sometimes you just need to observe a little longer or a bit more. Don't' just see the person as they communicate with you, watch how they communicate with others. Watch how others react to them. If this is a person with whom you have issues, watch their body language around those you know they like. Listen to their voice as they speak with others with whom they communicate well. Then observe how that other person responds to the one with whom you have issues. How does their voice sound? What is their body language saying? How are they standing or sitting that is different from the way you respond? For complicated relationships, surface observations just aren't enough.

You must be mindful of your goal as you observe your subject. What is it you want from the relationship? Being aware means you can't always focus on all things going on around them, but you need to choose just one or two things to observe for a while until you have a greater understanding of what they are saying with that gesture or expression. Once you know that, then move on to something else. Being mindful in your observations means you are determined to resolve the situation and improve the communications with that person.

Listening with Intent

Just as people observe others every day, they also hear them as well. The downside is you can hear someone, but if you are listening with a specific intent, you won't know what to do with what you hear. For instance, you can hear someone speaking, but if you are not listening with the intent to distinguish the person's rate of speech when they are talking or the volume of which they speak with a plan to identify their personality type, then you hear only part of the message.

When listening with intent, you don't interrupt, you don't plan what you're going to say next while the other is still talking, and you don't speak over that person. In fact, you don't speak at all; you listen, and you listen with the intent of discovering the meaning behind the words and between the lines.

Giving Effective Feedback

Sometimes providing effective feedback is nothing more than mimicking a person's rate or volume of speech. At other times, useful feedback means adopting an open, relaxed stance to reflect what you would like to see the other person do as well. Then there are times effective feedback means adjusting your personality traits a bit so that you don't make the other person uncomfortable or annoyed. If your message is garbled because your body language, gestures, and expressions are different from your words, then you need to bring clarity to the conversation by providing congruent feedback.

Of course, there are times where you don't want people to read what you are thinking, and in that case, effective feedback will be that which masks the way you feel. It is not about hiding your feelings, but more liked controlling them. It's not beneficial to you or anyone else if you always reveal every single thought and feeling. There are times you need to bury your emotions a bit so that your communications don't expose you or put you in a vulnerable position. In these cases, effective feedback is NOT revealing what you don't want another to know.

Practice these three key elements to connectivity and others will not only feel connected to you, but they will be more supportive of your ideas and suggestions. It's a way to get what you want without emotional outbursts and unreasonable demands. You get your way because you are an outstanding communicator. You get the support of others because they like you and because you GET them. You achieve success in your personal and professional life because you connect with others and they with you, and all because of the few strategies you've learned from these pages. Don't look now, but you've just practiced the three key elements to connectivity: mindful observation, listening with intent, and providing effective feedback.

Chapter 6: The Beauty of Successfully Analyzing Others

What a thrill it is to learn to analyze others and stop the anxiety of wondering how someone feels about you or what they think of your ideas or suggestions. Learning how to read someone's body language is as exciting as learning how to understand the author's meaning in a book or interpret a foreign language. What will help you to continue practicing and improving your analytical skills is to understand that you don't become an expert at reading others overnight. It takes time, practice, and a willingness to adopt good listening and observation skills to become an exceptional communicator.

There are tremendous payoffs that come from successfully analyzing others. The better you get, the more friends you'll have because people gravitate to those they like. The more you practice the strategies learned in this book, the better you'll get at reading people and adjusting your behaviors and language to match others. Soon analyzing one's body language and gestures will become second nature to you, and you'll wonder why you failed to notice the distinctive messages the body sends long before now.

Many aspects of your life will improve along with your communications. You'll have opportunities offered, and doors opened that were previously always out of reach. You'll see the world differently because the world will see you differently as well. Your confidence and self-esteem will raise with your increased ability to accurately analyze others. People will gain a new appreciation of you, and you'll be asked to participate in work projects or on teams whose members before may not have chosen you as a player.

There's magic in excellent communications, and that magic is making meaningful, long-lasting relationships. You'll look back on those people who you once considered the "beautiful" people and suddenly realize that you have joined their ranks. It may sound far-fetched, but our entire lives revolve around our ability to connect with others by speaking their language, by understanding the message they are sending, and by offering feedback that supports and enhances others.

One of the best feelings you can create in another person is that they are better off for having known you, for having kept company with you, and that's what learning to analyze people can do. People will leave your presence feeling good about spending time with you. You will leave the company of others without concern that your message wasn't understood or appreciated. Analyzing others is a work of art—a work of beauty—a treasure of information to be studied, enjoyed and shared.

Conclusion: Congratulations on Your Read

Thank you so much for purchasing this book!

I hope reading *How to Analyze People: How to Master Reading Anyone Instantly Using Body Language, Human Psychology, and Personality Types* will help you to improve your personal and professional communications significantly.

The next step is to put these strategies to work in your life to create great relationships.

Thank you and good luck on your new skills of analyzing people.

Persuasion

Psychology of Selling – Secret Techniques Only the World's Top Sales People Know to Close the Deal Every Time

Introduction

Congratulations on purchasing *Persuasion: Psychology of Selling – Secret Techniques Only the World's Top Sales People Know to Close the Deal Every Time* and thank you for doing so. Any salesperson who has spent an hour with a potential customer only to have them bail at the last minute has no doubt wished for the ability to control the minds. While direct mind control still isn't possible, the power of psychology allows you to unlock the next best thing, persuasive sales techniques that can dramatically improve your conversions in an extremely short amount of time.

The following chapters will discuss everything you need in order to take your sales game to the next level, starting with a wide variety of psychological sales triggers you can start taking advantage of today. Next, you will learn all about the power of reverse psychology and how it can be used to get potential customers to sell themselves on specific products.

From there, you will learn all about the power of the social proof and how it can be used to mitigate potential risk about your product or service, whatever it may be. Then you will learn all about the importance of being an authority and how you ensure that your customers can see you as one for your niche. Finally, you will learn about the importance of body language and how you can maximize yours to supercharge your sales.

There are plenty of books on this subject on the market, thanks again for choosing this one! Every effort was made to ensure it is full of as much useful information as possible, please enjoy!

Chapter 1: Powerful Sales Triggers

Reciprocity: Reciprocity is the idea that if you give your prospective clients something that they perceive as valuable they will feel obligated to give you something in return. If you tend to feel uncomfortable if you owe someone something, this is likely why and it is also why most businesses that are trying to sell you something start off the encounter by offering you something to drink. While this can be a powerful tool in the right situations, it is important to be aware that it won't work on everyone as some people have an entitlement mentality which means they naturally expect other people to defer to their desires, so any hope of reciprocity goes out the window.

Unfortunately, you often won't be able to tell which of your potential customers has an entitlement mindset, which means you need to come up with something that costs you far less than its perceived value as you will be giving it out to everyone out of the gate. At the very least you will develop a generous reputation in your chosen niche which can often end up being far more valuable in the long run anyway.

To understand why the concept of reciprocity can be so powerful, consider a scenario where you and a friend you haven't seen in a while go out to catch up and you enjoy a lengthy dinner, including both an appetizer and dessert. When the bill comes, you insist on paying, despite your friend's protests over the cost, and you then go your separate ways. As this is not an uncommon scenario, it is not hard to imagine what happens next, your friend will call you up and invite you out to a similarly priced meal, their treat.

If they didn't, odds are they would begin to feel psychologically uneasy, and their unease would continue to grow if you continued doing additional nice things for them before they had a chance to reciprocate. The only way they can psychologically even the scales is by doing an equally nice thing for you that equates to more than the total of the things you have done for them. In those who feel it, this need is nearly as strong in people they have just met as it is with people they have known for years, which is what makes this such a powerful sales tool.

Depending on the type of sales you are in, there are numerous different ways to go about activating a reciprocity response. If you are selling the type of product that people try before they buy, throw in something that is typically expensive when bought as a single unit, that grows cheaper in bulk and then continues lavishing other small freebies on them throughout the time you are talking. If you are working an online sales angle, you make a habit of regularly creating quality content that is useful without directly trying to sell anything in return. You could also offer free lead magnet products or an eBook that you have written on your chosen niche.

If you are dealing with a potential customer face to face, then you won't need to worry about mentioning your half of the equation as it will be implied throughout the interaction. However, if you are dealing with an online scenario then you will need to remind people of what you have recently done for them to ensure that this idea triggers the reciprocity response when you want it to. For example, if you were to give out a free eBook, at the end include a note thanking them for reading your free book and urging them that, if they enjoyed it, to click a link to share it with their friends.

Make them curious: Curiosity can be a powerful sales

motivator as it creates the type of mental itch that potential customers are eager to scratch. The key, then, lies in connecting the action that you want them to take with the mystery that you have created. A classic example of this can be seen in the original marketing campaign for BluBlocker sunglasses from the late 80s and early 90s. These ads pioneered what is now a common concept for all types of infomercials, real people trying a product in real time and talking about how impressive it is.

While this trope is extremely tired today, at the time it served to dramatically increase interest, and sales, for what was ultimately a middling, polarized pair of sunglasses. While the commercials could have simply shown how a polarized lens affects the camera, by removing this key piece of information from the equation it left viewers no choice but to order their own pair by mail, and they did, to the tune of more than five million pairs in the first two years alone.

Curiosity is a particularly powerful tool when it comes to online sales, starting with its ability to keep them reading regardless if they are looking at a report, blog post, email or sales letter. You can build curiosity through an email, and even inject more when you feel the content itself could use a little boost. Building anticipation in the introduction is particularly effective for reports, newsletter and blog posts. Simply include a hint of what is going to be learned in the process, in an exciting way, of course, and let curiosity do the rest. As an example, can you honestly say that you wouldn't at least skim an article that starts off talking about an exercise that many of the world's most elite militaries have been practicing regularly for more than 200 years?

Another practical approach is to start of by telling the first part of a compelling story before working the rest of it into the rest of your article. Not finishing the story right away increases the reader's curiosity and makes them more likely to at least read through parts of the rest of the piece to find the other parts of the story. This is why you are going to want to break it up into several chunks as otherwise the reader will just assume it is at the bottom and skip there.

As an example, assume you start off by telling the heart warming story of Janet, the mother of four who lost more than 100 pounds and saved her life using a common diet plan and your product, of course. Rather than outlining everything all at once, you can comment on how surprising Janet's plan was and noting that the details are outlined inside, along with other things she used to make her wonderful transition.

Whetting the reader's appetite for what's coming is an effective tool that works well in any report, article or sales letter. For example, you could return to Janet from earlier and explain how she used the same secret that the Hollywood elite uses to shed weight on the quick, a secret that you will explain as soon as you say some other stuff instead.

Another option is to make people more curious about the product or service you are selling directly. For example, if you are selling a weight loss shake, you could say something like, you won't believe how the inches will literally melt away thanks to our patented formula. Assuming you throw in the research to back up the claims, you can be sure that many people will be interested in finding out more.

Handle objections: Depending on the item you are selling, there is a good chance that even as you are winding up to your pitch, your potential clients are already working out reasons in their head that they shouldn't listen to you. These buzzkill thoughts are generally categorized as objections and it is your job to handle them properly or you will miss out on countless sales.

One of the most common objections that you will hear day in and day out is that the price of the product is too high, regardless of whether or not the person you are speaking with can afford it at the current rate. This can easily be countered in most cases by demonstrating the additional value that the product brings to the table compared to other, cheaper, competition. If there is specific reasoning behind the cost, then frankly explaining why the price is so high is also a valid tactic.

For example, the price difference on this model is primarily due to the additional quality of the parts which have been shown to last nearly twice as long as those put out by the cheaper brand. If you are having trouble justifying higher prices, start taking a closer look at ads for products from companies like Bentley, Mercedes, Armani, Rolex and the like and take what you see to heart as the same principles apply to most luxury products. In this case, even the term luxury products is an improvement over, say, needlessly expensive showpieces.

When dealing with a luxury product, one response you are going to hear on the regular is I can't really afford it right now, I really shouldn't, or some variation thereof. This type of response isn't saying that the product is too expensive, its that the potential customer has reservations about spending the money here versus elsewhere, which is a far more manageable objection to overcome. Adding scarcity to the mix is a good way to get the sale as it not only shows that other people are biting, it adds urgency to the sale as well as the idea then becomes if you don't buy now you will never have another opportunity.

The alternative to this is the argument that the price is too cheap, the thought process here being that if the product or service you are selling is noticeably below the average then there must be a negative reason for it. As such, it is important that you bring up the price in these instances as the potential customer is likely wondering about it anyway. For example, "Now I know what you're thinking, price that low there must be something wrong with it. I assure you this is not the case, with this price you still get the full package, plus our industry leading warranty which should put to bed any lingering concerns."

Often times, if you can regularly price your product at a point than is lower than the industry standard, you can also find a way around this reluctance by offering limited time sales that roll around at least once a month, not only does this add urgency to mix, it also helps potential buyers think they are getting a deal as well. For example, if you hired a professional service to generate this level of content you can expect to pay upwards of $500, if not more. However, if you are one of the first 100 people to use this code then you can get full rights to this content for just $50. Phrasing like this justifies the low price and the impulse purchase all at the same time.

Another viable alternative is to compare the purchase price to something else that most people regularly purchase or at least know the price of. For example, for the price of two cups of coffee from a coffee shop, you can get industry leading tips. But that $10 to use and invest in your future today.

If you come across the objection of a potential customer not being sure about the efficacy of your product or service, all you need to do is offer up some type of guarantee as to the customer's satisfaction. Keep in mind, however, that offering less than a complete money-back guarantee will not only not get the results you are looking for but will also lead potential customers to think something fishy is certainly going on. When it comes to the guarantees, go big or don't bother.

While knowing common objections and how to get around them is useful, you will likely find it even more useful to sit down and take a look at your product or service through the eye of the customer and brainstorm a list of every possible objection that you can think of, no matter how ridiculous you might think it is. Only by being prepared for every contingency will you be able to reliably break down the objections you come across in the field in a useful way.

Be credible: There was a time in the distant past where every transaction a customer had with a salesperson wasn't completely coated in a fine sheen of distrust. Consumers, whether digital or IRL are so used to being told partial truths and fabrications that in order to penetrate their shield of distrust you are going to need to do something to prove your credibility upfront. What this means is that you need to give them a reliable reason to believe you over everyone else who is trying to sell them something.

Examples of positive opening credibility statements include things like:

Why should you believe what I have to say? One irrefutable fact, the numbers don't lie. Using the system that I am now sharing with people like you I earned more than $2 million dollars without leaving my house.

I've lost nearly 100 pounds using this diet plan and kept it off for more than a decade. What's more, I've helped more than a thousand people lose at least 50 pounds as well. This diet plan works, its only a question of if you want it to work for you.

I've been in this business for more than 10 years and in that time have created campaigns that have grossed more than 1 billion dollars combined, including my last client whose product has since generated more than $200 million worth of sales.

What you are doing here is giving your potential customers a verifiable reason why you are qualified to sell them whatever it is you are trying to sell them. This can be experienced in a given field, specific results from the product in question, an impressive degree, awards given out be well-known groups, anything that will break down the wall of disbelief enough to let your other efforts start to work their magic.

Understand the power of fear: When it comes to motivating people to do something without thinking through the full ramifications of their choice, there are few better options than good old-fashioned fear. This isn't groundbreaking news, everyone including politicians, corporations, bosses and even your parents use fear to generate the desired action because it is easy to find a fear that resonates with a large group of people and because it is extremely effective when done properly.

When it comes to using this fact to increase sales, the type of fear that you should be aiming to tap into is known as the fear of missing out, more commonly known by the acronym FOMO. The acronym is typically used to describe those who are constantly looking at their smartphones for fear of missing out on something better that is going on somewhere without them. With sales, it applies to those who can't bear the thought of missing out on a particularly good deal regardless of what the specifics surrounding that deal actually turn out to be.

You can naturally funnel this fear to boost your sales by creating any one of numerous different limited offers. For example, you can limit the offer to a set number of people before then sweetening the pot even more for the first hundred customers who order in the next hour. Limited time discounts are also effective, but only if they are greater than 30 percent, deals of less than that will typically only be successful if the products you are working with have a history of only going on sale very rarely. Other options include:

- Seasonal sales
- Holiday sale
- Grand opening sales
- Introductory offers
- Early bird sales
- Sales where the amount of the discount decreases each day
- Flash sales
- Limited offer coupons
- Anything else that naturally implies a fear of missing out on an amazing deal.

Depending on the product or service that you are selling, you may also find success when it comes to reminding people of their fears. One of the most obvious examples of this type of thing is advertising for insurance companies where they should the true cost of some catastrophic event before showing how great the insurance company made things in the end. While this is an extreme example, a wide variety of products and services can play into this type of fear-based marketing in one way or another. For example:

While there is money to be made in cryptocurrency, the window for unmitigated profit is closing fast, buying this book will help you get in while the getting is good and take control of your financial future today.

Sure, you don't need to try this diet product, you can close this window and go on about your day, embarrassed by how you look, always thinking people are laughing at you behind your back and unlucky in love. Or, you could try this product and watch the pounds melt away thanks to our proprietary fat burning formula.

Be consistent: Everyone likes to think of themselves as consistent in their thoughts, beliefs and actions, especially those who are especially flighty and unreliable. You can use this fact to boost your sales by using what is known as the foot in the door technique. It's simple, all you need to do is get the potential customer to do you some small favor early on, let you borrow a pen perhaps, or get you a bottle of water if you are in their home or office. Then, later in your presentation, you ask them to do you a much larger favor, which they will be more inclined to do in order to appear consistent.

This psychological trigger is actually so powerful that it has been studied by scientists who have found the results to be disturbingly effective. First, they asked a group of people in a random neighborhood to put a large sign in the middle of their front yard and about 80 percent of people said no.

Next, they went to another neighborhood and started out by asking homeowners to put a small placard in their window to promote some benign local activity. All told, about 90 percent of the people tested agreed to put the placard in their window. After a few weeks, when the researchers came back with the signs, this time a full 60 percent of the test subjects agreed to put the signs up in their yards. Keep in mind how this can be adapted to your personal sales techniques and the potential for a dramatic increase in sales is high.

Chapter 2: Take Advantage of Reverse Psychology

Inoculation Effect

In the early 1960s, a man named William McGuire developed a theory to describe the process by which people become immune to related attempts at persuasion over a prolonged period of time. He dubbed his theory the Inoculation Effect and discovered that one way that resistance to persuasion develops most effectively is if the subject is warned that attempted persuasion is about to occur.

Over the years there has been plenty of evidence to support this theory, starting with a famous study of children who were heavily educated about the marketing tactics of cigarette companies, specifically those aimed at young people. While the study took several years to come to fruition, the results were extremely promising, all of the students showed higher than average resistance to the pressures of smoking at one year, two years and ten years down the line.

As a salesperson, you can take advantage of this fact by understanding that you are naturally going to need to work harder to attract customers as they have all been constantly inundated by toothless marketing practices practically since birth. Specifically, what you can do is put some reverse psychology into play and tell people something they never expect to hear from a salesman, the truth. This will often catch the potential customer so off guard that they drop their defenses almost completely.

Warn them about the competition: If you know that your potential customer is waffling between you and one of your competitors, and you don't have anything left with which to seal the deal, you can instead mention how you are always a straight shooter, while some of your competitors have been known to sweeten certain products that may have little known deficiencies or that bait and switch tactics are common with these types of products, "just so they know." It is important to only discuss minor sales tricks and ensure that they are nothing that you have tried on the client as well, remember, honesty isn't just the best policy if you hope to use this tactic, it is the only policy.

Consider what sets you apart from your competition: If you start out by explaining to your potential customer how you are different from your competition in one key way or another, it will also naturally inoculate your potential customer against common industry standards. This method is particularly useful if you have a clear demarcation point from your competition that can be clearly understood even by those who are completely unfamiliar with your industry.

If you are selling catering services for fancy parties, perhaps you have found a way to cut costs that allows you to not charge fees for flatware and china, so you can casually mention that most other companies tend to charge outrageous fees for such things. Then, even if the customer doesn't bite right away, if they go and get prices elsewhere, they will be on the lookout for the charges that are sure to make you look good by comparison.

Offer less: These days, choice is king. Customers who feel the need can customize virtually everything they buy online in ways that are perfect for them. While this is sure to be the case for some potential customers, others don't want to do the research themselves, or care enough about your product or service to want quality, without giving to much thought to the specifics. For customers like these, having too many choices can result in analysis paralysis where they literally end up frozen with indecision and end up walking away empty handed as a result.

These customers still want to feel in control of the process, but not to the point they have to make any tough choices. In cases like these, you are going to want to be prepared to offer potential customers who start looking glassy-eyed a package that contains exactly three options. This type of presentation shows that you, as the expert, have hand-picked the best of the best to provide the customer to pick from the choices you have already made for them.

Give them an out: Most potential customers go into any interaction with a sales person assuming they are going to get a high-pressure sale. As such, you will often find great results by simply backing off this tactic and ending your pitch with something along the lines of you know your product isn't for everyone, so you understand if they need some time to think things over. If they were already planning on buying, it is unlikely this is going to cause them to rethink their position, while also cutting down on the potential for buyer remorse besides. For those who are on the fence, it shows that you are confident enough in your product and your business to let it do the talking for you, increasing customer confidence as a result.

Disqualify your client: This technique can require a bit of careful balancing but can be very rewarding when things work out. Essentially, it requires that you offer the base model of your product, while at the same time dangling the deluxe version just out of reach. It tends to be most effective on those who you can determine to have something to prove. Young couples are often a good choice, as are those who are typically referred to as new money. For example, if you were selling mattresses to a young couple, you may walk them past the fancy memory foam models to a variety of quality box springs. When they inevitably ask why they were shown the other models, you simply explain that these are the models that tend to be in the price range of couples just starting out. While it won't work every time, if you can hook them properly you can virtually guarantee a deluxe sale.

Rate the attitude: Another useful technique is to ask the potential customer to rate their attitude towards the product after you are finished with your pitch. Assuming they come back with something in the 7 range, then they will expect you to tell them the reasons that they should be even higher. As such, you can lower their defenses by instead telling them that you are surprised as you expected their response to be lower, somewhere around three or four. As they now feel as though they have to explain themselves, the potential customer will then start elaborating on what they like about the product, working themselves closer and closer to a sale in the process.

Ask additional questions

One problem that many sales people have, especially those who are just starting out, is that they talk far more than they listen. If they opened their mouths to ask questions instead of spouting fact, then they would likely close far more sales. While a high-pressure salesperson might never stop pitching, a more effective salesperson instead listens to as much as the customer has to say as possible, while using what are known as reverses to keep the conversation slowly moving towards the sale.

A reverse is the name given to the strategy of asking questions in response to any question that the potential customer has.

There are countless different reverses that you can put into rotation, but you are sure to find the following useful on a regular basis. When using this method, it is important to keep in mind that potential customers rarely ask the question they really want to know up front, which means you might need to do some digging to get to where you need to be. As such, plan on needing around three questions to get to the root of each real question.

By three questions in, you should be able to determine the emotional set of the potential customer which is what influences their decision to buy or walk away in the moment. To understand how the rule of three works, it is first helpful to understand how a potential sale is lost by not using it. For example

Potential customer: Do you have any more of this model?

Salesperson: Yes sir, I can get one for you if you like.

Potential customer: I wonder if they make a lot of them?

Salesperson: I'm not sure, I know we sell a fair amount though.

Potential customer: Oh, never mind then, I only buy exclusives.

While there is nothing to say that the salesperson couldn't find another in with this potential customer, it does add far more pressure to the close than would otherwise be the case. Now, consider how the exchange could have gone if the salesperson used the rule of three.

Potential customer: Do you have any more of this model?

Salesperson: I think there might be another around somewhere, why do you ask?

Potential customer: I was just curious how many they make.

343

Salesperson: I suppose that makes sense, may I ask why that's important to you?

Potential customer: I prefer to buy exclusives.

In this scenario, the salesperson now has infinitely more flexibility when it comes to dealing with the customers true needs. What' s more, he is now under no pressure to close and is free to lead the customer to a purchase.

It is important to keep in mind, however, that questions alone can sometimes rub people the wrong way. This is why you will want to pad out your questions with softening statements that create an atmosphere where the potential client feels as though they can let their guard down and give a straight answer. Useful softening statements include

- This seems really important to you
- That is a good point
- I'm very glad you asked
- Good question

Using softening statements like these, while speaking in a calm, relaxed tone, will help the potential customer open up to you, making it easier for you to surface your questions in a way that feel inoffensive. If the potential customer seems to be moving too fast for your rule of threes questions to do their work, you can pump the breaks by using a reverse such as, "That's a good point, but I'd like to backtrack before we get too far." If they seem to be really putting the pressure on you can simply ask them why they are putting so much pressure on you, getting to the root of that answer can make things proceed far more smoothly for everyone.

Likewise, if you and the potential customer are largely in agreement except for one sticking point, rather than dancing around it you should speed right into it by stating that you have a problem, outlining the problem, and then asking the potential customer if there is anything to be done about it. If there is, great, if not, at least you didn't waste any more time on a sale that was going nowhere.

If there is a lull in the discussion, you can simply ask the potential customer to ask you any additional questions they have about the product or service. Rather than answering their question directly, you can then follow up with a second question along the lines of, "That's a great question, what made you think of that one?"

In addition to manufacturing questions you can answer, it is important that you also get into the habit of hearing the questions that the potential customers don't ask. For example, if they respond that the price is too high, you could go on the defensive, or you could say, softly and with assurance "which means..." Don't be afraid to let the ellipses dangle in this instance because as the silence grows the potential customer will have no choice but to chime in which is when productive dialog can begin.

Another common refrain that many sales people hear is something along the lines of, "You always do this to me." As this is a loaded statement at the best of times, the best response is to try and break down exactly what the potential customer is getting at, which can be done simply by asking "Do what to you?"

Keep in mind that you never really know what a potential customer means until they ask. In fact, as such, a statement like the price is too high, might not even be an objection, simply a sign of the stress the have of taking on a new monthly expense. If this is the case, then the price is high could mean that the potential customer is ready to make a deal, or it could mean that the price is high, and a negotiation is going to need to take place before any forward movement can occur. Once again, without asking you have no way to know.

With the previous examples, reversing eliminated all the confusion between the salesperson and the potential client. It also has the ability to make it possible for the potential client to offer your solutions that you would not have thought of otherwise. This can be done by simply asking the question, "If you could magically solve this problem, how would you go about doing so?"

Once the question is asked, it gives the potential client the freedom to describe what it is they are really looking for, without feeling bound by any constraints both real or imagined. If they still don't seem to be opening up, assure them this conversation is off the record, regardless of whatever it is you are talking about. Despite the fact that this is largely meaningless 99 times out of 100, you will be surprised at how effective it is at loosening lips.

While reversing is going to be a great way to get to a true question, if the potential customer asks the same question twice, then it is important to not make them repeat themselves a third time. While you can't count on customers to be direct, if you do find yourself dealing with one, don't beat around the bush, you will both be better off for it.

Chapter 3: Using Social Proof

To understand social proof, consider a scenario where you are in an unfamiliar city and are looking for a place to eat. If you find two restaurants across the street from one another, and one is extremely busy while at the same time the other is virtually empty, which one do you choose? The answer is obvious to anyone, the busy diner will be chosen virtually 100 percent of the time. The answer as to why this is the case can be explained through the concept of social proof.

When used correctly, a social proof can be one of the most powerful persuasive tools in your arsenal because it connects the persuasiveness of the given thought or behavior directly to the way that others are perceived to respond to it. Furthermore, with an understanding that many people are engaging in an idea or activity, the brain then naturally lowers the perceived risk of engaging in it as well. This is the reason that books that Oprah likes to end up being bestsellers, why there are five (six?) Transformer movies and why cigarettes were able to weather decades of open association with cancer before their usage rates started dropping.

Social proof is also responsible for creating the types of social norms that lead to enforced standards of behavior that are virtually impossible to break free from. A great example of this is the standing ovation. It only takes one person to follow the first person to stand to trigger an avalanche of people who all felt the need to spontaneously express the same emotion.

Social proof and sales

Luckily, you can use this same idea to convey to your potential customers that buying your product isn't just the safe or smart thing to do, it is the thing that everyone else is doing to. This can be especially useful with products that many people are naturally going to assume have a higher associated risk. The higher the perceived risk, the less likely the buyer is going to move in a positive direction on their own and the greater the likelihood that a social proof push can send them over the edge in a good way.

In fact, many businesses are already in the habit of using social proof as a means of increasing their audience's desire for a given product or service. As an example, the Ford Motor Company recently gave away a number of Ford Focus cars to popular YouTube influencers under the assumption that the positive response from said influencers would drive consumer interest in the cars. It worked, the next quarter interest in the Focus from the 18-35 demographic was up 22 percent.

While Red Bull is synonymous with energy drinks in 2018, when the concept of energy drinks was first coming to America it was a much more difficult sell. To utilize social proof, the marketing firm in charge of promoting the drink filled trash cans in Los Angles and New York with empty Red Bull cans to convince passersby that people, more influential than they were, were apparently consuming Red Bull at a frankly unhealthy pace.

The concept of social proof is great because it is just as effective for you as an individual salesperson as it is for big businesses. To activate your own social proof, all you need to do is reference your past customers more regularly through the use of phrases such as, "so many people," "my other clients tend to," "most organizations in your situations, or name-dropping customer names that your current client is likely to know.

Another viable alternative is to offer potential customers a number of success stories, ideally in the client's own words and with pictures. This type of personal touch demonstrates that real people, like your potential customer, have gone ahead and taken the plunge which will make them more likely to do the same. When you share how your customers are benefiting from what you are selling, you will then motivate even more potential customers to follow the trend because everyone else is doing it.

When it comes to harnessing the positive power of social proof, it is important to keep in mind that similarity is key. A substantial amount of research has been done on how the impact of the social proof can be magnified when the other people in question are from a peer group that the potential customer connects with on a personal level. As such, if you can prove to potential customers that customers in their same situation have purchased before, you will compound the effects of social proofs even more.

Types of social proof

There are five primary types of social proof, keep the following in mind and consider which will work naturally with the products you are selling.

1. *Certifications:* Any credible third-party entity which can certify you as a trustworthy source. Think things like the Better Business Bureau of the Health Department.

2. *Friends of the potential customer:* The most influential peer group for a potential customer is always going to be their friends. As such, any social media data that you can harvest has the potential to be put to very good use.

3. *Lots of other people:* If the potential customer doesn't know anyone who is doing what you want them to, then the next best thing is going to be a whole bunch of random customers together instead. The bigger the number   the   better.

4. *Celebrities:* While once upon a time the definition of a celebrity was relatively static, these days interests are so specialized that every niche is going to have its own celebrities or social media influencers. As such, if you want to impress your target audience then you are going to need to reach out to the names that they will be impressed   by.

5. *Experts:* As with celebrities, it is worth your while to reach out to experts in your chosen niche and offer them the opportunity to endorse your product or service.

Using social proof successfully

Online reviews: Get more online reviews, and use them more effectively

Online reviews are becoming more and more important for converting prospects into customers. In fact, 74% of customers say positive reviews make them trust a company even more, so it's fair to say that your potential customers take note of your reviews.

In order to ensure that when customers leave online reviews they only have great things to say, the first thing you will want to do is ensure your online presence is tip top and that your previous customers can easily leave reviews for the products or services they purchased. You may always want to offer incentives for existing customers to leave reviews as few things drive online sales these days than online reviews. If you aren't a big online person, the bare minimum you are going to need here will include a variety of social media profiles including Facebook, Pinterest and Instagram. You will also want to ensure that you have a Yelp and My Business page of Google if you have a physical location.

With the required infrastructure in place, you will then want to ensure that you follow up with all of your customers while the experience of using your product or service is still fresh in their mind. Customers are much more likely to respond positively to a request for a review if you strike while the iron is hot. Most businesses fail to ask for the review, so this is a supreme opportunity to take advantage of and create social proof. You can even automate this step.

Once you start seeing a steady stream of positive reviews, it is important to make sure that potential customers have as many opportunities to see them as possible by posting each and every one on social media. Not only does this keep you generating a steady stream of content which will keep you in your customers' minds, it helps to reinforce the idea of your positive social proof. If the reviews you receive are not so great, don't try to hide them as they always have a way of popping up again. Instead, you should put as much time as possible into correcting the mistake in question and doing whatever you can to make it right. Not only are you more likely to regain the lost customer, other customers are going to see the lengths you went to in order to correct the issue and decide to give you their business as a result.

Take more photos: Photos are the currency of the internet these days which means that providing plenty of pictures of happy, real, people using your products or services is a great way to improve your social proof. In fact, adding photos to existing testimonials is a great way to get an even greater boost. A recent study showed that the picture can even be nonsensical and still increased trust among viewers a measurable amount.

To take advantage of this fact, you are going to want to either take pictures of the happy customers yourself or make a point of mentioning that many customers send in pictures of themselves enjoying the product or service and ask that they do the same as well. If you can get people to include pictures with their reviews themselves, then great, otherwise you may want to add your own in response, when possible. This will help to visually reinforce the trustworthiness of the review itself and also increase the odds that it will go viral.

Share relevant anecdotes: Sharing stories of previously satisfied customers is a simple and effective way to increase sales. In fact, studies show that a good story is likely to make the potential customer more empathetic, trusting and all around more open by literally releasing a chemical in the brain, known as oxytocin, that does just that. In contrast, breaking the same story down into a series of facts about the product is shown to make the customer quicker to question what is being said.

Finding social proof without testimonials

While testimonials are great if you are just starting off and you don't have a wealth of potential customers to choose from this doesn't mean you can't still take advantage of the social proof. Consider the following alternatives to help give your products or services some extra credibility right from the start.

Social media testimonials: Social media is such a part of everyday life that people are used to substituting social media posts for real interactions and this extends to customer testimonials as well. It takes far less effort to ask someone for a positive tweet than a traditional review and you can feature it the same in the end. This can extend to generally nice things that people say about you on social media as well. While you will want to replace them with more relevant details later on, when you are first starting out everything helps build up a general feeling of social proof and every little bit helps.

Industry statistics: Show them that the things you're telling them weren't made up by you. You can find industry statistics to show to them and prove the issue you solve. For instance, if you were trying to prove to people how effective email marketing is, you could show numbers which prove that the things you are saying come from third parties. Feature quotes from industry experts that back up what you're telling people.

Most of the time, you can find these industry stats with Google searching and some surfing around. In some fields, there are sites which combine stats into beautiful reports. For instance, in the world of marketing, there are sites like MarketingCharts.com which regularly publish charts showing various stats relevant to the world of business and marketing.

Borrow trust from third parties: You can borrow the social proof that third-party organizations have built by placing the seals of organizations you are a part of or those that show your website offers secure checkouts, every little bit helps.

List notable appearances: Surely, if you've appeared in notable podcasts or blogs in your niche, displaying those logos with an "as seen on" on your site can show credibility. The same goes for any mentions in major media. It is important to be careful with this sort of thing, however, as it is easy to abuse it without much effort. Some people likely just make up media mentions counting on the fact that nobody will look it up. Or they will use some press release service that puts a bit of PR onto a major press site. They'll then use that site logo as if they were featured there, not telling.

Building up your initial list of testimonials

While dealing with alternatives is effective in the short-term, your goal should be to acquire some real testimonials as soon as possible. Luckily, there are several easy ways to do just that.

Give it away: A great way to get reviews on a new product is to give it away to a small group of people. You will get plenty of useful feedback on your product, the best of which you can use for testimonials, and they will get to keep the test product, it is a win/win. You can make these types of testimonials even more effective by including relevant niche influencers in your free samples as well. It is important to not go overboard with this process, however, as if you give away your product too regularly then it will only serve to devalue the product for those unlucky few who didn't get it for free.

Try blogger reviews: For every profitable blog out there, there is roughly a dozen that is trying everything they can to find a niche they can monetize. Regardless of what niche you are a part of, you can be sure that bloggers in that niche like free stuff, enjoy expressing their opinions and are always looking for new topics to write about to avoid irrelevance. As such, all you need to do is to reach out to these types of bloggers and offer them a copy of your product in exchange for a review which can be used as a testimonial assuming everything works out according to plan.

If you follow this approach for legal reasons, you need to ensure that they disclose that fact. But, if all goes well, you're going to have an entire blog post featuring and reviewing your product. If the review is good, you can get several quotes from it to use as social proof and/or a review on your landing page.

Consider case studies: Depending on what you are selling, you may find case studies an effective way to generate testimonials. You can then take on a small group of clients, for free, and then work closely with them in order to find out the difficulties they are having with your product or service, so things proceed as smoothly as possible. In addition to getting useful, personalized testimonials you may also get plenty of useful information for the next version of your product.

Chapter 4: Be an Authority

As previously discussed, many customers don't want to think through a complicated metric of potential decisions, they just want someone they trust to tell them what to do. The most notable example of this was the Stanley Milgram experiment where a man in a white lab coat told participants that they were to administer electric shocks to a person in another room. By the end of the study, a disturbing 65 percent of participants continued "shocking" the person in the other room, despite their pleas for mercy all the way to a point they were told could be fatal, as long as the person in the lab coat told them to continue.

While you certainly shouldn't take any potential power fantasies to such extreme lengths, you can use this same idea to build your overall credibility to the point where potential customers are practically falling over themselves to give you their money. Broadly speaking, the best way to do this is going to be by

Logos: Logos can be thought of as the reasoning behind the conclusions that potential clients should draw as a way of making it seem obvious that they should listen to whatever it is you are saying about the items you are selling. The trust that you establish by being an authority is particularly important for logos as it lends additional credibility to the things you say.

Pathos: Pathos can be thought of as the result of logos and is your main goal as it can be seen as the swaying of emotions that comes with a powerful argument. Changing a potential customer's pathos is easier once you have built up a relationship that, again, is primarily built on the trust that is gained from you being seen as an expert or authority on the topic in question.

Ethos: Ethos can broadly be thought of as selling yourself or establishing your credibility in the niche in question. Depending on what your niche is, this may or may not be something that you already have. Even if you already have the knowledge, you won't be considered an authority until you share that knowledge to the point that the public perception of the topic considers you a common source. This is something that will only build with time and cannot be rushed, remember slow and steady wins the race.

Understanding authority

With so much on the line, it can be easy to see while building your authority in a specific niche can be so important to both your short and long-term results. Unfortunately, this is often easier said than done as becoming an authority is like having the right of way while driving, it isn't something you can take, it is only something that other people give you. Having the title bestowed upon you is a mix of creating the right type of content, building the right social media image and having great SEO.

In many situations, the word expert and the word authority are often used interchangeably; this is not the case with sales, however, as being an authority is everything and being an expert is much worse than simply getting second place. In this case, an expert is someone who knows a lot about a certain niche while an authority is the person that all of the experts agree is the first stop for information. To put it another way, authorities aren't authorities because they say they are, they are authorities because when they make declarations in regard to their niche of choice, other people listen.

Benefits of being the best

The benefits of being an authority for you chosen niche are much the same as being an authority in any other situation when you speak, other people listen. This is because those who know you are an authority are naturally going to assume you know what you are talking about for a given situation. It doesn't take much to see how this can translate directly into additional sales when given a little extra push. If you can reach the status of authority for your niche, then you will be able to set the tone for the niche as a whole, along with legions of fans that will be willing to automatically agree with whatever you say.

If it seems like those you are giving niche authorities too much credit, stop and take a moment to consider someone who you believe to be an authority in your niche of choice. The odds are better than average that you listen to what this person has to say about everything, and you likely give little extra thought to the process while doing so. This is not to say that you are wrong, after all, you but your faith in this person for a reason, it just goes to show what reach these types of people have.

Trust is crucial

The key to building your eventual authority empire is going to be trustworthiness, not just sometimes, or when it is convenient, but each and every time no matter what. Taking the time to earn the trust of every potential customer you come into contact with is crucial as you are going to want to ensure that those who can say a bad word about you are very few and far between. This is not a short process, especially if you are working in a crowded niche, but the results are going to be well worth it in the end. However, once you have that trust, something as simple as selling a cheap but ultimately shoddy product and then recommending that your followers purchase it will be enough to ruin it forever, don't take this chance, treat the trust of your customers as sacrosanct.

Grow your reach

While it should be easy for your actual customers to think of you as a credible source at this point if you want to truly become an authority figure you are going to need to branch out substantially. Your goal during this phase should be to spread throughout the niche as completely as possible to the point that whenever anyone who is interested in the niche interacts with it, they can't help but see your name. This means you are going to want to spend time on forums talking about the niche and answering the questions that other people might have. Whenever you are able to do so successfully, you can then credit the information to your website, link included.

You will also want to join social media groups for sellers and bloggers in the niche so that you can get to know your competition as well. Not only will this allow you to get an inside look at their strengths and weaknesses, nothing says you are an authority figure like getting a guest spot on someone else's blog. As anyone who runs a blog can tell you, coming up with enough unique content every week to remain relevant can be a serious chore which is why, assuming you have proven yourself to be a reliable source of information in the community, any blogger should be happy to allow you to run a guest blog.

Once you have access to your competition's customers, you are going to want to do your best to take full advantage of the situation. First, you are going to want to ensure that the content you create is cream of the crop, buy a professional post online if you have to, just provide something that people are going to be interested in reading. End the post on a natural stopping point but offer those who are interested in more a follow up on your own site, link included. Finally, seal the deal by providing a coupon code in the post that is good for a serious discount on your own products as well. People will come to your site assuming you are an authority and additional conversions will follow.

Chapter 5: Use Body Language to Promote Sales

The exact percentage of communication that body posture accounts for is up for debate. What isn't up for debate is that it's incredibly important for displaying trust. As such, if you are looking for some help when it comes to closing deals, one of the easiest ways to start is by controlling the things you say with your body.

Open up: A defensive, closed body posture automatically tells those around you that you are tense, nervous and unwilling to come to a mutually beneficial agreement. This isn't a secret science either, these are common body language cues that you can bet money (your commission) on that your potential customers can read as well, even if this is just subconsciously.

What's worse, once they are aware of them, most potential customers will start mimicking them, and their related behaviors as well. Closed body posture gives them the signal that there's something to worry about and they'll fell ill at ease and much more resistant to persuasion. The fix, luckily, is quite simple. If you're concerned you may be displaying a defensive body posture, all you need to do is sit up straight so that your spine is aligned, and your shoulders are squared. At the same time, you are going to want to breathe deeply, place your hands on your legs, with your palms up. While this isn't a natural position, it is an important part of the overall whole.

Opening up your posture in this way will also serve to improve your mental state by decreasing the amount of the hormone cortisol that your body produces. Cortisol is responsible for stress levels so in this case acting and outwardly appearing to be calm and collected will make you feel this way as well, relaxing your potential customers in the process.

Watch your eye contact: Be careful with your eyes as making too much eye contact can be seen as antagonistic or off putting while making too little says you are not interested in the conversation you are having. A good rule of thumb is to make eye contact while either party is speaking unless you are both looking at an object that the conversation is in regard to. Be careful to avoid excessive blinking as this is known to be a sign of nervousness that can easily be interpreted as you are lying.

Watch your smile: Practically everyone you meet can spot a fake smile which means that if you are having a hard time closing sales, your smile might be to blame. There are 26 muscles that are used to smile, and not all of them can be controlled, even with practice. As such, if you are faking a smile, only those muscles directly under your control will activate, leaving a whole in your smile that can't be filled.

For most people, this manifests in a discrepancy that you can see it in the eyes and in the cheeks. For those who fake smile to potential customers, you're sending the message that you aren't being honest. And if that's the case, what else aren't you being honest about?

Luckily, the answer to the fake smile is also simple: start smiling for real.

How to give a genuine smile on-command:

- Look at something that makes you laugh right before your video.
- Watch yourself trying on different smiles in the mirror.
- Visualize things that really make you smile.

- Practice smiling with other salespeople. Often, just the knowledge that you're giving off a phony smile leads to dramatic improvements.

The next time you record a sales video, ask yourself: what am I communicating with my body language? If you can open your posture, keep eye contact, and give off a more radiant, genuine smile, then you're well on your way to building trust with your prospects. Remember, no important relationship survives if trust is totally lost and neither do deals.

Watch the handshake: For many people, a quality handshake is one of the most important aspects of body language, bar none. This is hardly surprising, after all, the handshake is the very first interaction that you will have with a potential customer and it can set the mood for the whole interaction. Some potential customers will have a very strong grip while others will be rather limp-wristed. Regardless of where they fall on the spectrum, if you fall on the other end then you can risk making the other person feel uncomfortable, which is why the first rule is always to wait and see how the other person responds before committing to one type of handshake or the other.

Watch the body positioning: You can draw a lot of conclusions about your potential prospects by the way they sit and stand, and they will be doing the same to you. As such, your best bet is typically to mimic their body language, as long as it is not defensive. This means you are going to want to do things like crossing your arms, leaning forward, scratching their neck, etc. While you shouldn't mirror them so much that it is obviously, following their cue is a great place to start.

Once you have matched their movements for a time, you can then get a good idea if they are on board with what you are selling by switching to your own mannerisms at a point late in the game and seeing if they start mimicking you instead, if they do then they may as well have already signed the deal.

Consider the tone, not just the content: While meeting with potential clients, it is important to the way they say things, as much as it is what is being said. Tonality is made up of two different parts, known separately as pace and volume. To ensure you get off to a good start with knew potential customers, you are going to want to match both. This means you are going to want to speak quietly to reserved customers and be brash with those who tend to only use their outdoor voices. A disconnect in either way will make them feel uncomfortable and can potentially cost you the sale as a result.

It is also important to pay close attention to the pace they are setting for the conversation. The pacing of their speech is often going to be a function of what part of the country, meaning that those who are used to a slower back and forth may find it hard to follow a fast talker and those who are used to some speed might get bored with a conversation that proceeds more leisurely. Practice speaking at different paces naturally and be ready to switch as needed.

Mistakes to avoid

Touching your face: Touching your face can be seen as disrespectful to your potential client as you have to shake their hand when the meeting is finished. What's worse, it is also considered a sign that you are lying about whatever it is you are discussing.

Not aligning your shoulders: Pay attention to what the potential customer's shoulders are doing, the further your shoulders are from one another, the more disinterested they are going to assume you are in whatever it is that is going on at the moment.

Scratching your head or neck: Any type of movement around the back of the head or the neck is thought to indicate that you are unsure of what it is you are talking about. Scratching an itch at the wrong time when talking about pricing, for example, can easily make your potential customer think that your numbers are fake.

Arousing suspicion: Standing with your hands in your pockets or behind your back will make the other party inherently trust you less as they will instinctively feel as though you are hiding something. The same goes for gesturing at odd moments or at anything other than chest height or above as gestures below this line cause the same natural inclination in the other party.

This doesn't mean that you should simply stand with your arms stiffly at your sides and never move them, as this will make you look suspicious as well. Unfortunately, this is what is likely to happen if you start thinking about your gestures too closely which is why it is recommended that you simply try and act as casual as possible and hope that your calm confident nature is reflected in your hand and arm movements.

Conclusion

Thank you for making it through to the end of *Persuasion: Psychology of Selling – Secret Techniques Only the World's Top Sales People Know to Close the Deal Every Time*, let's hope it was informative and able to provide you with all of the tools you need to achieve your goals, whatever it is that they may be. Just because you've finished this book doesn't mean there is nothing left to learn on the topic, expanding your horizons is the only way to find the mastery you seek. Remember, your competition is always going to be out there learning new and improved ways of making sales and if you don't dedicate yourself to doing the same you are ultimately going to end up being left behind.

While, in some instances, knowing about the topics discussed in the proceeding chapters will be enough to allow you to put them to use, many of the strategies will require practice in order to use them properly. As such, it is important to approach them with the idea that you will need to improve them as you would any other skill, slowly and with care. This is not to say that they will not be useful before they are at full strength, on the contrary, they can be used effectively right out of the gate, as long as you know what it is you are doing from the start. Don't have unreasonable expectations for yourself early on and you will find the success you seek in time.

Thank you!

Before you go, I just wanted to say thank you for purchasing my book.

You could have picked from dozens of other books on the same topic but you took a chance and chose this one.

So, a HUGE thanks to you for getting this book and for reading all the way to the end.

Now I wanted to ask you for a small favor. **Could you please take just a few minutes to leave a review for this book on Amazon?**

This feedback will help me continue to write the type of books that will help you get the results you want. So if you enjoyed it, please let me know!

CPSIA information can be obtained
at www.ICGtesting.com
Printed in the USA
LVHW100826070920
664728LV00011B/113

9 781951 030414